Legal Life Writing:
Marginalized Subjects and Sources

T0374590

Edited by

Linda Mulcahy and David Sugarman

WILEY Blackwell

This edition first published 2015
Editorial organization © 2015 Cardiff University Law School
Chapters © 2015 by the chapter author

Blackwell Publishing was acquired by John Wiley & Sons in February 2007. Blackwell's publishing programme has been merged with Wiley's global Scientific, Technical, and Medical business to form Wiley-Blackwell.

Editorial Offices
350 Main Street, Malden, MA 02148-5020, USA
9600 Garsington Road, Oxford OX4 2DQ, UK

For details of our global editorial offices, for customer services, and for information about how to apply for permission to reuse the copyright material in this book please see our website at www.wiley.com/wiley-blackwell

Registered Office
John Wiley & Sons Ltd, The Atrium, Southern Gate, Chichester, West Sussex PO19 8SQ.

Library of Congress Cataloging-in-Publication Data
Legal life-writing : marginalised subjects and sources / edited by Linda Mulcahy, David Sugarman. – 1
   pages cm. – (Journal of law and society special issues)
   Summary: "Legal Life-Writing provides the first sustained treatment of the implications of life-writing on legal biography, autobiography and the visual history of law in society through a focus on neglected sources, and on those usually marginalized or ignored in legal biography and legal history, such as women and minorities. Draws on a range of sources and disciplinary approaches including legal history, life-writing, sociology, history, art history, feminism and post-colonialism, seeking to build a bridge-head between them. Challenges the methodologies employed in conventional accounts of legal lives. Aims to ignite debate about the nature of the relationship between socio-legal studies and legal history. Aims to enlarge the fields of legal biography, legal history, history and socio-legal studies, and to foster a closer and more inter-disciplinary dialogue between these disciplines"– Provided by publisher.
   Includes bibliographical references and index.
   ISBN 978-1-119-05216-6 (paperback)
   1. Women lawyers–Great Britain–Biography. 2. Women lawyers–Biography. 3. Practice of law–Great Britain–History. 4. Practice of law–History. 5. Law–Great Britain–History. 6. Law–History.
   I. Mulcahy, Linda, 1962- editor. II. Sugarman, David, editor.
   KD472.W65L44 2015
   340.092'520941–dc23
                     2015009301

A catalogue record for this title is available from the British Library.

ISBN: 978-1-119-05216-6

Set in the United Kingdom by Godiva Publishing Services Ltd
Printed in Singapore by C.O.S. Printers Pte Ltd

Contents

Contents

JOURNAL OF LAW AND SOCIETY
VOLUME 42, NUMBER 1, MARCH 2015
ISSN: 0263-323X, pp. 1–6

Introduction: Legal Life Writing and Marginalized Subjects and Sources

LINDA MULCAHY* AND DAVID SUGARMAN**

'Life writing', from biographies of people to biographies of objects, is an increasingly popular field of scholarship in which the approaches adopted range from in-depth scholarly accounts to hagiography.[1] Despite this, a review of the literature reveals that the bulk of legal biographies produced have focused on charting the lives of the elite; most often white, male, heterosexual judges and barristers. There have been notable exceptions, including Mary Jane Mossman's *The First Women Lawyers*, Clay Smith's *The Making of the Black Lawyer*, and Patrick Polden's account of early female barristers,[2] but these remain in the minority. The implications of this for the field of socio-legal studies are extensive. Neglect of the lives of those whose entry to the legal profession was delayed or whose progress was hindered by virtue of their colour, gender or beliefs facilitates the promulgation of conventional views about the experiences and voices that are rendered authoritative and legitimate in the scholarly community. It also

* Department of Law, London School of Economics, Houghton Street, London WC2A 2AE, England
l.mulcahy@lse.ac.uk
** Law School, Lancaster University, Lancaster LA1 4YN, England
d.sugarman@lancaster.ac.uk

1 R.G. Parry, 'Is legal biography really legal scholarship?' (2010) 30 *Legal Studies* 208.
2 M.J. Mossman, *The First Women Lawyers: A Comparative Study of Gender, Law and the Legal Professions* (2006); J. Clay Smith Jr., *The Making of the First Black Lawyer 1844–1944* (1993); P. Polden, 'Portia's progress: women at the Bar in England, 1919–1939' (2005) 12 *International J. of the Legal Profession* 293. See, also, P. Polden, 'The Lady of Tower Bridge: Sybil Campbell, England's first woman judge' (1999) 8 *Women's History Rev.* 505; B. Babcock, *Woman Lawyer. The Trials of Clara Foltz* (2011); A.F. Logan, 'In Search of Equal Citizenship: the campaign for women magistrates in England and Wales, 1910–1939' (2007) 16 *Women's History Rev.* 501; H. MacQueen, 'Scotland's first women law graduates: an Edinburgh centenary' in *Miscellany VI* (2009) 221, and the work undertaken by the LSE's Legal Biography Project: <http://www.lse.ac.uk/collections/law/projects/legalbiog/lbp.htm>.

impacts on what we are able to direct our students to read, and points to the limited role models available to them in their own careers.

This collection provides the first sustained treatment of legal life writing (as broadly conceived). It aims to ignite debate about the nature of existing legal, historical, and socio-legal scholarship through the exploration of three key themes. The first of these relates to the nature of the relationship between socio-legal studies and legal history. Socio-legal scholarship has tended to give legal history short shift. A key question posed by contributors to this collection is whether this intra-disciplinary tension can be resolved by the emergence of discreet revisionist legal histories or whether the adoption of a socio-legal perspective requires a fundamental rethinking of what constitute authoritative subjects, methods, and sources.

These issues are addressed in **David Sugarman**'s scene-setting article. He describes and analyses some of the ways in which legal life writing has been enlarged to embrace a wider range of subjects, sources, and methods, and explains and justifies it as an intellectual project. He considers some of life writing's difficulties, shortcomings, and dilemmas, suggesting models that can assist the enterprise to go forward, and provides insights into the question of what legal life writing adds. The purpose of his article, and that of the collection as a whole, is to advance an emerging perspective: a broader, more pluralistic, democratic conception of legal life writing that transcends the traditional stark dualisms between internal and external legal history, top-down and bottom-up approaches, and legal history and socio-legal studies. Sugarman argues that legal life writing demonstrates the value of historical thinking as a means to comprehend law, politics, and culture, and that it can supplement the study of law. He concludes that legal life writing can help legal historians and socio-legal scholars to develop new skills and embrace a wider range of participants and audiences, thereby enhancing their ability to engage with public issues and public history.

The second major theme of the collection is the problem of silences in the existing literature. All of the contributions highlight the potential for the stories of those placed at the boundaries of law and the legal system to produce radically different accounts of law's empire and legal phenomena. In particular, the collection interrogates the ways in which the experiences of female or working-class judges, lawyers, spectators of trials, and academics disrupt existing orthodoxies of how lawyers are, and ought to be. While some of the biographies presented in this collection focus on individual lives, others present a complete or partial group biography (Auchmuty, Moran, Mulcahy). Group biography has proved valuable in allowing scholars to focus on the common characteristics or experiences of a group for which individual biographies of members are simply not traceable. They are also of value in their own right. While biographies of the great and famous tell us much about the exceptional, group biography can often reveal much more about the everyday ways in which social mores and public attitudes directed and constrained behaviour. Group biography allows us to explore the broader

2

political dynamics of biography that can often only be hinted at when we focus on the individual life.

Specific articles in the collection complement these general discussions by providing detailed accounts of particular actors whose stories have remained largely untold. Included in this category is **Fiona Cownie**'s work on Claire Palley, the first woman to hold a Chair in Law at a United Kingdom university. This article reminds us that even when biographies of women have been written, they have generally concentrated on female legal practitioners or judges, rather than academics. It is noticeable that despite the significance of Claire Palley's appointment as the first female professor of law in the United Kingdom, little is known about the circumstances surrounding her appointment and the responses to it or, indeed, the woman. Drawing on educational biography and in-depth interviews with Palley, Cownie explores why it took until 1970 to appoint a female law professor and, more particularly, what it was about Palley which made it likely that she would be singled out in this way.

The challenge of discovering the particular qualities that make it likely that some will succeed where others fail is taken up in **Catharine MacMillan**'s study of Judah Benjamin. MacMillan considers how a young man who might have been marginalized in society because of the circumstances of his birth, ethnic origin, and religious identity rose to prominence in law, politics, and business in both the United Kingdom and the United States. Unlike other articles in this collection, the challenge of writing a biography here is not caused by the lack of attention to the subject during his lifetime but his own determination to thwart those determined to write his life story.

Playing with the notion of outsider/insider, MacMillan is keen to draw attention to the fact that Benjamin possessed two key characteristics that were likely to aid his success in the societies of the time: he was white and male. It is argued that both attributes were important preconditions for success, without which all discussion of personal attributes would be rendered meaningless. He also possessed considerable intellect, the capacity for hard work, and exceptional skills as an orator. Despite these advantages, it is clear that the fact that Benjamin was Jewish meant he was the subject of anti-Semitism and was labelled as exotic. A major contribution of MacMillan's work is the way in which she presents us with a multi-dimensional account of a subject whose identities and abilities were manifold. Unlike many other accounts of the marginalized in this collection, Benjamin's difference is not always equated with disadvantage. Rather, it is argued that his outsider status was sometimes a positive attribute in the life of a man who crossed professions, classes, legal jurisdictions, and cultures.

The focus on gaps in the existing literature has also been extended in this collection to cover other academics who have been much written about from a particular perspective in ways which have obscured their broader contribution to law and the public sphere. **Mara Malagodi**'s essay on the life of

3

Ivor Jennings, one of Britain's most prominent constitutional law scholars of the twentieth century, falls squarely into this category. Malagodi contends that while Jennings is mainly known for his work in the 1930s on English public law, his work in South Asia during the early years of the Cold War allows us to see the man and his work through a very different lens. This alternative account of Jennings's constitutional legacy explores the interface of orthodox accounts of the 'Occidental Jennings' with an analysis of the neglected 'Oriental' experiences of this influential intellectual. Most importantly, it reveals the ambiguous relationship between constitutionalism and democracy in Jennings's constitutional work overseas, and the impact of his postcolonial work on his views of constitutionalism more generally.

The final theme to emerge from the collection is an exploration of the methodologies employed in legal life writing. Biography is generally acknowledged to be something of an epistemological minefield. The serendipity of discovery, the limitations of having to work with what has been preserved, and the difficulty of working with resources not necessarily produced with biography in mind make this a time-consuming and problematic form of legal scholarship. To these problems can be added the particular issues involved in researching the marginalized. By definition, those who have been barred from entry into, or effective participation in, the legal world rarely occupy a prominent position in the official reports of cases or commentaries which form the basis of much legal scholarship. The result is that we frequently have to work with materials relegated to the 'private sphere'. This raises important questions about whether legal biography is possible in such situations and the alternative sources to which it is legitimate to turn in the course of constructing accounts of a marginalized but important life. The political significance of this question for socio-legal studies should not be underestimated. Claims that these lives cannot be adequately charted because of insufficient information about them inevitably leads to a double marginalization: that which occurs during the lifetime of the subject and that which occurs when revisionist accounts of lives subsequently rendered important are attempted by scholars.

A number of articles in this collection explore the alternative sources that can be turned to in order to fill the gaps in existing knowledge. **Rosemary Auchmuty**'s article on the process of researching the life of Miss Bebb, who in 1913 challenged the Law Society of England and Wales for their refusal to admit women to the solicitors' profession,[3] raises a series of important questions about what is possible when there are significant gaps in public accounts of a person's life. It considers, for instance, whether sources such as turn-of-the-century novels set in women's colleges are valuable in helping us to understand what college and university might have been like for early

---

3 R. Auchmuty, 'Whatever happened to Miss Bebb? *Bebb v The Law Society* and women's legal history' (2010) 31 *Legal Studies* 199.

4

women law students or when establishing likely paths of activity. In addition to posing questions of whether these alternative sources constitute legitimate substitutes for public records, Auchmuty's work also asks whether it is important to seek out these sources in order to place the broader significance of a life and choices made in the context of the times. In particular, it raises critical questions about the ways in which all sources, even official ones, might be more imaginatively used than has been the norm in order to explore the extent to which information relating to networks of professional relationships and personal friendships allow conclusions to be drawn about lifestyle and even sexuality. Her argument is not just that these sources and techniques are useful for adding colour and context to otherwise bare accounts but that they are necessary, because a focus on public achievements will miss significant aspects of a woman's life – even, perhaps, its very essence.

Other articles take up the challenge of using visual sources in the production of legal biographies. In this vein, Leslie Moran and Linda Mulcahy both examine the use of images as a largely neglected source of data for researching the lives of the judiciary and public spectators in the trial. For **Leslie Moran**, image making and image management is of particular importance for elite groups such as the judiciary in the production of an outward, public face of legitimate authority as well as their self-regarding audience of peers. Images of judges also allow us to go beyond the individual biography of a particular subject to an appreciation of the way in which official images produce expectations of the judiciary as an institution. Moran does not propose that pictures should supersede other sources of data but, rather, that they are a neglected, sometimes poorly understood, and underused source of data to which socio-legal scholars could usefully pay more attention in their attempts to understand how authority is performed.

Linda Mulcahy develops these arguments about the importance of the image to socio-legal biography in her study of a much ignored legal actor, the trial spectator. She argues that although the spectator's critical role in rendering trials open is widely acknowledged to be fundamental to any progressive legal system, hardly anything can be gleaned about spectators and their demise from official transcripts of reports. Drawing on images of trials which appeared in Victorian and Edwardian popular journals and fine art, she argues that these images provide a rich data set which indicates that spectating was a popular pastime which was enjoyed by both men and women of the time, from a range of classes. It is argued that the primary importance of this data lies in the possibility it offers of producing a revisionist history of how women participated in the public sphere of the courts long before they were admitted as barristers, solicitors or judges. In addition, it raises an important methodological claim about the ways in which the image can be used by lawyers to understand the various ways in which the public have been managed and silenced in the courtroom. Rather than seeing the image as merely reflecting norms about what constituted appropriate behaviour in the public gallery, Mulcahy argues that certain images, most notably those produced by fine artists for the middle classes, were also complicit in the production of norms about how the spectator should behave.

One of the aims of this collection is to foster debate about marginalized legal lives and socio-legal approaches to the issues raised, but the articles published here mark no more than a beginning. Whilst there is much to be gleaned about race, class, and gender in this collection, there is much more to be said about those marginalized because of their sexuality or ethnicity. The seminar at which most of these papers were originally presented alongside those offered by librarians and curators made clear that there is considerable scope for the academic community to work much more closely with the keepers of visual and textual archives in identifying resources for future work on marginalized lawyers.[4] While each article in this collection represents an original contribution to knowledge, the whole is greater than the sum of its parts, in that it offers the promise of broadening the subjects, methodologies, and sources of legal life writing so as to free it from the traditional confines of accepted scholarly questions and methods. It is contended by the editors that legal life writing can and should be 'flipped' and reconstituted so that, rather than being a handmaiden of the elite, it becomes a 'dangerous supplement'[5] to 'black-letter', socio-legal, and historical scholarship.

If, by the end, we have persuaded you that legal life writing (as broadly conceived) can enhance our understanding of law and society, and the lives of individuals, groups, institutions, and objects, and their relationship to society, and that it is a fundamentally inter-disciplinary genre, offering exciting and challenging opportunities for closer collaboration between scholars of law, legal history, socio-legal studies, and museum archivists (amongst others), we will have succeeded.

4 This was a seminar that was jointly organized by the Socio-Legal Studies Association, Institute of Advanced Legal Studies, British Library, and the LSE Legal Biography Project in the summer of 2013.
5 The supplement is 'dangerous' argues Derrida because it is not fully assimilable. It remains outside, challenging the completeness and the adequacy of that which is within. See, J. Derrida, *Of Grammatology* (1976) 144–5 and P. Fitzpatrick (ed.), *Dangerous Supplements. Resistance and Renewal in Jurisprudence* (1991).

JOURNAL OF LAW AND SOCIETY
VOLUME 42, NUMBER 1, MARCH 2015
ISSN: 0263-323X, pp. 7–33

From Legal Biography to Legal Life Writing: Broadening Conceptions of Legal History and Socio-legal Scholarship

DAVID SUGARMAN*

This article describes and analyses how legal life writing has grown to embrace a wider range of subjects, sources, and methods – from eminent white male judges to women, minorities, displaced persons, and outsiders – and explains and justifies it as an intellectual project. It considers some of life writing's challenges, shortcomings, and dilemmas, suggesting ways forward. The aim is to advance an important, inter-disciplinary perspective in the making: namely, a more pluralistic, democratic conception of legal life writing, which offers new ways of advancing legal history and socio-legal scholarship, encouraging inter-disciplinary dialogue. It is argued that legal life writing demonstrates the value of historical thinking in comprehending law, politics, and culture; it can also supplement the study of law, helping legal historians and socio-legal scholars to develop new skills and embrace a wider range of participants and audiences, thereby enhancing their ability to engage with public issues and public history.

No species of writing seems more worthy of cultivation than biography, since ... none can more certainly enchain the heart by irresistible interest, or more widely diffuse instruction to every diversity of condition ... I have often thought that there has rarely passed a life of which a judicious and faithful narrative would not be useful ...[1]

* *Law School, Lancaster University, Lancaster LA1 4YN, England*
d.sugarman@lancaster.ac.uk

My thanks go to Léonie Sugarman for her helpful feedback. I am also indebted to the Institute of Advanced Legal Studies, University of London, for its long-standing support of my research.

1 S. Johnson, *Rambler* No. 60, 13 October 1750.

I.

At its best, life writing, such as biography and autobiography, illuminates the shifting interplay between agency, circumstance, and the material conditions prompting behaviour. It not only appeals to a universal human interest in gossip, but answers a need within us to understand each other better. It also raises intriguing and profound issues concerning every aspect of reading, and writing, a life. Great life writing is unsettling, challenging the way we look at the world, and inspiring us to develop new ways of knowing. It humanizes. It goes to the heart of our individual and shared existence. The dramas that comprise biography and autobiography are histories that speak to the state of our souls and the state of our world. As Virginia Woolf put it, biography can provide not only an account of a person's outer life, but also an insight into their 'inner life of emotion and thought'.[2] Most compelling of all, it tells us how it is to be inside our skins. Hence, pursuing in print the life of others may provide inspiration and encouragement,[3] especially at times of adversity.

These are very broad claims. And they are claims that could equally be made of other forms of writing and of great art.[4] Nonetheless, they are some of the good reasons why legal historians and socio-legal scholars should take legal life writing seriously.

Certainly, biography and autobiography are booming.[5] Artists, philosophers, politicians, historians, and even economists, from Beveridge[6] and Keynes[7] to Thatcher[8] and Wittgenstein,[9] have all attracted a steady stream of high-quality biographies. At first blush, the contrast with British legal

---

2 V. Woolf, 'The New Biography' (1927) reprinted in *Collected Essays Volume Four* (1967) 229, at 230. This concession to the power of biography appears in an essay primarily concerned to demonstrate biography to be a failed attempt to accomplish a task that only fiction can carry out successfully. For a valuable critique of Woolf's hostility to biography, see R. Monk, 'This Fictitious Life: Virginia Woolf on Biography, Reality, and Character' (2007) 31 *Philosophy and Literature* 1.
3 S. Bartie, 'Histories of Legal Scholars' (2014) 34 *Legal Studies* 305.
4 S. Sharma, *The Power of Art* (2009) at 6–13.
5 'Top Selling Biographies and Autobiographies since 2001' *Guardian* 7 February 2013, at <http://www.theguardian.com/news/datablog/2013/feb/07/biographies-autobiography-nielsen-2001>. The prevalence of biography is paralleled by the current popularity of another poor relation of academic history, genealogy. In an age where individual identity seems increasingly homogenized, and individual agency feels limited, family history, like biography, constitutes 'real history', telling us new things about the past and our identities, and suggesting new ways we might write about it: see, A. Light, 'In Defence of Family History' *Guardian*, 11 October 2014. See, further, the discussion of life writing in section V, below.
6 J. Harris, *William Beveridge* (1977).
7 R. Skidelsky, *John Maynard Keynes* (2013).
8 C. Moore, *Margaret Thatcher* (2013).
9 R. Monk, *Ludwig Wittgenstein* (1991).

8

biography is striking. Today, the once popular biographies of illustrious judges – and the mainstay of legal biography hitherto – appear to be in decline. Apparently, they are selling less, and certainly fewer are published today than in the previous two hundred years. Perhaps they have been eclipsed by a different notion of 'celebrity'. Perhaps, also, contemporary judges and lawyers are less colourful and publicly visible, and have become more professionalized, bureaucratized, and corporatized and, hence, less special than their counterparts of yore.[10] A decrease in deference, changes in the working practices of Parliament and the Bar which make it more difficult to practice law *and* politics, the fewer number of lawyers in the House of Commons, and the institutional and professional separation of law and politics,[11] underpinned by an increasing commitment to the separation of powers, may have contributed to the waning of judicial biography.[12]

Writing at the turn of the twentieth-first century, Philip Girard opined that 'the genre [of judicial biography] in England has run out of steam'.[13] One could also point to the invidious comparison between the quantity and quality of legal biography in the United States and, to a lesser extent in Canada, relative to Britain. However, change is in the air. High-quality legal biography by British academics, pioneered by Heuston and Stevens in the 1960s and 1970s, has grown and established a small, marginal, but discernible niche in the world of scholarship, albeit a precarious one.[14] And for the first time, it is legal and allied scholars, rather than judges and lawyers,

---

10 A. Paterson, *The Law Lords* (1982) and *Final Judgment. The Last Law Lords and the Supreme Court* (2013); K. Malleson, *The New Judiciary* (1999); R. Stevens, *The English Judges* (2002). A parallel process of bureaucratization and corporatization has also been observed of the contemporary legal profession: Y. Dezalay and D. Sugarman (eds.), *Professional Competition and Professional Power* (1995); H. Sommerlad, 'Managerialism and the Legal Profession' (1995) 2 *International J. of the Legal Profession* 159; H.W. Arthurs and R. Kreklewich, 'Law, Legal Institutions and the Legal Profession in the New Economy' (1996) 34 *Osgoode Hall Law J.* 34; R.L. Abel, *English Lawyers between Market and State* (2004).

11 D. Howarth, 'Lawyers in the House of Commons' in *Law in Politics, Politics in Law*, ed. D. Feldman (2013) 41.

12 Paradoxically, the increasing separation of law and politics in the United Kingdom has occurred co-extensively with the dramatic increase of judicial intervention in politics in the United Kingdom and continental Europe in recent decades, mirroring earlier trends in the United States: see Paterson, op. cit., n. 10; Malleson, op. cit., n. 10; Stevens, op. cit., n. 10; C. Guarnieri and P. Pederzoli (eds.), *The Power of Judges* (2002).

13 P. Girard, 'Judging Lives: Judicial Biography from Hale to Holmes' (2003) 7 *Australian J. of Legal History* 87, at 106. On the dearth of Irish judicial biography, see T. O'Malley, 'Judicial Biography and the Beauty of Tourists' (2011), at <http://www.extempore.ie/2011/03/31/judicial-biography-and-the-beauty-of-tourists/>.

14 R.F.V. Heuston, *Lives of the Lord Chancellors, 1885–1940* (1964) and *Lives of the Lord Chancellors, 1940–1970* (1987); R. Stevens, *Law and Politics: the House of Lords as a Judicial Body, 1800–1976* (1979). See, also, R.F.V. Heuston, *Judges and Biographers* (1967).

9

that are receiving most attention. Women and foreign-born émigrés – groups who were neglected hitherto – have begun to receive sustained biographical treatment. Some of the pre-eminent concerns of earlier generations of legal biography – such as elaborating the 'great men' of the law as instructive professional role models, offering amusing and anecdote-filled biographies that bring to life lawyers and their practices, and the interplay between top-court judges and high politics – have in important respects been supplemented, if not replaced, by a more sustained attention to intellectual biography[15] and social history. Work illustrative of this biographical turn includes Auchmuty on Gwyneth Bebb, Beatson and Zimmermann on German-speaking émigré lawyers in twentieth-century Britain,[16] Dukes on Kahn-Freund, Duxbury on Pollock, Lacey on Hart, Parry on Hughes Parry, and Prest on Blackstone.[17] Institutional initiatives at LSE[18] and Cambridge[19] also indicate that an effort is under way to sustain legal biography in Britain as never before. We may be witnessing a turning point.

In this article, I describe and analyse some of the ways in which legal life writing has been enlarged to embrace a wider range of subjects, sources, and methods. I seek to explain and justify it as an intellectual project, consider some of its challenges, shortcomings, and dilemmas, suggest some ways forward, and provide insights into the question of what legal life writing adds. In addressing these matters, my main focus is on Britain, although I do call attention to some of the exemplary Canadian and American scholarship.

My goal is to advance an important inter-disciplinary perspective in the making: namely, a broader, more pluralistic, democratic, conception of legal life writing that transcends the traditional stark dualisms between internal and external legal history,[20] top-down and bottom-up approaches,[21] and

15 This pre-occupation with intellectual history parallels the dominant trend in recent American and Canadian judicial biography.
16 See, also, G. Lewis, *F.A. Mann* (2013).
17 R. Auchmuty, 'Whatever happened to Miss Bebb?' (2011) 31 *Legal Studies* 199; J. Beatson and R. Zimmermann (eds.), *Jurists Uprooted: German-Speaking Émigré Lawyers in Twentieth Century Britain* (2004); R. Dukes, 'Constitutionalizing employment relations; Sinzheimer, Kahn-Freund, and the role of labour law' (2008) 35 *J. of Law and Society* 341, and 'Otto Kahn-Freund and Collective Laissez-Faire: An Edifice without a Keystone?' (2009) 72 *Modern Law Rev.* 220; N. Lacey, *A Life of H.L.A. Hart: The Nightmare and the Noble Dream* (2004); R.G. Parry, *David Hughes Parry* (2010); N. Duxbury, *Frederick Pollock and the English Juristic Tradition* (2004); W.R. Prest, *William Blackstone* (2008).
18 LSE, at <http://www.lse.ac.uk/collections/law/projects/legalbiog/lbp.htm>.
19 Eminent Scholars Archive, at <http://www.squire.law.cam.ac.uk/eminent_scholars/>.
20 On the distinction between internal and external legal history, see R.W. Gordon, 'Introduction: J. Willard Hurst and the Common Law Tradition in American Legal Historiography' (1975) 10 *Law & Society Rev.* 9.
21 On 'top-down' and 'bottom-up' histories see, for example, G. Eley, *A Crooked Line: From Cultural History to the History of Society* (2005); E.P. Thompson, *The Essential E.P. Thompson* (2001); P.N. Stearns, 'Social History Present and Future' (2003) 37 *J. of Social History* 1.

legal history and socio-legal studies. I also hope to demonstrate that legal life writing, broadly conceived, offers new ways of advancing legal history and socio-legal scholarship, and of encouraging inter-disciplinary dialogue between them, and also with other fields and audiences.

II.

The reasons for the limited acceptance of biography and other forms of life writing within the academic discipline of law are both specific to that discipline and also reflect the problematic status of biography within and beyond academia.[22]

Life writing is a multi-disciplinary enterprise at odds with the notion of law as a singular field of education and scholarship. It is historical, and a peculiar branch of history and the humanities. The dominant tradition of internalist, doctrinal legal scholarship and education created after c.1850 – and externalist, socio-legal scholarship and education constructed since c.1965 – were largely forged in opposition to history.[23] The modern academic discipline of law commonly regarded history as a rival from whose clutches law had escaped[24] to establish both an autonomous subject, and the desired professional legitimacy for university law teachers, in the face of sceptical universities and a largely hostile legal community.

'Law in context' and socio-legal studies were similarly constituted in opposition to that strand of legal historicism that uncritically celebrated the common law, that emphasized continuity and de-emphasized change, that privileged early history and 'origins' over modern history and 'effects', that judged legal success in terms of narrow, self-serving technical categories,[25] and that neglected the history of law as the lay public experienced it – that is, its social history. It was this vein of legal history (lawyers' legal history) that remained an important feature of British legal education, especially in first-

---

22 See, also, R.G. Parry, 'Is Legal Biography really Legal Scholarship?' (2010) 30 *Legal Studies* 208. L. Kalman, 'The Power of Biography' (1998) 23 *Law and Social Inquiry* 479, which includes valuable reflections on the hazards of writing judicial biography.

23 D. Sugarman, 'The Legal Boundaries of Liberty: Dicey, Liberalism and Legal Science' (1983) 46 *Modern Law Rev.* 102; 'Legal Theory, the Common Law Mind and the Making of the Textbook Tradition' in *Legal Theory and Common Law*, ed. W. Twining (1986) 26; '"Great Beyond His Knowing": Morton Horwitz's Influence on Legal Education and Scholarship in England, Canada and Australia' in *Transformations in American Legal History II*, eds. D.W. Hamilton and A.L. Brophy (2011) 504.

24 History and law were combined at the University of Oxford during 1850–1872 and at the University of Cambridge between 1868 and 1872. For some it was a marriage made in hell. Most dons welcomed the divorce, especially the historians.

25 M.J. Horwitz, 'The Conservative Tradition in the Writing of American Legal History' (1973) 17 *Am. J. of Legal History* 275.

11

year courses on the English legal system and its texts, until at least the final decade of the twentieth century.[26] It was a common hostility to history that united internalist, law-in-context, and externalist legal scholars, and which partly explains the marginalization of legal history[27] and, therefore, legal biography in orthodox and socio-legal scholarship.

Law's resistance to history has occurred in the face of law's central dependence on historical explanation. Law and history have always been joined at the hip in a relationship of '... intimate antagonism. Lawyers have always needed history, appealed to it for authority, and made significant contributions to writing it.'[28] Moreover, historical explanation has played a major role in British legal scholarship, during the Enlightenment, the late-nineteenth and early-twentieth centuries and the late 1970s to the mid-1980s, but its influence has fluctuated, its rise has prompted backlashes, and its ascendency has tended to be relatively short-lived.[29]

In addition, the details of the day-to-day practice of judges, lawyers, and jurists often seem trivial, repetitious, and boring even to those whose living depends upon them; to outsiders, the specifics are potentially interesting only when aggregated and used as guides to underlying structures or tendencies, 'a task demanding the patience and skill to pick jewels out of mountains of junk'.[30]

Legal biography has an image problem, which perhaps also explains why socio-legal and other scholars have tended to keep it at arm's length. I have already touched on the conservative tendencies of lawyers' legal biography.[31] To this should be added the inaccurate, inadequate, and undisclosed sources used by some of the most popular works of the genre during the nineteenth-century heyday of judicial biography, and the confines of conventional legal biography with respect to subject matter, sources, and frames of reference.

26 R. Cocks, 'History in eclipse?' in *The Life of the Law*, ed. P. Birks (1993) 257; D. Sugarman, 'Beyond ignorance and complacency: Robert Stevens' journey through lawyers and the courts' (2010) 16 *International J. of the Legal Profession* 7.

27 On the heterogeneity of legal history, see M. Lobban, 'The Varieties of Legal History' (2012), at <http://www.cliothemis.com/The-Varieties-of-Legal-History>. On the value of legal history, and the arguments for contextual approaches to legal history, see J. Phillips, 'Why Legal History Matters' (2010) 41 *Victoria University of Wellington Law Rev.* 293.

28 R.W. Gordon, 'The Past as Authority and as Social Critic' in *The Historical Turn in the Human Sciences*, ed. T.J. McDonald (1996) 339, at 339. See, also, D. Sugarman, 'Introduction: Histories of Law and Society' in *Law in History: Histories of Law and Society Vol. I*, ed. D. Sugarman (1996) xi, at xiii.

29 For a more detailed discussion, see D. Sugarman, 'Law' in *The Blackwell Companion to the Enlightenment*, eds. J.W. Yolton et al. (1991) 275, at 276–7; Sugarman, op. cit. (2011), n. 23; D. Rabban, *Law's History* (2013).

30 R.W. Gordon, 'The Devil and Daniel Webster,' (1984) 94 *Yale Law J.* 445, at 446.

31 This includes its long-standing preoccupation with 'greatness', which is an essentially ahistorical pursuit: see L. Przybyszewski, 'The Dilemma of Judicial Biography or Who Cares Who Is the Great Appellate Judge?' (1996) 21 *Law & Social Inquiry* 135.

The bulk of legal biographies have focused on the lives of the elite; most often white, male, higher-court judges.[32] Women,[33] artisan and working-class society, people of colour, and other 'outsiders' tend to receive short shrift, as do lower-court judges,[34] court officials, litigants,[35] the diverse audiences of the law beyond the judiciary and lawyers. While the history of law firms has added considerably to our understanding of legal practice, and the interplay between the public sphere and the private sphere in legal life,[36] the impact of these histories has been largely confined to the realm of business history. Consequently, legal biography has been largely cut-off from, and seen as irrelevant to, intellectual, social, and pictorial history, and the 'humanities turn' in socio-legal scholarship,[37] and from the new and challenging ways in which biography, autobiography and other forms of life writing can be discussed.[38]

---

32 Only a relatively small number of judges have been the subject of sustained, modern biographies: P. Polden, 'Judging Judges' in *Making Legal History*, eds. A. Musson and C. Stebbings (2012) 53.

33 See Auchmuty, op. cit., n. 17; R. Auchmuty, 'Early Women Law Students at Cambridge and Oxford' (2008) 29 *J. of Legal History* 63; P. Polden, 'Portia's progress: women at the bar in England, 1919–1939' (2005) 12 *International J. of the Legal Profession* 293; H. Heilbron, *Rose Heilbron* (2012). Nonetheless, women lawyers, judges, and law students have received more sustained biographical attention in Canada and the United States relative to Britain.

34 Polden's account of the idiosyncratic county court bench is an admirable exception to the tendency to neglect lower court judges: P. Polden, *A History of the County Court, 1846–1971* (1999).

35 For a suggestive exemplar, see C. Backhouse, *The Heiress vs The Establishment. Mrs Campbell's Campaign for Legal Justice* (2004), on a Canadian woman, with no formal education or legal training, who was the first woman to litigate her case in person before the Privy Council, and won.

36 For example, J. Slinn, *A History of Freshfields* (1984) and *Linklaters and Paines* (1987); V. Belcher, *Boodle, Hatfield and Co.* (1985); L. Dennett, *Slaughter and May* (1989). For a useful overview, see J. Slinn, 'The Histories and Records of Firms of Solicitors' (1989) 22 *Business Archives* 58.

37 For example, the following journals: *Yale Journal of Law and the Humani*ties, founded in 1988; *Law, Culture and the Humanities*, founded in 2005; and *Law and Humanities*, founded in 2007. There also exists a Law and Humanities blog at <http://lawlit.blogspot.co.uk/>. See, further, D. Feenan, 'Foreword: Socio-legal studies and the humanities' (2009) 5 *International J. of Law in Context*, 235–42. M.L. Williams, 'Socio-legal studies and the humanities – law, interdisciplinarity and integrity' (2009) 5 *International J. of Law in Context* 243.

38 Thus, biographies, obituaries, and eulogies are a rich source for investigating lawyers' professional identity, the myths lawyers generate in defence of existing professional structures, and the culture and mindset of the legal community: see W. Espeland and T.C. Halliday, 'Death Becomes Them: Commemoration, Biography and the Ritual Reconstruction of Chicago Lawyers in the Late 19th Century' (1990). Dictionaries of National Biography are invaluable research tools for legal life writing and a window on law's culture, nationhood, and national heritage, as are some of the biographies on Wikipedia. On obituaries, eulogies, and the legal press as research sources, see Polden op. cit., n. 32, pp. 60–2.

13

The problem is partly the general failure of legal education to provide even basic training in empirical and socio-legal research skills; also, Britain's undergraduate system of legal education does not benefit from students (and therefore faculty) trained in the human sciences, as occurs in the post-graduate legal education systems of Canada and the United States. Hence, the absence of the requisite skills to pursue this field of research is not peculiar to legal life writing, but affects socio-legal and law and humanities research too.[39] It also stems from the marginalization of historical research within the culture and institutional structure of the British socio-legal studies movement, in contrast to its counterparts in Australia, Canada, and the United Stateas.[40] One of the few exceptions to this tendency – and one relevant to our topic – is a shared and growing interest in the visual dimensions of law in legal history and socio-legal studies.[41]

The arrested development of legal biography should also be understood in the context of the problematic place of biography within the human sciences.[42] Academic regard for biography waxes and wanes over time; at least, within modern literary studies, biography is generally regarded as both popular and theoretically unexciting.[43] Some commentators have discerned a 'condescension towards biography ... For many ... biography seems a second-rate genre, beholden to its subject matter.'[44]

Furthermore, even when biographical source material is readily available, it may be fragmentary, elusive, scattered, and unreliable. There may be little

---

39 Compare H. Genn, M. Partington, S. Wheeler, *Law in the Real World. Improving Our Understanding of How Law Works* (2006).

40 The contrast is invidious: see, for example, J.K. Lowe, 'Radicalism's Legacy: American Legal History Since 1998' (2014) University of Virginia School of Law Research Paper.

41 See J.H. Baker, 'History of the Gowns worn at the English Bar' (1975) 9 *Costume* 15; R. Evans, *The fabrication of virtue* (1982); H.T. Dickinson, *Caricatures and the Constitution* (1986); A. Hunt, *Governance of the Consuming Passions: A History of Sumptuary Regulation* (1995); C. Douzinas and L. Nead (eds.), *Law and the Image* (1999); L. Mulcahy, *Legal Architecture* (2001); C. Graham, *Ordering Law: the Architectural and Social History of the English Law Court to 1914* (2003); P. Raffield, *Images and Cultures of Law in Early Modern England* (2004); D. Sugarman, 'Images of Law. Legal Buildings, "Englishness" and the Reproduction of Power' in *Rechtssymbolik und Wertevermittlung*, ed. R. Schulze (2004) 194; L. Moran, 'Judging Pictures' (2009) 5 *International J. of Law in Context* 255; P. Goodrich, *Legal Emblems and the Art of the Law* (2013); A. Musson, 'Visual Sources' in Musson and Stebbings (eds.) op. cit., n. 32, p. 264.

42 See M. Benton, *Literary Biography* (2009); T. Soderqvist (ed.), *The History and Poetics of Scientific Biography* (2007).

43 Autobiography tends to be regarded more highly than biography within modern literary studies, and has attracted scholarship addressing such issues as rhetoric, the use of linguistic models, and constructions of self-representation, rather than an emphasis on 'reality': see, R. Folkenflik (ed.), *The Culture of Autobiography* (1993).

44 C.E. Rollyson, *British Biography* (2005) 247.

14

or no surviving papers. Thus, biography and other legal life writing take us into a realm of evidential and interpretative uncertainty normally beyond the comfort zones of those trained in the certainties of the law. The connections, if any, between source material and lives are always complex and contradictory, and usually open to a welter of interpretations. And the reliability of sources such as private correspondence and interviews cannot be assumed. Whilst the reader expects:

> 'the truth' ... we know that that's a very complicated concept. There are always going to be things left out; there are always going to be things that are said differently by different biographers about the same person over a period of time.[45]

Life writing is perceived as an unstable and hybrid genre, incorporating as it does elements of both history and fiction writing. Biographies purport to be the life of the subject. However, they are the product of the biographies of the subject and the biographer. Thus, debate rages as to how much of the relationship between biographer and subject should be in the background, whether biographers should identify themselves closely with their subjects, and whether life writing is a branch of history or a branch of fiction, low voyeurism or moral education. For some, these questions necessarily lower the status of biography; for others, they are a refreshing badge of honesty, a healthy acknowledgement of the inevitable blurring of biography and autobiography, and that all life writing is a constructed narrative.

Biography has been criticized for inevitably simplifying a complex story, compressing and intensifying at a cost of rendering the story too smooth, so that alternatives, accidents, missed chances, and shading cease to count. It is a messy, eclectic, impure narrative form, often involving a contradictory assortment of approaches, and that there are as many kinds of biographies as there are lives.[46]

Conventional biography has struggled both to justify, and to transcend, the classically realistic biographies of yore in the face of those who entertain disturbing questions about conventional biographical practices:[47] 'self-reflexivity', the uncertainty over 'the real' and 'the fictional', ontological uncertainty, distrust of the structures of explanation – in short, post-modernism. Moreover, the increasing gulf between biography and the novel raises questions about what the contemporary reading public expects from its writers:

---

45 U. Vashist, 'The Life Biographic. An Interview with Hermione Lee' *The Literateur,* 21 June 2012, at <http://literateur.com/hermione-lee/>.

46 H. Lee, *Body Parts. Essays in Life-writing* (2005) 3.

47 M. Bradbury, 'The Telling Life' in *The Troubled Face of Biography,* eds. E. Homberger and J. Charmley (1988) 131; W.H. Epstein, *Recognizing Biography* (1987).

the novel and biography long co-habited within similar narrative structures . . . [Today, however,] the foregrounded story, the authorial presence, traditional chronological design, and the stately scene setting of the major biography are no longer typical of contemporary fiction.[48]

Life writing can be controversial, scandalous, and embarrassing – not least because it is often mixed up with personal loyalties, politics, and conflicting versions of history.[49] It almost invariably raises difficult issues of access to papers and persons, confidentiality, ethics, and acceptable tactics. Moreover, it may not be good for your academic career.[50] It is very time-consuming, labour-intensive, and expensive. Progress is often slow, especially where new approaches and new data are being explored. It fits ill within the current regime for assessing the quality of research at United Kingdom educational institutions.[51]

That biographers are regularly condemned and satirized as 'body-snatchers' by some of the lions of literature has also taken its toll. Henry James railed against 'post-mortem exploiters',[52] Kipling regarded biography as a form of 'higher cannibalism', Nabokov called them 'psycho-plagiarists', and Joyce had a horror of the 'biografiend'. Many have tried to have the last word on their posthumous reputations, the most popular method being to make a big bonfire. The most persistent arsonist was Sigmund Freud, who began consigning his personal papers to the flames at 29. 'As for biographers,' he said, 'I am already looking forward to seeing them go astray.'[53]

Of course, some of the giants of literature have also authored biographies and autobiographies. Moreover, life writing has undergone an enlargement of vision, adopting an increasing variety of perspectives, and addressing a larger range of sources than hitherto. It has been important in debates over subject and object, private and public, fact and fiction – debates which have

48 E. Homberger and J. Charmley, 'Introduction' in Homberger and Charmley, id.
49 Lee, op. cit., n. 46, p. 1.
50 'In the time [twenty years] that Gerald Gunther took to write his 818-page biography of Learned Hand, he might have written twenty (or probably more) law review articles averaging forty pages, and conceivably the contribution to legal scholarship would have been greater': R.A. Posner, 'Judicial Biography' (1995) 70 *New York University Law Rev.* 502, at 509.
51 This is likely to be the case for British scholars, given the Research Excellence Framework (REF), the new system for assessing the quality of research at United Kingdom educational institutions, and the role of 'impact' in assessing research excellence: see <http://www.ref.ac.uk/>. See, also, the brief but pointed comments of J. Baker, 'Reflections on "doing" legal history' in Musson and Stebbings, op. cit., n. 33, pp. 7–8. See, generally, P. Scott, 'Why research assessment is out of control' *Guardian*, 4 November 2013.
52 J. Stougaard-Nielsen, '"No absolute privacy": Henry James and the Ethics of Reading Authors' Letters' (2012) 1 *Authorship*, at <http://www.authorship.ugent.be/article/view/765/759>.
53 P. Theroux, 'The Trouble With Autobiography' *Smithsonian Magazine*, January 2011, at <http://www.smithsonianmag.com/arts-culture/the-trouble-with-autobiography-75464843/#kCy3BhjtG02zbf2G.99>.

16

proved especially important in feminist theory, including feminist theories of life writing. Indeed, autobiography has become a staple of feminist scholarship.[54] The excitement of biography and other life writing as a field of study is that it links together many different disciplines – including history, law, literature, sociology, feminism, race theory, queer theory, colonial and post-colonial scholarship, and cultural studies. Within each of these fields it explodes disciplinary boundaries and requires an understanding of other approaches, practices, and methods. It is an agent provocateur, difficult to pin down as a discrete genre, on the borderline of the public and the private, the academic and the popular, fact and fiction, the social and the personal, the literary and the everyday. Moreover, some of its supposed negatives – its hybridity; its instability; its relation to fiction; its inter-disciplinarity; its problematic status, theoretically and epistemologically; its somewhat different ideas of what a biography and other life writing is; that it is deeply rooted in the intellectual preoccupations of its moment of production; and that it challenges singular and stable notions of identity – can also be constituted as potential positives.

In the remainder of this article, I will indicate some of the ways that legal life writing has recently done more justice to its potential, and how that potential might be advanced and sustained.

III.

Lytton Strachey threw down the gauntlet when he turned the archetypal Victorian biography upside down in his classic, *Eminent Victorians.*[55] Challenging the dominant form of Victorian biography – 'Those two fat volumes, with which it is our custom to commemorate the dead'[56] – he gave a sense of the author and subject together, speaking directly to the reader rather than hiding in the background. His warts-and-all, psycho-logically-informed portraits revealed the complexities behind the men and women the public saw as saints and martyrs. Irreverence and wit were coupled with a sympathetic treatment of his subjects. And while he sought to puncture the pretensions of the Victorian age to moral superiority, he rejected the idea of fitting his subjects into a social or political theory. For Strachey, 'Human beings are too important to be treated as mere symptoms of the past.'[57]

Strachey conflated exemplary hagiographies and the protective practices of nineteenth-century 'Lives' with Victorian biography and, therefore,

---

54 L. Marcus, *Auto/biographical Discourses* (1994); T. Cosslett et al. (eds.), *Feminism and Autobiography* (2000).
55 L. Strachey, *Eminent Victorians* (1918).
56 id., p. 2.
57 id., p. 45.

17

understated the variety of life writing.[58] However, whilst he also gave posterity a licence to experiment with biography, few exercised it.[59] And when they did, they either did so cautiously and tentatively, or, were roasted for it. The spirit of Strachey rubbed off most on literary biographers,[60] who in a post-Freudian world, haltingly but increasingly focused on the public and the private aspects of a life, however revealing that might be. This contrasted with other disciplines and subjects, where perhaps expectations were more fixed, and where there appeared to be less leeway or variety in how a person's life is presented than in literary biography and the biography of obscure lives. Hence, the biographies of judges, lawyers, scientists, and allied professionals largely continued to focus on their subject's work – at least until the late twentieth century – by which time even the conventions of legal biography had changed. Monumental biographies of Holmes by G. Edward White and Learned Hand by Gerald Gunther[61] are good examples of the way judicial biographers in the 1990s strived to integrate the personal and the professional, even when this meant digging deep into the private lives of their subjects. Hence, Richard Posner in his review of the Learned Hand biography quipped that '[t]oday no biography can be thought complete without a chapter on sex'.[62] They also eschewed hagiography, adopting a realist perspective that punctured such romances, while advancing our understanding of the law.

By the mid-1990s, the renaissance of judicial biography in the United States was being actively touted,[63] since when the proliferation of judicial biography has extended to Australia and Canada.[64]

58 Warts-and-all biographies were advocated by Samuel Johnson and Thomas Carlyle: see Johnson, op. cit., n. 1 and T. Carlyle, 'Review', both reprinted in *Biography as an Art*, ed. J.L. Clifford (1962) 42, 82–3.

59 Historians have taken Strachey to task because he provided no references, used only secondary sources, and consulted no unpublished sources. Scholars have also made specific complaints about the sources he did use. Modern scholarship holds that some of these criticisms are well-founded, others less so. See, generally, M. Holroyd, *Lytton Strachey* (1994).

60 Such as biographies of poets, writers or playwrights.

61 G.E. White, *Justice Oliver Wendell Holmes. Law and the Inner Life* (1993); G. Gunther, *Learned Hand. The Man and the Judge* (1994). Their subtitles attest to the larger concerns and broader canvas that they adopted.

62 R. Posner, 'The Learned Hand Biography and the Question of Judicial Greatness' (1994) 104 *Yale Law J.* 511, at 518, cited by Kalman, op. cit., n. 22, p. 490.

63 G.E. White, 'The Renaissance of Judicial Biography' (1995) 23 *Rev. of Am. History* 716. While White detected a proliferation in the number of judicial biographies, Girard observed that the number of judicial biographies published in the United States, about three or four a year, had remained fairly constant over the last few decades and was largely devoted to Supreme Court judges: Girard, op. cit., n. 13, p. 88.

64 S. Burnside, 'Australian Judicial Biography' (2011) 57 *Australian J. of Politics and History* 221; on Canadian and Australian judicial biography, see Girard, id., pp. 97–106.

18

The principal approach currently adopted by American judicial biography is that of a branch of intellectual history.[65] Of course, the comprehensive study of a life opens up many layers of context and somewhat different ideas of what a biography is and who its audiences might be. Hence, judicial biography can contribute valuable depictions of a life in the law, judges as social beings, and can cast light on the law and the world beyond. Pnina Lahav's biography of Israeli Chief Justice Simon Agranat, is a case in point.[66] By exploring the interaction between Agranat's life and the larger context of the birth and development of the state of Israel, Lahav produces a wonderful portrait of a highly influential judge, and a nuanced interpretation of some of the key moments in the history of a nation, how they affected Agranat, and Agranat's impact on them.[67]

Not all judicial biography has adopted a nuanced approach to its subject matter.[68] In a review, Rande Kostal took aim at a biography of Canadian Supreme Court Chief Justice Brian Dickson, concluding that it was 'an up-market exercise in legitimation'.[69] He argues that Dickson's life is not critically evaluated so much as used to consolidate a political position. Every chapter and paragraph is calculated to convince readers of something external to the life and career of Brian Dickson, namely, that judicial review under the Charter is the most welcome innovation in Canadian politics since Confederation, and that the people should rest easy with the empowerment of elite judges.[70] Kostal brings a rare critical perspective to the enterprise of judicial biography, raising important and uncomfortable questions about the appropriate stance of scholarly biographers towards their subject matter, and the potential conflicts of interest arising from authorized biographies.[71] His comments echo those of historians in other fields, notably the history of

---

65 White recently described his conception of judicial biography as concerned, in part, with how a subject's life and work reflected the governing social and intellectual assumptions of various periods of American history: see 'Ted White Q&A: On Judicial Biography and "Great Man' History (or Not)?" (2012), at <http://legalhistoryblog.blogspot.co.uk/2012/03/ted-white-q-on-judicial-biography-and.html>.

66 P. Lahav, *Judgment in Jerusalem: Chief Justice Simon Agranat and the Zionist Century* (1997).

67 See G. Gunther, 'A Model Judicial Biography' (1999) 97 *Michigan Law Rev.* 2117; Kalman, op. cit., n. 22. Girard's award-winning portrait of Canadian Supreme Court Chief Justice Bora Laskin, while less a vantage point on a nation, nonetheless provides exceptionally well-contextualized accounts of the worlds of legal academia, labour arbitration, and the bench: P. Girard, *Bora Laskin* (2005).

68 See, for example, R. Kostal, 'Shilling for Judges' (2006) 51 *McGill Law J.* 199 and W. Kaplan, *Canadian Maverick: The Life and Times of Ivan C. Rand* (2009), both of which address Canadian judicial biography.

69 On the legitimation dimensions of biography, see M. Holroyd, *Works on Paper: The Craft of Biography and Autobiography* (2013).

70 Kostal, op. cit., n. 68, p. 208.

71 G.E. White, 'Authorized Judicial Biography: A Cautionary Tale' (2003) 7 *Green Bag* 2d 71.

19

science, who argue that historically insensitive writing perpetuates illusions about science, leading to utopian anticipations, and inevitable disappointment and misunderstandings.[72] In this regard, the field of legal biography would benefit from a consideration of the intellectual values, apart from historical ones, that can be adequately advanced by biographies, and the sort of biographies that would be required.

As was noted earlier, the recent renaissance of British legal biography has been largely directed at the lives and ideas of legal scholars, and, to a lesser extent, women lawyers. While the models underpinning this renaissance are varied, British legal biographers have tended to take their cue from the burgeoning field of biography, principally the biographies of British scholars[73] and literary figures, intellectual history, women's history, and feminism.

The earliest example of this new breed of legal biography – and the most important role model for subsequent biographies – is Nicola Lacey's *A Life of H.L.A. Hart*.[74] Lacey's biography of the most influential and widely-read British legal philosopher of the twentieth century gave its readers pause: the much-revered Hart turned out to have feet of clay, as she revealed aspects of Hart's life and work of which very few were aware. Hart was rendered strange and foreign, a mixture of 1950s Oxford and Woody Allen. Taking her cue from Ray Monk's biography of Ludwig Wittgenstein and Hermione Lee's *Virginia Woolf*,[75] Lacey illuminates the brilliance and the idiosyncrasy of her subject.[76] She gives us a cogent portrait of an archetypal 'tortured genius', and strives to demonstrate that Hart's ideas were shaped by his life, that his life was shaped by his ideas, and that his ideas and life were two sides of the same coin. In these respects, her approach echoes that of the best of recent American judicial biographies.

Other intellectual and personal influences are acknowledged by Lacey, including feminist theory, a more critical view of Hart's ideas, and a strong sympathy for Hart's wife, Jenifer.[77] Jenifer provided Lacey with unique access to Hart's unpublished diaries and letters to reveal intimate details about Hart's personal life, notably, the growing tensions in his marriage and his feelings about his sexuality. Lacey's close association with the Hart family, especially Jenifer,[78] and Hart's circle of friends, and the fact that

---

72 T.M. Porter and D. Ross, 'Introduction: Writing the History of Social Science' in *Cambridge History of Science, Vol. 7*, eds. T.M. Porter and D. Ross (2003) 1.
73 See, for example, K. Burk, *Troublemaker: The Life of A.J.P. Taylor* (2000); A. Sisman, *Hugh Trevor-Roper* (2009); F. Inglis, *History Man: The Life of R.G. Collingwood* (2011).
74 Lacey, op. cit., n. 17.
75 Monk, op. cit., n. 9; H. Lee, *Virginia Woolf* (1996).
76 Lacey, op. cit., n. 17, p. xix. For a valuable discussion of biography and intellectual elites, see S. Collini, *Common Reading* (2008) 283–98.
77 Lacey, id., pp. xvii–xx.
78 Lacey dedicated the biography to Jenifer Hart.

Lacey's was a de facto authorized biography[79] raised difficult issues, such as how successfully Lacey balanced engagement with detachment.[80] People will differ on whether and to what extent Hart's personal material, and the inner conflicts that they reveal, adds to our understanding of Hart's career (which it clearly does) and to characterizing his thought (where it seems to be of limited relevance).[81] Questions such as these demonstrate that a good biography is no easy undertaking. Despite the pitfalls and problems that confront biographers, especially those close to their subjects and their families, Lacey's achievement is considerable. As Hart's daughter, Joanna, observed:

> Lacey has succeeded not only in giving an accessible account of my father's work – which was a large part of my mother's motivation in wanting a biography written – but also in showing something of the complex emotional structures that underpinned and sustained his pursuit of philosophical knowledge.[82]

It is a biography that looks both inwards and outwards, bringing Hart's life and work, and the outside world, together.

IV.

Biography has played an important role in challenging the invisibility of women, the working classes and the poor, African-Americans, native peoples, post-colonial lives, queer and lesbian subjects, and minorities in history and society, and in speaking for hidden or alternative lives. These discrete genres of biography may of course overlap, and are changing rather than fixed entities. Today, they reflect the replacement of a single, authoritative version of the past with a multi-vocal alternative. We see authors, biographers, and institutions such as museums working on or with those previously silenced, spoken for or marginalized to reclaim ownership of their own and their communities' pasts.

---

79 In the sense that Lacey received the full support of Hart's family and enjoyed unique access to his personal papers.
80 T. Nagel, 'The Central Questions' (2005) 27(3) *London Rev. of Books* 12; G.E. White, 'Getting Close to H.L.A. Hart' (2005) 29 *Melbourne University Law Rev.* 317.
81 See Collini, op. cit., n. 76, p. 293. For differing answers to these questions see, for example, Nagel, id.; J. Ryan, S. Blackburn, and J. Waldron, and Nagel's response, all in 'Letters' (2005) 27(4) *London Rev. of Books* 17; A.W.B. Simpson, 'Stag-Hunter and Mole' *Times Literary Supplement*, 11 February 2005, 6–7; L. Green and B. Leiter, 'H.L.A. Hart and *The Concept of Law*' *Times Literary Supplement*, 11 March 2005, 15; A.W.B Simpson, 'H.L.A. Hart and *The Concept of Law*' *Times Literary Supplement*, 25 March 2005; L. Green and B. Leiter, 'H.L.A. Hart' *Times Literary Supplement*, 15 April 2005.
82 Ryan, id.

21

In the case of women's history, the biographical turn grew out of a feminist concern with recovering the many untold histories of women's lives, challenging historical assumptions about separate spheres and domestic priorities, and with highlighting 'difference' – that writing the lives of men and women is different. Biography has proved central in recovering the lives of the first women lawyers, judges, and law teachers, in exploring the contexts in which they gained admission to the world of the law, and the obstacles, challenges, choices, and possibilities that they confronted. A key theme in such work recently is that everything about practising in the law and beyond is affected in important ways by gender. Not only obvious matters like women's relations to the private sphere of the family, but everything – the market for clients, the definition of commitment, human, social, and cultural capital, legal education, job searches, shoptalk, and dress.

The use of biographies to give voice to those who have not been heard has been inspired, in part, by 'history from below' or social history, that seeks to take as its subjects ordinary people, and concentrate on their experiences and perspectives. Probably its most notable exemplar is E.P. Thompson's *The Making of the English Working Class*,[83] of which there are at least three aspects that are of potential value to legal life writing. First, it described the pressures of economic exploitation and political harassment that the poor experienced on a daily basis not as a series of generalizations, buried by terms such as culture and class, but itemized as a form of moral respect in order to appreciate the kinds of courage and sheer endurance needed to sustain others' lives. Secondly, it emphasized that the making of people and classes is an active process that owes as much to human agency as to conditioning. Thirdly, and perhaps most importantly, there is the famous statement of intent: to rescue those people whose experiences did not form part of orthodox historical accounts of the early-nineteenth century from the 'enormous condescension of posterity'.[84] The fact that their kind and what they stood for might be dead or dying, and that some of them would now be regarded as having been backward-looking, does not mean we should ignore them, for: 'In some of the lost causes of the people of the Industrial Revolution we may discover insights into social evils which we have yet to cure.'[85]

At some periods, women, Catholics, and Jews were barred from reaching the bench; in the case of women, few were able to receive the requisite

83 E.P. Thompson, *The Making of the English Working Class* (1963).
84 id., p. 13. See, further, H.J. Kaye, *The British Marxist Historians* (1984) 167; R.W. Gordon, 'E.P. Thompson's Legacies' (1994) 82 *Georgetown Law J.* 2005. See, also, Luke Fowler's excellent film documentary on Thompson, 'The Poor Stockinger' (2012).
85 Thompson, op. cit., n. 83, p. 13.

22

training. Lingering official prejudice extended well into the twentieth century and possibly continues still.[86] A history-from-below perspective has contributed to legal biographies on women,[87] 'failed', 'deviant', and 'outsider' judges, lawyers,[88] court and allied officials, litigants,[89] prisoners,[90] and law professors[91] – those individuals who because of their gender, class, race, religion, politics, and sexuality were excluded from the higher reaches of the legal community. Thus, biographical and allied work has begun to address the early history of women lawyers and law students, and the lives of lawyers who challenged the status quo.

Other approaches to legal life writing have further extended the character of legal biography in order to recover a view of the past that would otherwise be lost. Group biography is a case in point. The form is ancient, embraced by the likes of Plutarch[92] and John Aubrey.[93] The more 'scientific' version is called prosopography.[94] This form of collective biography investigates features of a group, such as servants, explorers, and clog dancers, that the researcher has determined has something in common (profession, social

---

86 R. Stevens, *The Independence of the Judiciary* (1993).
87 M.J. Mossman, *The First Women Lawyers* (2006). On Canada, see, for example, T. Roth, 'Clara Brett Martin' (1984) 18 *Law Society Gazette* 323; C.B. Backhouse, '"To Open the Way for Others of my Sex": Clara Brett Martin's Career as Canada's First Women Lawyer' (1985) 1 *Canadian J. of Women and the Law* 1; C.B. Backhouse, *Petticoats and Prejudice: Women and Law in Nineteenth-Century Canada* (1991). On England see, for example, Auchmuty, op. cit., n. 17; Polden, op. cit., n. 33. On the United States, see, for example, B. Babcock, *Woman Lawyer: The Trials of Clara Folz* (2012); for a searchable database on pioneering women lawyers in the United States and women's legal history, see <http://wlh.law.stanford.edu/>.
88 Thus, Wes Pue's pioneering research casts light on those barristers who threatened to expose the seamier side of the Bar in the mid-nineteenth century, and who were, therefore, ostracized by the profession: W.W. Pue, 'Exorcising Professional Demons: Charles Rann Kennedy and the Transition to the Modern Bar' (1987) 5 *Law and History Rev.* 135 and 'Rebels at the Bar' (1987) 16 *Anglo-American Law Rev.* 303. Other rebels proved more successful. Elliot Johnston, the first known member of the Communist Party of Australia to become a Queens Counsel, and later a Justice of the Supreme Court of South Australia, is the subject of Penelope Debelle's biography, *Red Silk* (2012). See, likewise, leftist barrister D.N. Pritt QC, *Autobiography* (1965–66) 3 vols.
89 Compare D. Watkins, 'Recovering the Lost Stories of Law' (2013) 7 *Law and Humanities* 68.
90 Compare P. Gready, *Writing as resistance: life stories of imprisonment, exile, and homecoming from apartheid South Africa* (c. 2003).
91 L. Star, *Julius Stone* (1992).
92 Plutarch, *Parallel Lives of the Noble Greeks and Romans*, a series of biographies of famous men, arranged in tandem to illuminate their common moral virtues or failings, written in the late first century.
93 J. Aubrey, *Brief Lives* (1680–1693).
94 See L. Stone, 'Prosopography' (1971) 100 *Daedalus* 46, which includes a classic treatment of the pitfalls and limitations of prosopography.

origins, and so on) by means of a collective study of lives. It has proved a valuable adjunct to the history of the legal profession,[95] and, to a lesser extent, to the history of the judiciary.[96] Of course, the nature and scale of the quantitative data can prove daunting – even in the age of super-fast computers. Moreover, prosopography has traditionally focused on the quantitative, rather than the qualitative, and has therefore tended to neglect or de-emphasize the intellectual, philosophical, and cultural dimensions of the group under scrutiny.[97] Certainly, it used to be thought rather dusty and academic but now 'group lives' are thriving as a popular and mould-breaking biographical genre.[98] The current tendency is to address a few lives to reveal a past we might otherwise overlook. Women figure prominently in this genre, both as authors and subjects: Norma Clarke[99] reclaims unsung female intellectuals of the eighteenth century by investigating the lives and writings of six leading female authors Dr Johnson knew well and regarded highly, their relationships with Johnson, with each other, and with the world of letters and the restrictions, obstacles, and opportunities available to women of talent in the eighteenth century; Patricia Fara[100] pairs women scientists with better-known brothers or husbands to demonstrate that while women may have been excluded from the traditional historical record, they were not excluded from scientific activity in the eighteenth century, despite the pronouncements of those who declared women were unscientific.

A theme can unite a group biography, as in Sebastian Faulks's study of three heroic failures.[101] Faulks was inspired by the hint that 'young or short lives are more sensitive indicators of the pressure of public attitudes than lives lived long and crowned with honours'.[102]

The second form of group history is the study of the tangled lives of small sets of people such as the Peabody Sisters (who were in many ways America's Brontes, and who played a central role in fashioning the thinking of their day);[103] the Bloomsbury Set;[104] and the Metaphysical Club, the

---

95 See, for example, D. Duman, *The English and Colonial Bars in the Nineteenth Century* (1983); W.R. Prest, *The Rise of the Barristers* (1986); E.W. Ives, *The Common Lawyers of Pre-Reformation England* (1983); J.H. Baker, *The Men of Court 1440 to 1550, 2 vols.* (2012). See, also, M. Stuckey, 'Antiquarianism and legal history' in Musson and Stebbings, op. cit., n. 32, pp. 223–7.

96 See Duman, id.

97 See D.J. Ibbetson, 'Common Lawyers and the Law before the Civil War' (1988) 8 *Oxford J. of Legal Studies* 142, at 147–8.

98 See, generally, J. Uglow, 'Writing Group Biography' (2005), at <http://www.jennyuglow.com/?page=Agroup> to which I am especially indebted.

99 N. Clarke, *Dr Johnson's Women* (2005).

100 P. Fara, *Pandora's Breeches: Women, Science and Power in the Enlightenment* (2004).

101 S. Faulks, *The Fatal Englishman: Three Short Lives* (1996).

102 Cited in Uglow op. cit., n. 98.

103 M. Marshall, *The Peabody Sisters* (2006).

104 L. Edel, *Bloomsbury* (1979); S.P. Rosenbaum, *Victorian Bloomsbury* (1987); Holroyd, op. cit., n. 59.

24

crucible out of which a new American philosophy, pragmatism, was constructed in the aftermath of the publication of Darwin's *Origin of Species* and the Civil War, to help people cope with the conditions of modern life.[105]

Inevitably, the family, in all its shapes and sizes, has figured prominently in such group histories. In the case of Annette Gordon-Reed's acclaimed, *The Hemingses of Monticello: An American Family*,[106] the sting is in the subtitle. This 'American family' is not the stereotypical 'American family' – white, wholesome, and centred on a married couple. Instead, Gordon-Reed's family are black slaves (the Hemingses) owned by Thomas Jefferson – an American Founding Father, principal author of the Declaration of Independence (1776), third President of the United States (1801–1809), and prominent Enlightenment figure. Jefferson had a long-standing sexual relationship with his slave, Sally Hemings, and was probably the father of all six of her children.[107] Since Gordon-Reed had already played a significant role in marshalling the evidence for Jefferson's paternity of some or all of Hemings's children,[108] the question now was what to make of it. By reconfiguring the story as an American family history, Gordon-Reed not only rescues the Hemings family from relative obscurity, and problematizes what we mean by 'family' in America, but also challenges the tendency to separate white/black/mixed race, slavemaster/slaves, and the 'founding fathers'/politics/law/social history of slavery. This family story is one that embraces black slaves and their white master as kin inhabiting the same house and the same history. Building on recent scholarship that regards the sexual politics of slavery as a constitutive aspect of the regime, *The Hemingses of Monticello* provides a unique opportunity to understand American slavery.

Gordon-Reed recognizes that 'The medium of biography is problematic in the context of slavery.'[109] So too is social history. 'For African Americans social history almost invariably overwhelms biography'; nevertheless:

> there is, in fact, no one context to consult in regards to Sally Hemings: she lived many ... the circle of her mother and siblings, her extended family, the larger enslaved community at Monticello, her community in Paris, his white family, and, finally, her own children.[110]

Transcending the confines of group biography, the *Hemingses of Monticello* is at once a group biography, a family history, a history of women, a legal history of slavery in Virginia, and a social history of a plantation.

---

105 L. Menand, *The Metaphysical Club* (2001).
106 A. Gordon-Reed, *The Hemingses of Monticello: An American Family* (2008).
107 A DNA study of 1999 confirmed a genetic link between Jefferson and Hemings descendants.
108 A. Gordon-Reed, *Thomas Jefferson and Sally Hemings: An American Controversy* (1997).
109 id., p. 83.
110 id., pp. 290–1.

Group biographies add further to our knowledge of, and sensitivity to, alliances and networks – local, national, and international – and to the ways they can be energizing, facilitative, and supportive, as well as elitist, exclusionary, and oppressive. Sometimes group biography adds something new and unexpected as well as complementing what we thought we knew. It is a genre that attracts because, as one historian put it:

> I have always thought that the linear idea of biography is limiting and not 'true to life', and people are defined by many of those who surrounded them – so accounts of siblings, classmates, groups of friends are just as illuminating as the single life.[111]

Of course, the difficulties that apply to biographies of single lives also apply to the writing of multiple lives – perhaps even more so. The relevant evidence is likely to be more unmanageable, producing an elegant but focused narrative may be more difficult, and there are also the inevitable imbalances of sources as between individuals within the group. The broken threads and loose ends that afflict all life writing are likely to be compounded.

That group lives can deepen our understanding of law's connection with society is evident from Kenneth Mack's *Representing the Race*.[112] He presents a poignant collective biography of the intersecting lives of African-American civil-rights lawyers during the era of segregation, and the dilemmas they faced in winning power and respect when that struggle required that African-American lawyers who claimed to or were thought to speak for, stand in for, and advocate for the interests of African-Americans were expected to seem as unlike the rest of their race as possible and to 'represent the core identity'[113] of the white-dominated, and almost entirely male, legal profession. Mack chronicles this paradox, beginning in the mid-nineteenth century, through the twentieth, and its persistence into the twenty-first.

While Mack's subjects embrace famous figures, they also offer fascinating portraits of many little-known African-American lawyers, such as Pauli Murray, a black woman who seemed neither black nor white, neither man nor woman, who helped to devise sex discrimination as a legal category; and Loren Miller, a mixed-race lawyer who, after realizing in college that he was

---

111 S. Tillyard, quoted in Uglow, op. cit., n. 98.
112 K.W. Mack, *Representing the Race: the Creation of the Civil Rights Lawyer* (2012). My discussion of this book relates only to its pertinence to legal life writing and socio-legal studies. For a more wide-ranging discussion see, A.V. Alfieri and A. Onwuachi-Willig, 'Next-Generation Civil Rights Lawyers: Race and Representation in the Age of Identity Performance' (2013) 123 *Yale Law J.* 1484; R. Goluboff, 'Lawyers, Law, and the New Civil Rights History' (2013) 126 *Harvard Law Rev.* 2312, and the response of K.W. Mack, 'Civil Rights History: the Old and the New' (2013) 126 *Harvard Law Rev.* 258; M. McCann, 'The Personal is Political: On Twentieth Century Activist Lawyers in the United States' (2013) 49 *Tulsa Law Rev.* 485.
113 Mack, id. (2012), p. 6.

26

black, became a Marxist critic of the 'legalism' of his fellow black lawyers, found himself broke, became a Democrat, and reconnected with those fellow black reformers he had previously repudiated.

One of the virtues of Mack's book is the serious attention it affords those civil-rights lawyers who failed, professionally and socially, as well as those who succeeded, and the ways their failure was both illuminating and important. Rather than traditional preoccupations with the appellate 'test case' litigation and 'high law' culminating in *Brown*,[114] Mack focuses on the experiences and practices of black civil-rights lawyers in ordinary legal practices coming face to face with white judges and lawyers mostly in lower courts. Mack's 'bottom-up' focus underpins his thesis that the law – or, more accurately, lawyers – construct race. It is a lens that is likely to engage socio-legal scholars concerned with: legal pluralism; the gulf between the law in the books and the law in action; 'cause lawyers' and the tensions they experience between doing good for their clients and doing good for themselves, in terms of status and material rewards;[115] and those who investigate 'legal consciousness', that is, people's routine experiences and perceptions of law in everyday life.[116] The tensions and frustrations that Mack perceives are probably generalizable to many different 'outsider' rights activists, such as lawyers for women, racial minorities, gay and lesbian communities, immigrants and the poor, as well as lawyers faced in balancing the demands of their professional and other identities. Mack's attempt to shed new light on the problem of representation echoes the contribution of feminist and allied scholars on the dilemmas of the politics of recognition.[117]

This kind of work demonstrates that ideas themselves are social. It also points to some of the ways in which biography and allied forms of life writing have sought to transcend an authorized collective memory, frequently linked to a linear narrative of progress, and render biography, and allied life writing, a site of pluralism and inclusion.

The space opened up by autobiography has been grasped by poor and ordinary people, women and people of colour and other minorities, thereby furthering the democratization of life writing. Critical race theory[118] has distinguished itself from conventional legal criticism by insisting on the

114 *Brown* v. *Board of Education*, 347 U.S. 483 (1954).
115 S.A. Scheingold and A. Sarat, *Something to Believe In: Politics, Professionalism and Cause Lawyering* (2004).
116 McCann, op. cit., n. 112. See, also, S.E. Merry, *Getting Justice and Getting Even: Legal Consciousness among Working-Class Americans* (1990); P. Ewick and S. Silbey, *The Common Place of Law: Stories from Everyday Life* (1998); D.M. Engel and F.W. Munger, *Rights of Inclusion* (2003); D. Cowan, 'Legal Consciousness: Some Observations' (2004) 67 *Modern Law Rev.* 928.
117 N. Fraser, 'Rethinking Recognition' (2000) 3 (May–June) *New Left Rev.* 107; N. Fraser and A. Honneth, *Redistribution or Recognition?* (2004); McCann, id., p. 492.
118 See G. Minda, *Postmodern Legal Movements* (1995) ch. 9; R. Dalgardo, *Critical Race Theory* (2012).

importance of auto/biography in shaping legal doctrine and practice.[119] Many critical race theorists have utilized biography and autobiography as literary devices in their criticism in order to demonstrate the relationship between form and content in legal thought. Taking its cue from American legal realism and critical legal studies, critical race theory contends that the person who makes a legal decision shapes legal doctrine and its application, and that legal discourse obscures how biography shapes their acts of judgement and their application of legal ideals. Critical race theorists have deployed auto/biography to make visible the hidden racial subjectivities that structure legal discourse and the false objectivity of American law. In perhaps the most well-known work in this genre, *The Alchemy of Race and Rights*,[120] Patricia Williams repeatedly reminds us that '[s]ubject position is everything in ... [the] analysis of the law.'[121] Abandoning the disembodied 'neutral' voice of conventional scholarship, she injects autobiographical accounts in an attempt to convey the complexity of her identity and exist-ence, exploring the terrain in which racism and gender oppression flourish, and sifting through her experiences to refine and expand our understanding of the processes through which race and gender oppression become estab-lished. Original and disquieting as this work is, it nonetheless raises difficult issues about the basis upon which scholarly assessment can be conducted: do we judge it as legal analysis or literature or both – especially given Williams's repudiation of traditional scholarly categories as well as the very idea of objectivity itself? In my view, it should not matter whether we characterize such work as memoir or law. The real question is whether work of this sort 'provokes us to think about old problems in new ways'.[122] This it certainly does.[123]

V.

The movement to enlarge the subjects, sources, and methods of auto/biography is most evident in the increasing popularity of 'life writing', a term embraced by Virginia Woolf,[124] but which did not take off until the 1990s, when the first life-writing courses were established,[125] and particu-

---

119 The 1980s and 1990s saw the rise of identity politics in the United States, and a surge in the number of creative and challenging autobiographical writings by people of colour: see, for example, D. Bell, *Confronting Authority* (1994).
120 P. Williams, *The Alchemy of Race and Rights* (1991).
121 id., p. 3.
122 L.S. Greene, 'Breaking Form' (1992) 44 *Stanford Law Rev.* 909, at 915.
123 Moreover, it has inspired other African-American female law professors, and others similarly situated, to give voice to the complexities of their lives on the record.
124 Lee, op. cit., n. 75.
125 The first life-writing course commenced at the University of York in the early 1990s, and was started by acclaimed biographer, Hermione Lee.

28

larly since the inception at the end of the 1990s of the first centres for life-writing research.[126]

Whilst at first blush the shift from auto/biography to life writing appears little more than an exercise in rebranding, life writing involves, and goes beyond, biography. It is a wide-ranging field, pluralistic in its approaches, agendas, and narratives and less constricted by convention than conventional biography and history writing. It brings together people interested in all aspects of narrative and all forms of auto/biographical representation. It uses life story as a primary source for the study of history and culture. It encompasses everything from the complete life to the day-in-the-life. It embraces the lives of objects and things (from cities, deities, and diseases to the River Thames and the Bayeux Tapestry) and institutions as well as the lives of individuals, families, and groups. While views differ on its nature and scope, life writing increasingly includes biography, autobiography, memoir, letters, diaries, personal essays, obituaries and eulogies, anthropological data, oral testimony, eye-witness accounts, visual images, and digital forms, such as blogs and email. It is not only a literary or historical specialism, but is relevant across the humanities, the social sciences, and the sciences.[127]

Life writing reflects changing attitudes to censorship and privacy, the rapid expansion of online access to a cornucopia of information, old and new, from Poor Law records and census data to the records of London's Central Criminal Court,[128] and the huge appetite for, and prevalence of,

---

126 The first United Kingdom centres on life writing were established at Sussex University in 1999 and Kings College, London, in 2007. Other life-writing centres now include the Centre for Life Narrative, Kingston University, London; the Centre for Narrative and Auto/Biographical Studies, University of Edinburgh, and the Oxford Centre for Life-writing. Amongst the leading centres beyond the United Kingdom are the Centre for Biographical Research, University of Hawai'i at Mnoa, and the Ludwig Boltzmann Institut für Geschichte und Theorie der Biography [History and Theory of Biography], Vienna. The principal periodicals in the field are very recent: *Life Writing* (2004); *Lifewriting Annual. Biographical and Autobiographical Studies* (2010); and the *European J. of Life Writing* (2012). See, further, A. Light, 'Writing Lives', *Cambridge History of Twentieth-Century English Literature*, eds. P. Nicholls and L. Marcus (2004) 751.

127 Recent areas of interest in life-writing studies include the relation of biography to scientific discovery. Life writing is also an integral part of studies relating to the Holocaust, genocide, testimony, confession, gender, memorialization and the politics of memory struggles, and apartheid.

128 'The Old Bailey Online' is a fully searchable edition of the largest body of texts detailing the lives of non-elite people ever published, containing 197,745 criminal trials held at London's central criminal court, at <www.oldbaileyonline.org>. See, also, T.G. Ashplant, 'Writing the Lives of the Poor' (2014) 3 *European J. of Life Writing* 1 on a joint Anglo-German project to construct an online corpus of letters and petitions written by paupers appealing for help (1770–1914), texts which reveal what the poor knew about the law and its administration; and P. Carter and N. Whistance, 'The Poor Law Commission: a New Digital Resource for Nineteenth-century Domestic Historians' (2011) 71 *History Workshop J.* 29. The latter details

history and confessional writing in wider culture – in the best-seller charts, TV, radio, and film, museums, memoir, and family and local history – and the transformation in the ways in which history is presented in these media. In some of its guises, life writing and the metamorphosis of museum presentation that has paralleled it, address the 'democratization' of life writing, and of mainstream museums, through social and cultural diversity, the representation of multiple perspectives, and reaching out to new communities. In this vein, it is about the democratization of the past.

The principal British sources on life writing[129] testify to its disparate nature and its efforts to engage with a greater variety of audiences and stakeholders. The topics examined[130] reveal life writing as an unruly category of narrative. It not only fills in gaps left by academic history, but it creates new evidence and concerns which may challenge academic or public policy narratives. It raises questions about what kinds of evidence count and how they should be analysed. And if evidence does count, how should it be brought into play and by whom? If it does not count, how might this be

the rich contents of 105 volumes of poor law union correspondence which were recently catalogued and digitalized, making it much easier to examine the administration of the workhouse system, developments in public health, crime, neglect and ill-treatment of paupers, Chartism and trade union matters, and much more. For an overview of recent uses of digital sources in the history of crime, see T. Hitchcock and R. Shoemaker, 'Digitalising History From Below: the Old Bailey Proceedings online, 1674–1834' (2006) 4 *History Compass* 1. See, generally, S. Alexander and A. Howkins, 'Digital Sources, Access and "History of a Nation"?' (2011) 71 *History Workshop J.* 1.

129 These sources include the British Library's National Sound Archives, which collects audio and videotaped interviews as well as carrying out its own programme of life-story recordings and includes a multitude of links to oral history organizations, archives, and project groups worldwide; the Mass-Observation Archive, a collection of writing by ordinary people about their experiences gathered from 1937 to 1949 and resumed in 1981, which has inspired novelists, documentaries, and a wealth of other publications; the Museums and Galleries History Group (MGHG), which promotes the study of the history and theory of museums and galleries, acts as a forum for considerations of the place of museum history within academic discourse, and its importance for current museum practice; and the Centre for Historical Record, Kingston University, London, which promotes collaborative research, knowledge exchange, and discussion between historians, archivists, curators, heritage providers, and the public.

130 Topics examined by researchers working in this genre include: 'The Making of Mr Gray's Anatomy – Biography of a Medical Textbook'; 'Autobiography and Film Adaptation'; 'The House as Self: Sir John Soane's Autobiography on Lincoln's Inn Fields'; 'Portraiture and Life Writing'; 'Academic Autobiography as Women's History: On the Intersection of Life, Scholarship, and the Disciplines'; 'The Master and the Apprentice: Identity Formation and Inculcation in the Autobiographical Novel'; 'Moving Forward by Looking Back: The Work of Autobiography in Adult Education'; '"Unlike actors, politicians or eminent military men": The Meaning of Hard Work in Working Class Autobiography'; 'Global Subjects. The Transnationalisation of Biography'; and 'Why Life Writing is Impossible'.

challenged? How do you ensure the quality of the history presented, and what do you mean by 'quality'?

Nonetheless, life history's varied intellectual agendas, its pluralism of approaches and narratives, its truth seeking, its diligence, its demythologizing, and its openness to other disciplines reflect the strengths of history in Britain and elsewhere today. What emerges from good life writing is a multi-layered, enormously complicated, interlocking picture of life stories that throws up the unexpected. The fractured lives of individuals and societies expose the rents in conventional life histories, notions of the family and family life, and challenge the founding stories of a 'nation', provoking a reworking of the past.[131] That these life stories have a popular as well as a historical resonance is evidenced by series such as 'Who Do You Think You Are?',[132] 'Secrets from the Clink',[133] and 'Voices of the Old Bailey'.[134]

VI.

So far I have largely focused on text-based material. But life writing also embraces the biographies of objects. This new focus directs attention to the way human and object histories inform each other; that objects do not just provide a stage setting to human action, but are integral to it; and that objects can have lives of their own.[135] Object biographies raise substantial methodological issues regarding narrative, structure, and chronology; the representation of change and improvement; the influence of objects in human lives, communities, and material history; and museum management.[136] They also interrogate the fundamental concept of 'life'. The popular success of *The Hare with Amber Eyes*,[137] which traces the journey of the carvings Edmund de Waal inherited through the generations of his family against the

131 Alexander and Howkins, op. cit., n. 128.
132 BBC 1, at <http://www.bbc.co.uk/programmes/b007t575>.
133 ITV, at <http://www.itv.com/presscentre/ep1week32/secrets-clink>.
134 BBC Radio 4, at <http://www.bbc.co.uk/iplayer/episode/b01380pf/Voices_from_ the_Old_Bailey_Series_2_Whose_Law_Is_It _Anyway/>.
135 A. Appadurai (ed.), *The Social Life of Things* (1986); C. Gosden and Y. Marshall, 'The Cultural Biography of Objects' (1999) 31 *World Archaeology* 169; L. Daston, *Biographies of Scientific Objects* (2000); S. Connor, *Paraphernalia: The Curious Lives of Magical Things* (2011); M. Kurlansky, *Salt: A World History* (2003).
136 K. Hill (ed.), *Museums and Biographies: Stories, Objects, Identities* (2012) examines for the first time biography – of individuals, objects, and institutions – in relation to the museum, casting new light on the context of museums of biography and autobiography, institutional biographies, object biographies, and museums as biographies/autobiographies.
137 E. de Waal, *The Hare with Amber Eyes* (2010). See, also, P. Byrne, *The Real Jane Austen: A Life in Small Things* (2013) which demonstrates the objects connected to Austen's life offer revealing insights into her inner thoughts.

31

backdrop of twentieth century history, and Neil MacGregor's *A History of the World in 100 Objects* and *Germany: Memoirs of a Nation*[138] suggest an intriguing new template for legal scholarship.[139]

While lawyers and law teachers regard law as principally text-based, it has a richer existence in the world. It is often developed, conveyed, and authorized through objects or images. From the symbolic to the mundane, law can be found in the objects around us. Similarly, the practice of law often relies on material objects or images, both as evidence and to ground authority. The biography of objects raises questions about what objects, rather than texts, tell us about the law and legal institutions, how legal objects are used to construct identity, and law's role in constituting particular spaces of possibility and constraint, and as a means of cultural construction.[140]

VII.

In this article, I have suggested that legal life writing is a heterogeneous field that offers new ways of advancing legal history and socio-legal scholarship, and of encouraging inter-disciplinary dialogue, both between them, and also with other fields and audiences. Legal historians and socio-legal scholars could learn from their colleagues involved in life writing, expand their skill-set, and embrace a wider range of participants and audiences, including librarians, archivists, curators, heritage providers, and the general public, thereby enhancing their ability to communicate and engage with public issues and public history.

Legal life writing has the potential to enhance many of the primary types of inquiry undertaken by legal historians and socio-legal scholars, including legal pluralism, rights consciousness, racial identity, citizenship, and the state. Moreover, its intellectual promiscuity – its interest in almost everything – enables life writing to transcend these concerns and speak to a broader version of 'law' and 'society' than is often used in legal and socio-

---

138 N. MacGregor, *A History of the World in 100 Objects* (2010), see <http://www.britishmuseum.org/explore/a_history_of_the_world.aspx>; N. MacGregor, *Germany: Memoirs of a Nation* (2014). MacGregor is Director of the British Museum and both books were successful BBC Radio 4 series.

139 It is a new genre that can build upon the growing interest in the visual dimensions of the law evident in both legal history and socio-legal scholarship referred to earlier in this article. See, also, J. Resnik and D. Curtis, *Representing Justice* (2011).

140 Amanda Perry-Kessaris constructed a mini virtual tour of objects at the British Museum exploring the theme of the 'rule of law'. The tour was based on the British Museum/BBC History of the World in 100 Objects project. See, also, J. Lezaun, 'The Pragmatic Sanction of Materials: Notes for an Ethnography of Legal Substances' (2012) 39 *J. of Law and Society* 20. A workshop, 'International Law's Objects: Emergence, Encounter and Erasure through Object and Image', will be hosted at Queen Mary, University of London, in April 2016.

32

legal studies, thereby enriching both the 'socio' and the 'legal' in socio-legal studies.[141]

Legal life writing enables us to reveal lives that we would never know if we refused to look beyond conventional notions of legal history, biography, and socio-legal studies. It can also provide a vital means of exploring the ways in which certain kinds of law and legal discourses and practices functioned for the English people as a form of covert political thought. It both grants us a privileged position from which we are able to look back at ourselves, and reminds us of the value of historical thinking as a means to comprehend law, politics, and culture, thereby providing a valuable supplement to the study of law.[142]

Finally, in questioning assumptions about the form of biography, emphasizing that form is as important as content, inspired in part by fiction writing, life writing suggests more vibrant alternatives to academic and other conventional writing, and that truthfulness and elegance can be finely poised.[143]

---

141 In his otherwise positive review of D. Feenan (ed.), *Exploring the 'Socio' of Socio-Legal Studies* (2013), Alan Hunt observed that: 'What is missing is the historical dimension' (in (2014) 41 *J. of Law and Society* 484, at 485).

142 The inter-disciplinary study of law and literature is of obvious relevance: see in I. Ward, *Law and Literature* (1995) and P. Hanifan, A. Geary, and J. Brooker (eds.), *Law and Literature* (2004).

143 The following is illustrative of this concern to explore different ways of telling a life story. Hermione Lee structured her biography of Virginia Woolf thematically, instead of chronologically. Lucy Hughes-Hallett's biography of Gabriele D'Annunzio, *The Pike* (2012), is written so as to give due weight to the contiguous but unconnected strands of life, and tries to avoid a homogeneous narrative. F. Prochaska, *The Memoirs of Walter Bagehot* (2013), is an imaginative reconstruction of the memoir Bagehot might have written, drawing on the author's extensive knowledge of Bagehot's life and his writings. Colm Tóibín and David Lodge have both published lightly fictionalized biographies of Henry James: C. Tóibín, *The Master* (2004); D. Lodge, *H.G. Wells, A Man of Parts* (2011). Not all these approaches have been well-received. In his *Lives in Writing* (2014), for example, Lodge defends the notion of 'bio-fiction', that is, lightly fictionalized life, in response to the critical response to his work on H.G. Wells.

JOURNAL OF LAW AND SOCIETY
VOLUME 42, NUMBER 1, MARCH 2015
ISSN: 0263-323X, pp. 34–52

Recovering Lost Lives: Researching Women in Legal History

Rosemary Auchmuty*

*Drawing on the research I undertook into the life of Gwyneth Bebb, who in 1913 challenged the Law Society of England and Wales for their refusal to admit women to the solicitors' profession, this article focuses on the range of sources one might use to explore the lives of women in law, about whom there might be a few public records but little else, and on the ways in which sources, even official ones, might be imaginatively used. It traces the research process from the case that inspired the research (*Bebb v. *the Law Society [1914] 1 Ch 286) through to the creation of an entry in the* Oxford Dictionary of National Biography *and what this means for women's history, emphasizing the importance of asking the 'woman question' and seeking out the broader significance of a woman's life in the context of her times.*

There are very few biographies of legal women in the United Kingdom. This is partly because very few such women have been considered important enough to merit the conventional type of study, based on their contribution to public life, but also because women's legal history has also not, until recently, been considered important enough for academic study. Para-doxically, what this really meant was that it was *too* important, for to reveal women's legal history too clearly would be to uncover the many mechanisms by which men have retained power for themselves in law and to give the lie to the vaunted equality of opportunity for men and women. Today, fortunately, no scholar need apologize for focusing on women; the problem is, rather, the paucity of information about those legal pioneers, for whom records have not been kept precisely *because* their lives were deemed

* *School of Law, University of Reading, Foxhill House, Whiteknights Road, Reading RG6 7BA, England*
r.auchmuty@reading.ac.uk

unimportant. This means we have to be imaginative in our search not only for source material but actually for women subjects to research, and to ask different questions of the public records that do survive and have been written up in the past.

As Karen Tani puts it, the task of historical scholarship is

> to continually assess and re-assess significance; to take existing categories and orderings and reconstruct them, so that raw data, new and old, becomes meaningful to today's consumers. It is especially the task of historians of women, since their data is so often cast into the 'unimportant' bin.[1]

Painstaking research by Patrick Polden,[2] Anne Logan,[3] Hector MacQueen,[4] and others has uncovered the names of many of the 'firsts' among English and Scottish legal women but, as they found, naming them is just the start; in trying to reconstruct what it was like to *be* one of these pioneers, and to fill in the context of their lives – not simply the public struggles and achievements but also, if possible, the private ones – the source problem is magnified a hundredfold, for *personal* records are so rarely kept. Even sizable archives like that of Helena Normanton (early woman barrister and contemporary of Miss Bebb) contain no personal papers.[5] Mary Jane Mossman's *The First Women Lawyers*,[6] which compares the experiences of early women lawyers in the United States, Canada, England, New Zealand, India, and some continental jurisdictions, benefited from a reasonably wide range of public sources, while for her North American case studies she was assisted by an increasing body of doctoral dissertations on early women lawyers. Nevertheless, the amount of effort in recovering these stories was prodigious and she had to ask different questions from the usual 'tale of progress' to reach the uncomfortable conclusion that admission to the legal profession was the *start*, rather than the *end*, of women's struggle for equality.

For what I actually found out about Miss Bebb, I refer readers to the substantive article in *Legal Studies*.[7] In brief, she studied law at Oxford, worked for some years in government service, brought the test case against the Law Society, married, and had a child, all the while playing an active role in a well-organized, persistent, and very public campaign (about which

1 K.M. Tani, 'Portia's Deal' (2012) 87 *Chicago-Kent Law Rev.* 569.
2 P. Polden, 'Portia's Progress: Women and the Bar, 1919–1939' (2005) 12 *International J. of the Legal Profession* 293–338.
3 A.F. Logan, 'In Search of Equal Citizenship: the campaign for women magistrates in England and Wales, 1910–1939' (2007) 16 *Women's History Rev.* 501–18.
4 H. MacQueen, 'Scotland's first women law graduates: an Edinburgh centenary' in *Miscellany VI: Stair Society* (2009) 221–65.
5 J. Bourne, 'Helena Normanton and the Opening of the Bar to Women', unpublished PhD thesis, University of London (2014).
6 M.J. Mossman, *The First Women Lawyers: A Comparative Study of Gender, Law and the Legal Professions* (2006).
7 R. Auchmuty, 'Whatever happened to Miss Bebb? *Bebb v The Law Society* and women's legal history' (2010) 31 *Legal Studies* 199–230.

the institutional histories are totally silent) for the admission of women to the legal profession, eventually won in 1919. But she died before she could be called to the Bar[8] and this accounted for her disappearance from history.

The present article focuses on the *method* and *process* of undertaking a biography of this type when the sources are elusive or absent, as is so often the case with women. It begins with a consideration of case law as a historical source, since my own research started thus. While legal scholars are uniquely qualified to understand the legal reasoning behind a judgment (something often misunderstood or ignored by non-legally-trained historians), they are apt to forget that judgments are products of their time, as susceptible of historical analysis as any other primary source (Who is speaking? For what purpose? Who is the audience? What is the context?). The article then considers how the biographer might move from the case to other, sometimes unexpected, sources, and how these sources can – indeed, *must* – be creatively used in order to elicit information not always apparent on their face, or able to be extrapolated or conjectured across to one's subject. It concludes with an assessment of the *significance* of this kind of biographical study, which extends above and beyond the telling of an individual life.

STARTING FROM THE CASE

My research was inspired by a case: *Bebb* v. *the Law Society*.[9] It is sometimes mentioned in history books but with little detail or context. The Court of Appeal decision is easy enough to find; it was reported in both the Law Reports and the Times Law Reports. Characteristically for the time, the reports are is quite short, though counsels' main arguments are included and all three justices pronounced. The summary of facts tells us nothing about the plaintiff except that she was a 'spinster', a description repeated faithfully by my students, with all its misleading connotations – Miss Bebb was 23 years old at the time – and, less forgivably, by Manchester in his *Modern Legal History*.[10] The Master of the Rolls mentions in his judgment that Miss Bebb was 'a distinguished Oxford student' (a clue to the biographer) '– and at least equal to a great many, and probably, far better than many, of the candidates who will come up for examination,[11] but', he adds, 'that is really not for us to consider. Our duty is to consider and, so far as we can, to ascertain what the law is, and I disclaim absolutely any right to legislate in a matter of this kind.'[12] In that disclaimer, of course, lies the reasoning behind

---

8 As Patrick Polden established (op. cit., n. 2), but he did not investigate the cause of death, which formed the basis of my own interpretation of her life.

9 *Bebb* v. *the Law Society* [1914] 1 Ch 286.

10 A.H. Manchester, *A Modern Legal History of England and Wales 1750–1950* (1980) 70.

11 As I subsequently discovered, she had a first from Oxford.

12 *Bebb*, op. cit., n. 9, p. 294.

36

the outcome. His fellow-judges agreed: 'We are not here to say what should be the law', Phillimore LJ states. '... Our function is to declare the law.'[13] Neither he nor Swinfen-Eady LJ says anything about Miss Bebb.

The era before the First World War is widely-regarded as a conservative one for judicial law-making.[14] J.A.G. Griffith, however, argued forcefully that judges in all periods have demonstrated judicial creativity when they wanted to and, further, that the notion of judicial neutrality is a myth.[15] Certainly, the spirited arguments of Miss Bebb's counsel, Lord Robert Cecil KC, suggest that a different outcome was not inconceivable. He drew on precedents of women in public life, persuasive practice in other common law jurisdictions, and the wording of the statute under consideration – section 2 of the Solicitors Act 1843 – which mentioned 'persons', and section 48, which said that words importing the masculine gender were to be taken as applying also to women. In her comparative study, Mary Jane Mossman notes that the same precedents were used by judges in other common law jurisdictions to justify *opening* the profession to women.[16] The fact that a woman was willing to challenge the law in England, and the fact that leave to appeal was granted, indicate that there was some will for change. People do not present themselves as test cases out of the blue. They nearly always represent a wider constituency, one that enjoys a measure of support and probably organization. In 1912, first-wave feminism was at its zenith, with a strong and active suffrage movement and votes for women seemingly just around the corner. I was keen to discover more about Miss Bebb and her associates and how she fitted into all this.

BIOGRAPHY IN JUDGMENTS

I am not the first person (it goes without saying) to want to find out more about the story behind a case. Brian Simpson famously explained how, confronted by the very first case he read as a law student,[17] his curiosity about the context stood in the way of his comprehension of the legal principle. Questions piled up in his mind:

> Who were these men? What on earth were they doing in the South Atlantic in a yacht? Why did it founder? Why did they not keep quiet about the whole affair, given the fact that the principal evidence against them had been consumed? Why just six months' imprisonment? What became of them afterwards? *Only, it seemed to me, by answering these questions could this weird case be undertood* (my emphasis).[18]

13 id., p. 297.
14 See, for example, R. Stevens, *Law and Politics: The House of Lords as a Judicial Body 1800–1976* (1978).
15 J.A.G. Griffith, *The Politics of the Judiciary* (2010, 5th edn.) part 3.
16 Mossman, op. cit., n. 6, p. 278.
17 *R* v. *Dudley and Stephens* [1884] 14 Q.B.D. 273.
18 A.W.B. Simpson, *Leading Cases in the Common Law* (1995) 9.

37

He noted, however, that this reaction – almost instinctive for a legal historian – was at odds with the prevailing legal pedagogy. Richard Ireland confirms:

> As lawyers, we often lose the people behind the law, the circumstances and personalities in the intensely personal dramas which eventually lead to the headnotes of our authorities. The more personal and contextual details, as Simpson reminds us, we are taught to consider as legally irrelevant.[19]

Law teachers who practise a socio-legal approach are torn. On the one hand, we try to wean our students away from the superfluous retelling of facts every time they apply an authority to a problem. On the other, we want them to be able to situate case law in its social and political context, if only to show how cases may be distinguished and the law developed. What matters, of course, is *which* facts are emphasized, and what is done with them.[20] A further problem is that many of the facts a biographer or historian might be interested in are not, in fact, those highlighted (or even mentioned) in the case report.[21]

The suppression of superfluous or 'irrelevant' facts in the study of case law arises from the attempt, which began towards the end of the nineteenth century with the production of the first law textbooks, to impose a form of scientific logic on the development of the common law. Legal reasoning became a process of finding (and, in some cases, writing back into past decisions) an evolving legal principle, while paring down the facts of cases to the bare distinguishable (or not) elements. It is easy to see why this happened: more and more cases were being decided, law reports were correspondingly more voluminous and comprehensive, legal education was expanding, and legal academics were trying to establish law as a subject for university study rather than simply a practical apprenticeship. The whole tenor of Victorian life was, in any case, conducive to the scientific approach. There is no denying that the appearance of textbooks greatly facilitated students' learning of law but the effect was to over-simplify, confuse and, at times, obliterate the historical context which had contributed to legal decisions and developments. When we look at some of the textbooks on the market today we can see this process of reducing law to an exact science raised to the highest and most regrettable level.

---

19 R.W. Ireland, 'Sanctity, superstition and the death of Sarah Jacob' in *Making Legal History: Approaches and Methodologies*, eds. A. Musson and C. Stebbings (2012) 300.

20 For a discussion of the importance of fact telling for feminists, see R. Hunter, 'An account of feminist judging' in *Feminist Judgments: From theory to practice*, eds. R. Hunter, C. McGlynn, and E. Rackley (2010) 36 and, for the application of these principles, see the judgments contained throughout this volume.

21 It is also true that the court and/or the report might get the facts wrong. See R. Auchmuty, 'The Fiction of Equity' in *Feminist Perspectives on Equity and Trusts*, eds. S. Scott-Hunt and H. Lim (2001); D. Watkins, 'Recovering the lost human stories of law: Finding Mrs Burns' (2013) 7 *Law and Humanities* 68.

That said, the omission of 'irrelevant' facts was not simply a textbook technique; it was also characteristic of the judgments of the time. The Court of Appeal judgments in *Bebb* illustrate this tendency. While facts have played a greater or lesser role in legal decision making at different periods and at the hands of different judges, it is clear that the more scientific the court's approach (that is, the more the judge simply applies the 'relevant' principle), the fewer facts will be revealed and the less we will be told about the particular circumstances of the litigants.

There are two reasons for this. First, giving details of the claimants' lives and situation is likely to engender empathy, if not sympathy, making an unfavourable verdict harder to deliver and justify. No wonder, then, that judges might avoid the uncomfortable detail. Second, information of this sort often serves to highlight the gap between the assumptions behind the principle relied upon and the reality on the ground, and thus raise doubts as to the suitability or justice of the principle itself. In Miss Bebb's case, for instance, the principle which caused her challenge to fail was the one that said that women had always been barred from public office. Yet Miss Bebb in the very year the case was heard, in 1913, was working (as I subsequently discovered) as an Investigating Officer for the Board of Trade, in which role she brought prosecutions against employers in the sweated trades. In other words, she was employed in the public sector doing exactly what a qualified solicitor would do. This went unmentioned in the judgment, lest the outcome be too clearly revealed as senseless and contradictory.

By way of comparison, let us briefly consider the use made of biography and context by that master of legal narrative, Lord Denning. Denning was a great judge partly because his knowledge of the law was so extensive he could conjure up a precedent for every result he wished to reach, but partly for his ability – and willingness – to advance the law in situations where he believed this would procure justice. His technique of starting his judgments by situating the parties and their actions in the context of their place and time marked a break from the earlier practice of ignoring biography and context, and it enabled Denning to do precisely what the judges in *Bebb* could not and would not do: to develop the law by (a) engaging sympathy for the unjustly-treated claimant (Denning by his own account single-handedly revived the equitable jurisdiction)[22] and (b) exposing the contradiction between a legal principle based on a particular conception of society and the reality of people's social circumstances at that moment in time. This helps to explain why Denning contributed so significantly to the development of rights for women in the 1960s and 1970s, because women's situation changed so profoundly across the twentieth century, beginning with the advances of the

---

22 Lord Denning wrote many wonderfully expressive accounts of his life and role in law making. See, among others, 'The rights of women' in his *The Changing Law* (1953) 79–98; *The Due Process of Law* (1980); and *The Family Story* (1981).

first-wave feminist movement of which Miss Bebb was part, and continuing with those of second-wave feminism which precipitated so many women into the courts during Denning's time as Master of the Rolls.

Here is one example, offered simply to show how, in different times and with different judges, Miss Bebb's case could have been decided differently. In *Williams & Glyn's Bank* v. *Boland*, Templeman J found the idea that Mrs Boland might have an overriding interest against the bank impossible in law and impracticable in practice (it would have 'almost catastrophic effects', he warned).[23] Lord Denning in the Court of Appeal, however, deftly disposed of these objections by exposing, while never actually saying so, the fact that Templeman's real objection was to the idea that women might have separate interests in the home from their legal-owner husband's. Such a notion was inconceivable to judges comfortable with the traditional image of breadwinner husband and dependent wife that had dominated British society up to the 1950s.

Noting the finding by both Stamp J in *Caunce* v. *Caunce*[24] and Templeman J in *Boland* that lenders cannot be said to have notice of occupying wives, Denning says:

> I profoundly disagree. Such statements would have been true a hundred years ago when the law regarded husband and wife as one; and the husband as that one. But they are not true today.[25]

And of course they were not. Mrs Boland, as Denning explained at the outset, was a nurse, married for 20 years to a builder. Both husband and wife worked (they had only one child) and both had contributed to the purchase of the home in dispute, as well as to a previous one. Denning sets out these facts at the very start (Templeman tells us absolutely nothing about Mrs Boland except that she is Mr Boland's wife) so that later he can reach a radical new understanding of the law by demonstrating that the denial of rights to women in her situation is contrived, out of step with modern circumstances (not to speak of common sense) and, indeed, unfair.

Let us now consider one more aspect of Denning's judgment technique, which demonstrates more than that of any other judge except, perhaps, Lady Hale, how biography and context can work for women litigants. Just as he generalizes from the individual litigant to women as a group, so Denning sometimes uses the reverse technique, starting from the general and ascribing this to the particular. While this is obviously very effective as a rhetorical device, it also enabled him to fill in gaps in the facts – the very

---

23 *Williams & Glyn's Bank* v. *Boland* (1978) 36 P & CR 448, at 454
24 *Caunce* v. *Caunce* [1969] WLR 286.
25 *Boland*, op. cit., n. 23, p. 560. This reference to the doctrine of coverture, largely abolished by the Married Women's Property Act 1882 (literally, almost a hundred years before), show all too clearly how old values die hard with those who benefit from them.

40

technique I was to use when trying to fill in the gaps in Miss Bebb's life. Templeman J, for example, observed in the lower court that Mrs Boland could have protected herself by entering a spouse's right of occupation (referred to as a Class F charge) on the Land Register. Lord Denning, not knowing precisely why Mrs Boland had not done so (but a clue may lie in the fact that this right only became available to wives with a beneficial interest in the property *after* the property in dispute had been purchased),[26] instead generalized as to how women like her *would have* behaved:

> But that amendment was of precious little use to her, at any rate when she was living at home in peace with her husband. *She would never have heard of a Class F charge: and she would not have understood it if she had.*[27]

This is patronizing, perhaps, but effective and, what is more important, probably *true* – and it is also, of course, the reason why overriding interests were introduced into the Land Registration Act 1925 in the first place: to protect those who would not think of registering their right. But the point I wish to make in this article is that sometimes, in trying to construct a life of someone for whom few records are available, the biographer may have to conjecture from the general to the particular.

GETTING BEHIND THE CASE

> Once you begin to ask intelligent questions about cases, questions directed to understanding the case as a historical event, it is fairly obvious that you have to seek for answers in sources other than law reports ...[28]

I wanted to find out more about Miss Bebb – her family background, her Oxford experience, her role in the trial, and her later life. So – where to start? The obvious place would be the Register of Births, Deaths, and Marriages at St Catherine's House, and to follow up with visits to the archives of her Oxford college, the Law Society, and her Inn of Court. But the truth is that, these days, we tend to go first to the internet, and this is what I did. Websites provide a valuable forum for genealogists, local history societies, independent researchers, and bloggers to publicize their work, in addition to leading us to published books, articles, and archives. But they need to be treated with

---

26 The ability to register a spouse's right of occupation was introduced in the Matrimonial Homes Act 1967, but applied only to wives with no interest in the property. Section 38 of the Matrimonial Proceedings and Property Act 1970 extended the right to wives with a beneficial interest. The Bolands, however, had bought their house in 1969. Moreover, Mrs Boland thought the property had been registered in joint names, as their previous home had been. Nothing was said in the report as to why she thought this. We can infer that, as in *Caunce* (op. cit., n. 24), neither the bank nor her husband had bothered to tell her.

27 *Boland*, op. cit., n. 23, p. 556, my emphasis.

28 Simpson, op. cit., n. 18, p. 10.

caution. The same ideas, the same stories get repeated endlessly and we can easily fall into the trap of seeing this as corroboration. Often it is not; it's just the same, possibly mistaken, source being repeated again and again – as I found. The story of Miss Bebb's legal challenge to the Law Society has been retold so often that I thought, writing my article, that I could skim over this bit – that a brief summary of what happened would do. In fact, although I called it 'a brief summary', the account ran to two pages because what was in the public domain seemed to me so misleading. This meant that, before I even embarked on finding out about my subject's life beyond her legal action (my initial goal), I had to check the facts of the case itself and revise existing accounts of the campaign that led to it. Even the public records had been misrepresented, and that was before I even got to the private ones!

This brings us to the second consideration of the legal biographer, which is equally crucial. Without sources, you can't really say much that is authoritative about your subject; but, even with them, you won't produce anything worthwhile unless you *ask the right questions* of your sources. Many short biographical studies – articles, say, like the one I was writing – present the known facts of the subject's life but fail to consider the questions that might immediately occur to the reader. Questions like, What was it *like* to be in that situation? How would that event have affected that person? In the absence of any direct reference, many scholars are loathe to 'speculate' (as they see it); and critics can be scathing about assertions like 'she must have …' or 'she would have …' (a criticism which, incidentally, never bothered Lord Denning).

So we have two problems: our 'facts' are not always true, as published accounts may be wrong, and our conjectures may not be founded in 'fact' – so we end up with maybe two sentences: birth, death, and a few achievements in between that can be conclusively 'proved' to have happened.

How biographers deal with these two considerations depends fundamentally on what their aims are in tackling this particular life. It is why one account can differ so greatly from another; it is why history is often described as a 'dialogue between the past and the present'; and it is why we train research students to come up with a research question. What do you want to find out? What is the issue for *you*? It isn't 'all I know about X' for a biography any more than it is for an answer to an exam or coursework question.

In my case, the research question was the title of my article: 'Whatever happened to Miss Bebb?' If you read any history of the English legal professions, she will probably rate a mention – or her case will – but that will be it. One mention; then she's gone. Now women get little enough attention in institutional histories, but Helena Normanton, Ivy Williams, other feminist pioneers – we can construct lives for them from other available sources.[29]

29 Both have entries, with attached references, in the *Oxford Dictionary of National Biography* (*ODNB*), at <www.oxforddnb.com>.

Miss Bebb, however, was just a case name. I didn't even know her first name when I started; she didn't appear in the *Oxford Dictionary of National Biography* or *Who's Who*. But even once I discovered this, and something about her background and education, I still could not understand why more was not heard of her subsequently. So I set myself the task of finding out.

ASKING QUESTIONS THAT MATTER

I do think that telling the story of any human being's life is worth doing, especially a woman's, since women have been (as Sheila Rowbotham put it in her pioneering book more than 40 years ago) *Hidden from History*[30] for so long. But a life on its own is not always interesting in itself; sometimes I read an account and think (I am sorry to say), '*So what?*' Individual life accounts are useful source material for social historians who can aggregate experiences and make generalizations or offer them as examples, but they are not necessarily fascinating on their own.

After some research, I was able to establish why Miss Bebb disappeared from legal history. She married, so she changed her name; then she died before she had qualified as a lawyer, so she dropped out of the story altogether. So I answered my question.

But was this enough? No – the 'So what?' question remained. But by then I knew enough about her life to be able to make a bigger argument about women's place in history generally. Once I found out that she had died in childbirth, I recognized that, unlike most other pioneer professional women who had been able to pursue their careers largely because they did not marry (like Ivy Williams) or did not have children (like Helena Normanton), the fact that Miss Bebb had wanted both a career and a family was actually her undoing. The penalty she paid for this choice, which men did not have to make, was not simply a professional but a biological one. She died because women, unlike men, bear babies, and because maternal health care was not a high priority in early twentieth-century Britain. Mothers suffered, mothers died; maternal mortality, though sad, was routine. In this sense, then, Miss Bebb stood for a much larger group of women, because what happened to her happened *because she was a woman*. Indeed, everything in her life was different *because she was a woman*. Different from what? From the normal human story – the usual history of the professions or public life: *the story of the male experience,* a world in which women were excluded or treated differently, and into which we were eventually subsumed, as if nothing had happened.

So one of the questions any historian or biographer must ask (whether researching a male or female figure) is the *woman question*. You must ask,

---

30 S. Rowbotham, *Hidden from History: 300 Years of Women's Oppression and the Fight Against It* (1973).

does this statement, law or situation apply to both sexes or only to men? If to both, how would their experiences of the same phenomenon be different? If only to men, where are the women? What was happening to them?

Miss Bebb, for example, was among the second generation of women who were admitted to Oxford. In theory, she could have had the same education as men; she certainly had the same teachers and sat the same exams. But of course her experience of Oxford was totally different from the men's. She lived in a small, poor women's college (which was nevertheless an intensely stimulating environment for a girl at the time). She got her first, but could not be awarded a degree. She studied law, but could not become a lawyer. We are fortunate that the editorial policy of the multi-volume *History of the University of Oxford* has been to include women at every point; this is one secondary source that responded to feminist critics, and I found it invaluable for details of degree courses, personnel, and university and college practices.[31] But the sweep is so broad that one cannot rely on it for specifics – in particular, what was it like for Miss Bebb? She wrote no accounts of her life: no diaries, no memoirs. Where can we look for source material for women's 'different' experience, where none appears to exist?

EXPLORING THE RANGE OF SOURCES

I became interested in Miss Bebb as a consequence of research I did on early women law students at Cambridge and Oxford.[32] In the course of *that* research I discovered that there had originally been four prospective litigants against the Law Society, all Oxbridge law students or ex-students, and Miss Bebb was chosen (for reasons we can only conjecture at) to bring the test case. I followed up all four but, where the other three women's careers could be established with relative ease, Miss Bebb's life – apart from that brief appearance – eluded record. This piqued my interest.

The former Women's Library in London, now relocated to the London School of Economics, holds the scrapbooks of two of her fellow-litigants, Nancy Nettlefold and Maud Ingram.[33] A record not only of the celebrated case but of the entire campaign for women's entry into the profession, these collections of newspaper cuttings, invitations, programmes, and transcripts are a wonderful resource, immediate and moving. Not all biographers will have access to such a scrapbook or to private papers containing such

---

31 See, for example, J. Howarth, '"In Oxford but ... not of Oxford": the women's colleges' in *The History of the University of Oxford. Vol VII: Nineteenth-century Oxford, Part 2*, eds. M.G. Brock and M.C. Curthoys (2000) 248.

32 R. Auchmuty, 'Early women law students at Cambridge and Oxford' (2008) 29 *J. of Legal History* 63.

33 Later Mrs Crofts. She became a solicitor and wrote *Women Under English Law* (1925).

materials, but it must be stressed here that newspapers, both national and local (and sometimes trade journals too), are among the most useful and valuable sources available to us. Newspapers tell us what is *news* and, crucially, they tell us how it is presented to the public – with all the errors, misunderstandings and biases of which we must be conscious, as in all sources. They may offer rare photographic glimpses of your subject, while cartoons, editorial comments, and letters to the editor provide critical viewpoints. We are fortunate in this electronic age that more and more newspapers are being indexed and made available online.

But the problem with the Women's Library scrapbooks was that they only took Miss Bebb's story up to 1920, when women were admitted to the legal profession. To find out about the rest of her life, I sought out the birth, death, and marriage certificates of Miss Bebb and her daughters. These are the building blocks of biography and, in the case of the marriage and death certificates, were to provide the essential clues to Miss Bebb's fate. But taking such sources on their own, in the absence of amplifying diaries, letters or reminiscences, sets up a rather individualized narrative. Poor Miss Bebb, what bad luck, she died in childbirth. A personal tragedy.

Of course it wasn't just like that. She died because of a public failing: her medical care was poor. It was poor because there was no National Health Service then and, crucially, because maternal health was not a government priority. It was poor because, even though the condition she died from was known and doctors might have been able to save her, she chose to have her baby in a nursing home (as middle-class women did) rather than a public hospital. I found statistics in Jane Lewis's still unsurpassed account of women in England at this period[34] comparing the maternal mortality rate in middle-class Chelsea and working-class Hackney; the survival rate was better in Hackney, precisely because public hospitals were staffed by honorary consultants who knew what they were doing. I used these to extrapolate that the risk for middle-class women in childbirth, unlikely as it might seem, was actually *higher* than for their working-class sisters at this time. Thus Miss Bebb is not just one unlucky individual but, in this situation, one of many people against whom the scales were weighted in terms of both gender *and* class.

I use this example to illustrate the technique I used for filling out the bare details of Miss Bebb's life. With no personal records to turn to, I fell back on context. This is where asking the right questions intersects with finding useful sources. Throughout my account, I kept asking myself: What would it have been *like* for her? You can never really get inside your subject, and I certainly never felt that Gwyneth Bebb and I had much in common beyond our gender and our feminism. But I could still try to reconstruct her life in the context of the society in which she moved.

34 J. Lewis, *Women in England 1870–1950* (1984) 117–18.

45

Many years ago I wrote a chapter in a book on lesbian history entitled 'By Their Friends We Shall Know Them'.[35] Lesbian history was in its infancy then, a product of second-wave feminists' call for sexuality to be freely chosen (the seventh demand of the Women's Liberation Movement) and its insistence that sexuality was socially constructed, not inborn. Lesbian feminists recognised that patriarchal societies were sustained by what Adrienne Rich termed 'compulsory heterosexuality'[36] which included, alongside the categorization of homosexuality as deviant and perverted, the suppression of all knowledge of same-sex relationships and non-heterosexual lifestyles in the past. My chapter was a study of women's friendship networks in Lambeth, where I lived at the time, intended to demonstrate that if you could identify some lesbians in history and then studied who they socialized with (these were all women in public life so there were plenty of sources for their lives), you could formulate a pretty good idea of which other women were lesbians at the time, in the absence of other evidence. If one woman lived with another, but had previously lived with a different woman who now lived with ... that sort of thing. I was not concerned to 'prove' anything, rather, to suggest possibilities excluded in past accounts.

I used the same technique for Miss Bebb. If I couldn't find out anything first-hand about her, I would investigate her associates; and they might cast light on her own circumstances. I could *extrapolate* from what they said about the context in which she moved, to *conjecture* what her own experience might have been.

For her schooldays there was nothing; the school no longer exists. But an Oxford women's college at that time is a goldmine, because the colleges all have extensive archives. Not only that, but the women's colleges, like the men's, were populated by outstanding women, many of whom became prominent in public life and wrote memoirs or had biographies written about them. It was not difficult to find half a dozen accounts of life at the Oxbridge women's colleges in this period (there was also an institutional history of St Hugh's itself, which did not mention Miss Bebb) and I used these to try to reconstruct atmosphere, customs, and rituals. For her law studies, which were shared with the men students, there were biographies of legal scholars to draw on (Holland, Dicey, Geldart, Vinogradoff and, especially, Holdsworth), as later there were biographies of the judges in the *Bebb* case and the leading politicians in Parliament (such as Lord Buckmaster and Lord Robert Cecil) who endorsed or opposed the various reforming Bills. The *Oxford*

---

35 R. Auchmuty, 'By Their Friends We Shall Know Them: The lives and networks of some women in North Lambeth, 1880–1940' in Lesbian History Group, *Not a Passing Phase: Reclaiming Lesbians in History 1840–1984* (1989) 77.
36 A. Rich, 'Compulsory heterosexuality and lesbian existence' (1980) in her *Blood, Bread and Poetry: Selected Prose 1979–1985* (1996) 23.

Dictionary of National Biography, with its helpful bibliographies, was a constant resource, for one entry led often to another. For instance, I discovered that Violet Markham, with whom Miss Bebb worked in the National Service for Women during the war, was a close friend of Jack Hills,[37] the solicitor MP who introduced the 1913 Bill to open the solicitors' profession to women in the wake of the failed court case. Another connection was Sybil Campbell, later to become the first woman professional magistrate,[38] who worked with Miss Bebb at both the Board of Trade and the Ministry of Food and became godmother to her daughter Diana.

I am sure that these connections are not accidental. Nor was it accidental that Miss Bebb went to work after finishing at Oxford with Clara Collet at the Board of Trade. It was not just that her legal talents would have been useful for the work; I feel sure that Miss Bebb must have known Miss Collet, because Miss Collet had studied law herself (at University College) and was a friend of one of the first women law students at Cambridge, who had been at school with her. The feminist world was a small one; probably everyone knew, or knew of, everyone else. This is important because advances for women are so often presented as the result of *individual* effort or, worse, concessions from above with no feminist input whatsoever.

In attempting to reconstruct Miss Bebb's experiences as a student at an Oxford women's college I drew on another type of source often overlooked by historians: fiction. 'College novels' form a distinct literary subgenre for both adults and young people, and those written for girls were at their most fashionable in the very years that Miss Bebb was at university. Elsewhere I have argued[39] that, while of course one must treat fiction as critically as any other source, the fact that it is 'not true' does not mean it can't be of assistance to the historian in capturing aspects such as shared assumptions, customs, and the atmosphere of the time and place. The background for girls' college novels was in any case always carefully researched by professional writers like L.T. Meade (the most popular writer for girls of the period) or, in other cases, drawn from the writer's own experience of college life.[40]

Be imaginative, then; look around the subject; immerse yourself in the culture and society of your period. Legal scholarship is too prone to cut itself off from the historical roots of our contemporary situation by confining itself to formal, abstract, stylized, dehumanized even, conventional legal sources. As law and literature scholars have long argued, literature can shed light on law since both are products of the same society and both are sources for its history.

---

37 Jack Hills's entry in the *ODNB* does not mention his support of women's entry into the legal profession. It focuses instead on his contribution to fly-fishing!
38 P. Polden, 'The Lady of Tower Bridge: Sybil Campbell, England's first woman judge' (1999) 8 *Women's History Rev.* 505–26.
39 R. Auchmuty, 'The Woman Law Student and the Girls' College Novel' (2007) 19 *Can. J. of Women and the Law* 37.
40 See, for example, L.T. Meade, *The Girls of Merton College* (1911); Mrs S. Stevenson, *Hilary: the Story of a College Girl* (1920).

47

Sir John Baker, doyen of English legal historians, has written: 'The historian, like the lawyer, has to find something above and beyond the sources – a story, a changing institution, or an evolving idea'. He goes on:

> We must have stored in the backs of our minds numerous questions arising from our own reading of the secondary literature, from our knowledge of what went on in other periods and places, and above all from the sources themselves. As we uncover more evidence, and try to sift out what is useful, we are simultaneously relating it to our older questions and formulating new ones, until now and again we see enough light to propose some answers. We never produce final answers, but we help to take the general understanding forward.[41]

This is true too for the biographer. However difficult and time-consuming the process of uncovering sources to piece together a life (and there is no denying that non-historians frequently underestimate and undervalue the effort involved in simply doing this), the end result is of little use unless the life is ascribed a significance. That is not to say that only the great figures of public life deserve to be recorded for posterity, as used to be received wisdom; ordinary people, people in the private sphere, people whose lives never came to anything much (all of which might be said of Miss Bebb) may still tell us something over and above the details of their own existence. Indeed, with some public figures whose biographies have been told, the significance lies not so much in how they carried out their public role as in how they got there in the first place. What did it take for X to reach the bench, or Y to become the first whatever it was? Sometimes the story is one not of merit and personal achievement but of political intrigue, family connections, or choices based on compromise. This is, regrettably, particularly true of many who have risen to positions of judicial or legislative power in this country.

When she came to edit *The Macmillan Dictionary of Women's Biography*,[42] Jenny Uglow (distinguished biographer of women) noted how difficult it was to select candidates, given that public achievement was the usual criterion for inclusion in a volume of this sort, when women had been so excluded and marginalized from public life. Obviously, some women *had* made their mark, and they were the people of whom biographies had been written or whom one might find in a standard history or reference work. They had to go in, but others were chosen because, although often omitted from those very histories, they had advanced women's position, so often considered irrelevant in mainstream accounts. Uglow also decided to include two other categories of woman, those who embodied stereotypes (such as witches and film stars) and those who had become legends, for whatever reason. She recognized that in putting together this motley bunch

---

41 J. Baker, 'Reflections on "doing" legal history' in Musson and Stebbings, op. cit., n. 19, p. 16.
42 J.S. Uglow (ed.), *The Macmillan Dictionary of Women's Biography* (1982).

48

she was not 'presenting a book which was representative of women's achievements' but 'compiling a book of deviants'.[43]

But even women in public life have private lives too, and those of us who seek to write more extended studies than the entries in a reference book do not have to focus on the one to the exclusion of the other. One of the things I appreciated about the recent biography of pioneer woman judge Rose Heilbron by her daughter was the space devoted to the subject's private life, particularly insightful when produced, as here, by a close family member.[44] Indeed, when writing about professional women in an era when women were constructed as responsible for domestic matters, one cannot really ignore the effect of this ideology on, on the one hand, their personal strategies for negotiating the two portfolios and, on the other, the opposition they faced from traditionalists who would exclude them from the public sphere altogether. From Miss Bebb to Rose Heilbron to today's aspiring young women lawyers, the struggle is the same, and this makes women's legal biography very much a dialogue between past and present.

CREATING HEROINES

Uglow described two motivations for researching women. The first, given women's exclusion or marginalization from historical accounts, is the need purely for information ('who were the women involved, where did they qualify, what did they go on to do'). The second, quite different, was 'a request for heroines'.[45] Women, she explained, did not always want to see themselves portrayed as 'passive victims'; heroines were especially important for young people, lest they grow up believing, as some of us were educated to believe, that only men had achieved – or could achieve – anything in public life.

Law, of course, is notorious for constructing women as passive victims (except where it wants to suggest they 'asked for it'), so we cannot be surprised when our students are affected by this bias. But the truth is that we have precious few legal heroines out there, and our students need to understand that this is largely because women *have* been victims – not always passive ones – of a system of patriarchal power massively stacked against us, not simply in terms of what we achieved (or not), but also in terms of how our achievements have been recorded (or not).[46] When I write my historical work I always have my students in mind – students for whom, as I realized recently when writing about the 1970s, I might as well have lived in the

---

43 id., p. viii.
44 H. Heilbron, *Rose Heilbron: The Story of England's First Woman Judge* (2012).
45 Uglow, op. cit., n. 42.
46 They should read D. Spender, *Women of Ideas (and what men have done to them)* (1983).

Victorian age, so distant seem the events and concerns of my own youthful feminism. For them it is often just 'back then', when women were unequal, the unspoken assumption being that *we are equal now* – so if women fail to achieve in this day and age it must be due to lack of merit or ambition or, employing that fashionable liberal notion, *choice*.[47]

Making someone into a heroine for posterity's sake carries a burden of responsibility. In the course of one's research one may well find what one perceives as flaws, contradictions, wrong decisions or inappropriate behaviour – our subjects are human, after all, and we all make mistakes – and we cannot edit these out, even as we attempt to account for them. Biographers must not falsify the account to fit a preconceived model of hero status, not just because we are not arbiters of correct feminist behaviour, but because we are not competent to judge what might have been the best course of action in circumstances we can only imagine. We may not feel particularly close to our subject; as I have said, I did not particularly identify with Miss Bebb. It is perhaps more difficult to be impartial when we *do*. When Barbara Babcock, herself a feminist pioneer (first woman appointed to the regular faculty at Stanford Law School, first woman director of the Public Defender Service in Washington, DC), tackled her biography of the woman who inspired the public defender service, Clara Foltz,[48] she had to steer a course at once sympathetic and critical through a tale of mistaken decisions and erratic changes of direction. The book's achievement is that we nevertheless end up feeling inspired by Foltz's resourcefulness, energy, optimism, and humanity.

Cornelia Sorabji, the first woman law student at Oxford and distinguished Anglo-Indian barrister, presents her biographer with a similar range of contradictions: was she or was she not a feminist? Whose cause did she serve?[49] Sorabji chose not to align herself with the British women's movement or Indian nationalism, yet she worked all her life for women and strove to break down the barriers to women in the legal profession. Who knows what routes she would have taken had she not been faced with the need to fit in, to be accepted and unthreatening in a racist, misogynistic society, simply to be able to accomplish the work she had been trained to do? Sorabji's life incidentally raises other challenges for the biographer. There is no shortage of primary source material, as she wrote voluminously. But her fascinating autobiography *India Calling*[50] is, as scholars have discovered, fanciful and unreliable to the point of fictitious.[51] Lawyers, while accustomed to

---

47 On 'choice', see A. Diduck, 'What is family law for?' (2011) 64 *Current Legal Problems* 287–314.

48 B. Babcock, *Woman Lawyer: The Trials of Clara Foltz* (2011).

49 S. Gooptu, *Cornelia Sorabji. India's Pioneer Woman Lawyer: A Biography* (2010).

50 C. Lokugé (ed.), *India Calling: The Memories of Cornelia Sorabji, India's First Woman Barrister* (1934).

51 A. Burton, 'The *Purdahnashin* in Her Setting: Colonial Modernity and the *Zenana* in Cornelia Sorabji's Memoirs' (2000) 65 *Feminist Rev.* 145; Mossman, op. cit., n. 6, ch. 5.

50

weighing legal testimony, tend to abandon their critical sense outside the legal forum, taking for granted the idea that a published life is more or less 'true'. But truth is relative (this is the reverse point of my remarks about college fiction above), and there is a long tradition of fictionalized female autobiography encompassing, for example, writers as distinguished as Gertrude Stein[52] and Ann Oakley.[53] Again, we need to understand the motives for this, which may well lie in (among other factors) the hostile environments in which women are forced to operate.

COUNTERING THE MYTH OF CONTINUOUS PROGRESS

One of the most persistent myths I sought to attack in the Bebb article was the myth of continuous progress. It is true enough that things are generally better for women now than they were in Miss Bebb's time, but it has certainly not been a steady uphill climb nor, crucially, an inevitable one, and things are not perfect yet. Institutional histories, especially legal ones, tend to set down a record in which the time is right for reform, attitudes have changed, those in power are benevolent. What gets left out is the steady, decades-long campaigns conducted by *feminists* (that dreadful word), female *and* male. And what also gets left out is the steady, decades-long resistance of the ruling group of legal men, supported no doubt by many women, reluctant to share their power.

Consider how the entry of women into the legal profession, if mentioned at all, is dealt with in the standard texts. Here is Manchester in his standard text, *Modern Legal History*:

> After the First World War, and the dramatically changed role which women played during the course of that conflict, society began to take a radically different view of women's proper role in society. In 1919 the Law Society resolved that women might be admitted to the profession.[54]

If I had a penny for every time women's legal advances were ascribed to changed social attitudes I would be a rich woman today. Yes, I always want to say when confronted with such accounts, attitudes changed – but *why?* Because the men suddenly decided it would be a good idea to let women in? Or might it be because women fought a long, arduous battle to convince them? You would think that the achievement of the vote and entry into the legal profession would somehow be linked in people's minds to the 50 years of first-wave feminist campaigns for precisely these goals. You would

52 G. Stein, *The Autobiography of Alice B. Toklas* (1933).
53 A. Oakley, *Taking It Like a Woman* (1984). On autobiography as fiction, see L. Stanley, *The auto/biographical I: The theory and practice of feminist auto/biography* (1992). For a legal example, see M. Weait, 'Imagining Ivy Williams', at <http://www.academia.edu/169684/Imagining_Ivy_Williams>.
54 Manchester, op. cit., n. 10, p. 71.

imagine that the advances in gender equality that took place in the 1970s, 80s, and 90s might be due, perhaps, to the second-wave feminist campaigns for equal pay, against discrimination at work, against domestic violence, and so on. But no. Law is offered to students as a series of top-down reforms responding to, at best, individual challenges like that of Miss Bebb; at worst, those unmotivated shifts in public opinion.

Cutting each generation off from its history is the most effective means of disempowering them: believing that equality has been achieved, young women are destabilized when they encounter persistent discrimination; every battle has to be re-fought; every wheel re-invented. Here again, what happened in Miss Bebb's lifetime has been replayed over different issues in my own. This is, then, the final question that biographers must ask of their sources: *why* did all this happen in the way it did? Who was responsible, and who stood in the way, and, again, *why*?

CONCLUSION

When the *Dictionary of National Biography* was being revised in the last years of the twentieth century, a welcome decision was made to include many more women and representatives of minority interests beyond the great white men of the nineteenth-century volumes. When it became clear that the editors were interested not simply in those who had succeeded in public life, but also in those through whose efforts important social changes were progressed, I was emboldened to write and suggest that Miss Bebb might be suitable for inclusion. The editors accepted my suggestion and invited me to write the entry.

This was a woman whose contribution to the legal profession had been ignored or dismissed by the institutional histories because it was deemed *unimportant* and whose contribution to feminism had been overlooked and forgotten because her early death robbed her of the chance to be England's first woman barrister. This was a woman who left no records, not even a will; whose 'voice' is only preserved in the transcript of the *Bebb* trial in the Chancery Division and in extracts from speeches in newspaper accounts (all formal settings); and whose life had to be painstakingly reconstructed from a few public records, a great deal of extrapolation and some shameless conjecture. But, given that the *ODNB* is often scholars' first port of call if they want to find out about an individual, my account of Gwyneth Bebb's life has become an important resource for future researchers. More than that, I am proud to have created, in the sense I have described, a heroine, someone for future legal campaigners to find, admire, perhaps; even to emulate, in the face of women's continued struggles for justice and equality.

JOURNAL OF LAW AND SOCIETY
VOLUME 42, NUMBER 1, MARCH 2015
ISSN: 0263-323X, pp. 53–73

Watching Women: What Illustrations of Courtroom Scenes Tell Us about Women and the Public Sphere in the Nineteenth Century

LINDA MULCAHY*

This article provides a revisionist account of the role of women in the legal system in the latter decades of the nineteenth century. Contrary to assertions that women played no role in trials other than as defendants and witnesses for most of our legal history, it suggests that women were much more active in the public sphere of Victorian law courts than previously envisaged. Drawing on depictions of trials in popular visual culture and fine art, it also reveals how images of the active female spectator challenged the emergence of new codes of behaviour which sought to protect the masculine realm of law from corruption by the feminine. It is argued that images have much to reveal about the socio-legal dynamics of trials and the ways in which fine art has been complicit in the construction and reconstruction of behavioural codes in the courtroom.

Women did not enjoy the freedom of incognito in the crowd. They were never positioned as the normal occupants of the public realm. They did not have the right to look, to stare, scrutinize or watch.[1]

INTRODUCTION

Open justice is widely acknowledged to be an essential feature of modern legal systems in democratic states yet very little is known about the people

* Department of Law, London School of Economics, Houghton Street, London WC2A 2AE, England
l.mulcahy@lse.ac.uk

The author would like to thank Lynda Nead, Niki Lacey, and David Sugarman for their very helpful comments on earlier drafts and to express her thanks to the British Library and Tate Britain for allowing her to reproduce the images contained in this article.

1 G. Pollock, *Vision and Difference: Femininity, Feminism and the Histories of Art* (1988) 71.

53

who attend courtrooms to observe trials.[2] Socio-legal scholars have paid a considerable amount of attention to judges, jurors, lawyers, litigants, and witnesses but much less consideration has been given to those who sit at the margins of the court and perform the important task of rendering justice 'open'. While constitutional theorists and human-rights lawyers have focused on the right of observers to attend trials and the importance of limiting exceptions to the principle of open justice, they have given much less thought to the exact nature of the functions that spectators perform once they are there. This article attempts to fill this gap in existing scholarship by presenting a group biography of spectators in the latter part of the nineteenth century. It does so with particular reference to the female spectator. Three key questions are posed in this work. How have spectators and their role in the legal process been conceptualized? How have ideas about what constitutes acceptable behaviour in the spectators' gallery changed over time? What part has visual culture played in determining who should sit in the public gallery?

As the editors of this volume argue in the introduction, histories of the legal system and profession have tended to be dominated by accounts of men. It is undoubtedly the case that women played a much more restricted part in legal proceedings than men throughout the nineteenth century. It was men who made law in parliament and an all-male judiciary who interpreted it. Women were directly and indirectly barred from taking office as barristers, solicitors, judges, jurors or clerks until the twentieth century.[3] Even criminality was associated with the masculine[4] as is apparent from the fact that women who stepped out of the role expected of them by murdering their husbands, lovers, seducers, and children were characterized as 'freaks, lunatics or rebels' by the press, court artists, judiciary, and even 'sober historians'.[5] With women denied the opportunity to participate in court proceedings as anything other than defendants or witnesses, spectating becomes a critical role for feminists to explore because it was one of the few roles that women could play in the trial. Whilst there is a burgeoning literature on pioneering women lawyers and judges, and the historical importance of the

---

2 Throughout this article I use the words observation, spectatorship, and audience as though they were synonymous.
3 The exception is the jury of matrons. The first female solicitor was admitted in 1922, the first female barrister was called to the bar in 1921, and the first female Kings Counsel was created in 1949. The first female juror was sworn in at the Old Bailey as recently in January 1921 and the first county court judge, Elizabeth Lane, was not appointed until 1962.
4 L. Zedner, *Women, Crime, and Custody in Victorian England* (1991); N. Lacey, *Women, Crime and Character: From Moll Flanders to Tess of the D'Urbervilles* (2008).
5 M. Hartman, 'Murder for Respectability: The Case of Madeleine Smith' (1973) 16 *Victorian Studies* 381, at 381; L. Nead, 'Visual culture of the courtroom – reflections on History, Law and the Image' (2002) 3 *Visual Culture in Britain* 119.

role of women litigants should also not be underestimated,[6] much less has been said about the ways in which women regularly participated in the public sphere by observing and evaluating what they saw in law courts.

Accounts of the interface between gender, modernity, and the city have tended to stress the many ways in which women experienced the metropolis differently from men in the nineteenth century. Considerable attention has been paid to the notion of separate spheres and to the ways in which it was the public sphere that came to be closely associated with the worlds of productive labour, politics, law, public service, and men.[7] Whatever the reality, the new social codes which emerged during this period expected women to confine, or aspire to confine, their activities to the private sphere of home, suburb, and prescribed spaces of bourgeoisie recreation such as the park, opera and museum. Art of the period played a particularly important role in drawing attention to the symbiotic relationship between representations of gender and space and to the ever-increasing ways in which women were subjected to the male gaze in the city. But contrary to Pollock's assertion at the beginning of this article, this study of women spectators suggests that the law court may well have been a place in which the dominant male gaze was reversed and women had the right to look, to stare, scrutinize, and watch the law in action. It offers the possibility of a feminist revisionist history of the Victorian legal system which draws attention to previously unrecognized patterns of participation in the public sphere amongst women.

In common with other articles in this collection, one immediate problem in pursuing this research has been the lack of official accounts of the spectator. The sources traditionally used by scholars to chart the lives of legal actors such as trial transcripts, reports, and private papers are largely silent on the subject of spectating. Observers are most likely to be discussed when they misbehave or intimidate other participants in the trial since it is only then that they become the subject of contempt of court proceedings and visible in reports of cases. Newspaper reports of trials also tell us remarkably little about the presence or behaviour of spectators, preferring instead to focus on the events leading up to the trial or the main protagonists in the courtroom drama.[8]

---

6 Unlike the civil and common law courts, the ecclesiastical or 'bawdy' courts during the Elizabethan era recognized the separate existence of women. In the 1570s the plaintiffs in half the cases brought before these courts, which dealt with disputes about marriage and sexual assaults, were women as were half the witnesses: see L. Picard, *Elizabeth's London: Everyday Life in Elizabethan London* (2003).

7 Pollock, op. cit., n. 1; E. Wilson, *The Sphinx in the City* (1991).

8 A review of the *Times*, from first issue to the present day, to determine the frequency with which the public gallery was mentioned in reports of trials, shows that references are negligible. See, also, Nead, op. cit., n. 5.

This absence of conventional legal sources has two implications for the way this study has been conducted. First, it has been used to justify the development of a group biography. Prosopography allows us to say something about the common characteristics or experiences of a group for which individual biographies of members are simply not traceable. Scholars are increasingly recognizing the importance of this approach in helping us to trace uncharted lives alongside accounts of eminent individuals who are extensively written about.[9] The gap between the ordinary and celebrated is particularly obvious in the field of legal biography where much has been written about well-known barristers and judges and much less on other key actors such as court clerks, ushers, and solicitors. While the biographies of the great and famous tell us much about the exceptional, prosopography can often reveal a considerable amount about the everyday ways in which social mores and public attitudes directed and constrained behaviour.

Secondly, the lack of conventional sources has prompted an exploration of visual resources to fill the gaps left by legal texts. The field of visual jurisprudence and explorations of the complex relationship between law and art are still in their infancy[10] but sketches of trials, sentencing, and courtroom incidents have been extremely popular throughout history and provide a rich source of data for socio-legal researchers. In contrast to legal and press reports, illustrations of trials provide us with an incomparable amount of information about the presence of spectators, especially women. Moreover, these images are not just important because of the lack of textual sources. I argue here that images of legal proceedings have the capacity to tell us things about the operation of the legal system that lawyers have failed to acknowledge. Perhaps most importantly, I suggest that rather than seeing art as a channel through which meanings about law are conveyed, socio-legal scholars should be more alert to the ways in which art has been implicated in the production of those meanings.

In the section which follows, the question of what is expected of spectators and how this has changed over time is explored. The article goes on to consider how messages about what constituted appropriate behaviour in the public gallery have been conveyed to the general public and women in particular. It will be argued that an analysis of trials depicted in fine art suggests that certain codes of behaviour emerged in the nineteenth century which attempted to discourage women from entering the courtroom. These are compared with illustrations in the realist style, directed at working-class

---

9 K. Verboven, M. Carlier, and J. Dumolyn, *A Short Manual to the Art of Prosopography* (undated), at <http://prosopography.modhist.ox.ac.uk/images/01%20 Verboven%20pdf.pdf>.
10 See, most notably, A. Young, *Judging the Image: Art, Value, Law* (2005); M. Valverde, *Law and Order: Images, Meanings, Myths* (2006); C. Douzinas and L. Nead (eds.), *Law and the Image: The Authority of Art and the Aesthetics of Law* (1999).

56

audiences, which suggest that these codes were largely prescriptive rather than descriptive. The thesis I pursue is that aspirations to new codes of feminine behaviour, represented and promoted by depictions in fine art of law courts, played a significant role in discouraging middle-class women from attending courts. Far from treating spectators as noble protectors of open justice, as constitutional and human-rights lawyers would have us imagine, the images discussed suggest the highly nuanced ways in which public participation in trials began to be discouraged in late modernity. In contrast, populist images of trials indicate that the working classes may well have remained less sensitive to the new social and legal codes which emerged in this period than the middle classes who were generally charged with the creation and maintenance of new codes of behaviour.

CONCEPTUALIZATIONS OF THE SPECTATOR: REGULATOR OR GAWPER?

A very noble place has been reserved for the spectator who is frequently characterized as the guardian of open justice and the rule of law.[11] The centrality of the common law norm that legitimate legal process should be seen as synonymous with open justice is said to go back hundreds of years,[12] and is now widely reflected in constitutional documents across the globe, such as Article 6(i) of the European Convention on Human Rights. Indeed, it is treated as something of a truism that among the many factors contributing to the moral integrity of proceedings is the fact that trials are expected to be held in public places in which spectators unconnected with the trial are able to observe justice being done.[13] Contemporary debate about secret courts and the opening up of family proceedings to the press suggests that the principle of open justice continues to be central to notions of the fair and legitimate trial.[14] Despite this, a closer examination of the concept of open justice reveals that there are a host of ways of thinking about the function of the spectator.

---

11 See, further, *Scott* v. *Scott* [1913] A.C. 417; *DE* v. *AB* [2014] EWCA Civ 1064; *Bank Mellat* v. *HM Treasury* [2013] UKSC 38; [2013] 4 All E.R. 495; *Al-Rawi* v. *Security Service* [2011] UKSC 34; [2012] 1 A.C. 531.
12 See Lord Halsbury in *Scott* v. *Scott* [1913] EWCA Civ 1064.
13 P. Roberts and A. Zuckerman, *Criminal Evidence* (2004).
14 See, further, J. Brophy and C. Roberts, '"Openness and transparency" in family courts: what the experience of other countries tells us about reform in England and Wales' (2009), at <http://www.nuffieldfoundation.org/sites/default/files/Family_Policy_Briefing_5.pdf>; Ministry of Justice (MoJ), *Confidence and confidentiality: Openness in family courts, a new approach* (2007; Cm. 7131); Department for Constitutional Affairs (DCA), *Confidence and confidentiality: Improving transparency and privacy in family courts* (2006; Cm. 6886).

At the most basic level, spectators legitimate the trial by being able to attest that justice was meted out to particular individuals, on a particular day, by particular people with a specific result. In England and Wales, a key function of the ceremony and ritual attached to the 700-year-old system of Assizes was to attract the attention of the public to legal proceedings so that they could mark the day and place of adjudication. Observers can also render the trial authoritative by symbolic acknowledgements of the authority of the judge. Members of the public gallery do this each time they stand at the entry and exit of a judge. In addition, the presence of spectators can also symbolize the fact that justice in democratic states is administered in the name of the broader community. The expectation that all those connected with the manor would attend manorial courts and the ability of the monarch's itinerant judges to fine those local Justices of the Peace who did not attend the Assizes were practices which reflected the importance of decisions being imbued with community support and the recognition of certain community members as stakeholders in the decision. Herman has argued that, in the aftermath of the Norman conquest, holding courts in the open air was seen as increasingly consistent with the idea that crimes were not just an offence against the victim's family or clan but against the whole community. She suggests that it is only with the signing of the Magna Carta that public opinion began to coalesce behind the idea that the right to public trial was an individual right.[15]

These conceptualizations of the spectator have considerable political power but there is a danger that they encourage us to imagine the spectator as little more than a silent witness or passive recipient of law. Much more important to the modern concept of open justice developed by Bentham is the contention that spectators are also there to scrutinize the activities of the judiciary.[16] At one level this might take the form of observers evaluating whether the judge has facilitated fair process. In a more radical guise it requires that spectators are given access to the same information as decision makers in order to evaluate whether the right outcome has been achieved. It has been suggested that the emphasis on performance in the adversarial model of the trial reflects a belief that trials are not just mechanisms for conveying information to fact-finders, but are also forums in which the evidence which unfolds in court can evaluated by those who observe. This vision of the active spectator has recently been recognized in *R. (on the application of Guardian News and Media Ltd)* v. *City of Westminster Magistrates' Court*[17] in which the Court of Appeal determined that the

---

15 S.N. Herman, *The Right to a Speedy and Public Trial: A Reference Guide to the United States Constitution (2006)*.

16 J. Bentham, *Rationale of Judicial Evidence* (1827) in *The Works of Jeremy Bentham, Vol. 6*, ed. J. Bowring (1843).

17 *R. (on the application of Guardian News and Media Ltd)* v. *City of Westminster Magistrates' Court* [2012] EWCA Civ 420.

purpose of the open justice principles was not simply to deter impropriety or sloppiness by the judge hearing the case but to enable the public to understand and scrutinize the justice system of which the courts were the administrators. Viewed in this way it could be argued that a system that does not protect the right of the public to critically scrutinize, affirm or condemn judicial process or outcome can hardly be called public in the proper sense.[18] It also means that trials in which the public cannot hear or understand all that goes on, cannot access or view written evidence or have poor views of the main participants may be considered illegitimate.

References to the rights of the individual to attend, scrutinize, and evaluate legal proceedings can often serve to mask the fact that facilitating spectatorship has also been used by the state as a way of disciplining the people. In its most benign form, this can be seen in Bentham's suggestion that spectating can be seen as a way to educate the public about morality and the operation of the legal system. Foucault's work offers a more malign vision of spectatorship as providing the state with important opportunities to reaffirm their right to punish the populace. For him, the significance of legal spectacles like public hangings and the adversarial trial was that they engendered a fear of law and legitimated state violence.[19]

Conceptualizations of the public have not been limited to jurisprudential debate. Far from recognizing the spectator in legal proceedings as noble protectors of fundamental liberties, popular and political discourse has often typified them as being motivated by a morbid curiosity in the pain of others rather than pursuit of civic ideals. Legal proceedings are often treated as a form of popular entertainment and public fascination with notorious trials has always been part of their lure.[20] The testimony of key witnesses, the arrival of the defendant, the deliberations of the jury, and the passing of sentence by the judge all provide dramatic highpoints and sustain interest in legal drama.[21] It has been argued that the association between law and entertainment may have been disapproved of by the political elite but it has been tolerated because of the educational value of proceedings in engendering fear of law and authority.[22]

Nineteenth-century trials were very different from those of today. In her seminal account of courthouse architecture, Graham argues that 'sociable courts', in which spectators actively participated in trials, were the norm up until the latter part of the nineteenth century.[23] Courts held in market halls

18 A. Duff et al., *The Trial on Trial, Vol. 3: Towards a Normative Theory of the Criminal Trial* (2007).
19 M. Foucault, *Discipline and Punishment: The Birth of The Prison*, trans. A. Sheridan (1977); M. Foucault, *Spectacle of the Scaffold*, trans. A. Sheridan (2008).
20 A. Delgado, *Victorian Entertainment* (1971); Nead, op. cit., n. 5.
21 J. Grossman, *The Art of Alibi: English Law Courts and the Novel* (2002); Nead, id.
22 R. Malcolmson, *Popular Recreations in English Society 1700–1850* (1973).
23 C. Graham, *Ordering Law: The Architecture and Social History of the English Law Court to 1914* (2003).

were commonly open to the surrounding streets, allowing passers-by to intervene in proceedings as they went about their business.[24] Moreover, many rooms in which trials were held hosted more than one court at a time, allowing spectators to wander at will between the spaces set aside for adjudication and around and among other participants.[25] Reflecting on the Assizes in the nineteenth century, Lewis argues that the courts of the era were very far from being the quiet spaces of today and that spectators regularly booed, hissed, and applauded their favourites.[26]

There has always been a risk that encouraging spectators to attend trials carried the risk of entertainment taking precedence over civic duty with the result that those who were seen as being in need of instruction might be impervious to the messages about law and order that modern states hoped to convey. As Fischer-Taylor concludes in her study of the Palais de Justice in mid-nineteenth-century Paris, commentators became increasingly concerned that spectators were 'treating the trial as an entertainment for themselves, distancing the debate between the rights of the defendant and those of society, and thereby evading application of its stern moral lesson to their own lives.'[27] Charting a similar trend in England, Graham asserts that this resulted in attempts to discipline spectators by containing and silencing them.[28]

The state's interest in encouraging spectatorship certainly appears to have waned in late modernity when the public galleries of courtrooms are more likely to be empty. In England and Wales we have moved from a position in which courthouses in the eighteenth century often accommodated hundreds of spectators to the present position in which the Ministry of Justice recommends that just 25 seats should be reserved for onlookers.[29] New disciplinary techniques developed by the state in the nineteenth century, such as an organized police force, offered much more sophisticated ways of controlling the masses and disseminating information about the implications of breaking the law. Elsewhere, I have argued that one way in which the marginalization and silencing of the spectator was achieved was through shifts in architectural and design practices which increasingly placed the public in dedicated seats at the margins of the courts.[30] Architects of new purpose-built courts in the early nineteenth century found a variety of new ways of herding the public in dedicated

---

24 C. Brookes and M. Lobban, *Communities and Courts in Britain* (1997).
25 Graham, op. cit., n. 23; see, also, L. Mulcahy, *Legal Architecture: Justice, Due Process and the Place of Law* (2011).
26 J. Lewis, *The Victorian Bar* (1982).
27 K. Fischer-Taylor, *In the Theater of Criminal Justice: The Palais de Justice in Second Empire Paris* (1993).
28 Graham, op. cit., n. 23.
29 MoJ, *Court Standards and Design Guide* (2010).
30 Mulcahy, op. cit., n. 25.

circulation routes which rendered it unnecessary for them to access large sections of the courthouse. By the time the Report of the Commissioners for the Royal Courts of Justice was published in the latter part of the nineteenth century, the idea of the spectator as someone who interrupts the business of the court had become a dominant narrative.[31] In their submission to the Commissioners, the Joint Committee of the Bar and Solicitors complained that one of the chief inconveniences in court was the presence of members of the public who daily took seats in the court 'not with any view to the particular business before the court, but merely as a place where they can spend their time'.[32] In his authoritative work on the Royal Courts of Justice, Brownlee confirms that the new Royal Courts of Justice in the Strand completed in 1882 were largely planned to limit the movement of the 'dirty' public.[33]

The remainder of this article attempts to build on this emerging understanding of how spectatorship has evolved and changed and the part that popular conceptualizations of the female spectator have played in the demise of spectatorship. It does so by reference to what depictions of spectators in fine art and illustrated newspapers can tell us about the new behavioural codes about spectatorship that emerged in the Victorian era and the extent to which the female spectator was distinguished from the male. It is argued that visual culture plays a critical role in the construction and performance of socio-legal identities and that images and not just texts can provide us with essential clues about prevalent expectations of people according to their status, gender, and wealth. Moreover, it is contended that important messages about law were not only generated by the legal system but in contemporary representations of it by artists who worked outside of it and reached a much larger audience. The suggestion is not that artists and illustrators acted as handmaidens of the legal system in conveying messages about what judges and others thought spectators should and should not do. Rather, this article attempts to reveal the symbiotic relationship of law and fine art in prescribing what constituted appropriate behaviour for the middle classes who dominated both spheres.

VISUAL REPRESENTATIONS OF SPECTATORS

Tate Britain has confidently asserted that paintings about trials were extremely popular during the Victorian period,[34] and a review of academic

31 Commissioners for the New Courts of Justice, *Report of the Royal Commission on Buildings and Plans for New Courts of Justice* (C. 290; 1871).
32 id., p. 64.
33 D. Brownlee, *The Law Courts: The Architecture of George Edmund Street* (1984).
34 See <http://www.tate.org.uk/art/artworks/solomon-waiting-for-the-verdict-t03614>.

and commercial image databases confirms the accuracy of this claim.[35] However, closer scrutiny suggests that the claim needs some refining since certain types of trial were clearly much more popular with artists than others. Numerous religious paintings, generally seen to be the most acceptable subject in fine art well into the nineteenth century, depict the trials of important figures such as St. Lawrence, Moses, St. Francis of Assisi, St. Stephen, St. Paul, and Christ before the law. High-profile historical trials, such as those of Charles I, Warren Hastings, Sir William Wallace, Queen Caroline, and Socrates were also fashionable, as were literary trials such as scenes from *The Merchant of Venice*.[36] Significantly, nineteenth-century paintings of contemporary trials were a rarity and when they did appear, they were more likely to depict the main protagonists in legal proceedings than spectators.[37] Much more numerous than fine-art depictions of trials were the many sketches, engravings, and watercolours produced for nineteenth-century books, pamphlets, journals, and newspapers.[38] Illustrated newspapers such as *The Graphic* and *Illustrated London News* regularly carried sketches of contemporary courtroom scenes, and other magazines such as *Punch, The Oxford Magazine*, and *Funny Folks* were known for their subversive and satirical cartoons.[39]

Two particular sets of contrasting images have been selected for more detailed scrutiny here in order to tease out the extent to which women took part in spectating in the nineteenth century and the different expectations of

35 Searches for images were conducted using the following image databases, portals, and online image collections: Artstor; AMICA; Courtauld Institute of Art online image archive; Artchive; Artcyclopedia; ARTstor; Beazley Archive of Classical Art and Architecture; British Library Images Online; Collage portal; LUNA Commons; Public Domain Images; Vads; Web Gallery of Art; The Fitzwilliam Museum; British Museum Images; The National Gallery; Royal Academy of Arts; Tate Collection; V&A Image database; The Wallace Collection; New York Metropolitan Museum of Art; and the Louvre.

36 See, for example, Fra Angelico, *St Lawrence on Trial* (1447–49), The Vatican: image available at <http:www.wga.hu/index1.html>; Giorgio da Castelfranco, *Moses Undergoing Trial by Fire*, 1502–05; Giotto Di Bondone, *Scenes from the Life of Saint Francis: 6. St Francis before the Sultan (Trial by Fire)* (1325); Rembrandt's *Ecco Homo* (1634); William Bell Scott, *The Trial of Sir William Wallace at Westminster* (date unknown); and Johan Zoffany, *Charles Macklin as Shylock* (c. 1768), The Tate.

37 But see, for instance, Lady Dorothy Stanley's *His First Offence* (1896), which depicts a child in the dock; John Morgan's *The Jury* (1861), Bucks Gallery; Vladimir Makovsky's *Verdict, 'Not Guilty', 1882* (1882), Tretyakov Gallery, Moscow; Nikolaj Kasatkin's *In the Corridor of the District Court* (1897), Sebastopol Art Museum; and Ludwig Bokelmann's *In the Courtroom* (1883).

38 Particularly worthy of note in this context are the 12 acquatints by Augustus Pugin and others produced for the three-volume *Microcosm of London* that was published in the first decade of the nineteenth century.

39 See, for instance, *Impeachment Ticket for the Trial of Warren Hastings* (1788), and the *Trial of the Sovereign* (1768–76), both of which are available from British Library images online.

62

them. The first of these took the form of images from *The Illustrated Police News, Law Courts and Weekly Record* (*The Illustrated Police News*), a publication, aimed at the marginally literate working class.[40] Not only was it one of Britain's earliest tabloid newspapers, published continuously from 1864 to 1938, it was also the first, and longest-running, Saturday penny newspaper. As its name suggests, it was dedicated to reporting stories about crimes and trials. *The Illustrated Police News* consisted of a front page illustrated with wood engravings and three pages of text. It reported stories which were often drawn from trials at the London police courts and illustrated them in highly dramatic ways. Headlines such as 'Young lady attacked by a bull',[41] 'Strange freak of a miner near Barnsley', 'Horrible cruelty to a cat',[42] 'A dog called as a witness',[43] 'A duel between nuns',[44] and 'Capital punishments of all nations'[45] will give the reader an indication of the tenor of the stories produced. Described as the most sensational newspaper of the mid- and late-Victorian era,[46] the sketches produced would have been familiar to large numbers of the working classes. The *Illustrated Police News* pioneered the mass publication of engravings from 1842 and its normal weekly circulation was impressive for the time. Sales are reported to have been in the region of 150,000 to 200,000 copies, with figures reaching 600,000 for special issues.[47]

Whilst the separate-spheres thesis continues to have considerable explanatory force in terms of what the Victorians middle classes considered to be ideal behaviour, attention has increasingly been drawn to the fact that working-class women experienced the new spaces of industrialization and the metropolis in very different ways from their middle-class counterparts.[48] An analysis of a popular newspaper provided an opportunity to shift the focus of scholarly work away from its obsession with understanding visual culture through the lens of high art.[49] Working-class women were present in the

40 F. Stout, 'Visions of a New Reality: The City and the Emergence of Modern Visual Culture' in *The City Reader*, eds. R. T. LeGates and F. Stout (1999).
41 *Illustrated Police News etc.* (issue 433), Saturday 1 June 1872.
42 *Illustrated Police News etc.* (issue 736), Saturday 27 April 1878.
43 *Illustrated Police News etc.* (issue 800), Saturday 27 September 1879.
44 *Illustrated Police News etc.* (issue 287), Saturday 14 August 1869.
45 *Illustrated Police News etc.* (issue 437), Saturday 29 June 1872.
46 S. Jones, *The Illustrated Police News: London's Court Cases and Sensational Stories* (2002).
47 J. Bondeson, *Illustrated Police News: Sensational Stories and Startling Victorian Images from the 'Worst Newspaper in England'* (2011).
48 E. Wilson, *The Sphinx in the City* (1991); M. Arnot and C. Usborne, *Gender and Crime in Modern Europe* (1999). Even in the context of middle-class women's use of space, commentators have explored their involvement in local government and philanthropic organizations, such as the Salvation Army and army lasses as examples of the many ways in which the notion of separate spheres was actively disregarded: J. Walkowitz, 'Urban Spectatorship' in *The Nineteenth-century Visual Culture Reader*, eds. V.R. Schwartz and J.M. Przyblyski (2004) 205.
49 Nead, op. cit., n. 5

public sphere in ways that middle-class women were not since they entered it to work as cleaners, cooks, dressmakers, clerks, shop assistants, and prostitutes. At the same time, it has been argued that the role of middle-class women in the public sphere may well have gone unrecognized. These different revisionist accounts of the public sphere as exclusively masculine have produced new stories of modernity which intersect with, and challenge, the concept of the public sphere as either wholly masculine or middle-class.[50]

The importance of class in determining how people occupied the Victorian public sphere makes it important to compare the impact of the sketches in the *Illustrated Police News* with other forms of representation to which the middle classes were more likely to be exposed. As a result, two celebrated oil paintings by Abraham Solomon were selected for comparison with the *Illustrated Police News*. Both images are painted in the narrative style and tell the story of the family of a man facing criminal charges. In the first of these rare treatments of a contemporary scene, *Waiting for the Verdict*, we see the group waiting exhausted and in despair while the jury adjudicates on his guilt. In the second, *Not Guilty*, we see their reaction as they are informed that there has been an acquittal. These paintings were amongst the best known, if not *the* best known, treatments of the subject in the Victorian age. They would have been well known to middle-class audiences who formed both the clientele of the newly emerging art galleries and the readership of the new illustrated magazines in which new art works were discussed. Both paintings were exhibited at the Royal Academy and regional art galleries and attracted the attention of numerous critics. A great number of replicas of the works were created[51] and both paintings were engraved in mezzotint for widespread reproduction. Such was the popularity of *Waiting for the Verdict* that it has been reported that copies of the print could be seen in inns and homes as late as 1925.[52] It was described as one of the greatest works of 1857[53] and a blockbuster success of the era.[54] By the 1870s, both paintings were being described as 'two very old favourites'[55] and several commentators suggested that it was through these two works and other examples of his later work that Solomon became a great exponent of the manners of the time.[56]

50 L. Nead, *Victorian Babylon – People, Streets and Images in Nineteenth-century London* (2000).
51 Geffrye Museum, *Solomon – A Family of Painters* (1986).
52 Tate Gallery, *Illustrated Catalogue of Acquisitions 1982–84* (1986).
53 'Waiting for the Verdict painting by Abraham Solomon from the exhibition of the Royal Academy' *Illustrated London News* (issue 864), Saturday 20 June 1857.
54 R. Treble, 'Abraham, Rebecca and Simeon Solomon' (1986) 128 (994) *The Burlington Magazine* 53–4.
55 'The International Exhibition' *Morning Post* (issue 30394), 9 May 1871, 6.
56 'Waiting for the Verdict' *Illustrated London News* (issue 864), Saturday 20 June 1857; 'Feuilleton of the Week' *The Lady's Newspaper* (issue 837), Saturday 10 January 1863, 175.

In order to explore how spectators were portrayed to working class audiences, a visual analysis of all of the images of trials contained in 1660 issues of the *Illustrated Police News* from its launch in 1864 until 1900 was undertaken.[57] It soon became clear that despite its full title, the newspaper was more likely to focus on the events leading up to a crime than on legal proceedings but representations of the trial were still common. Illustrations of courtroom scenes fall into three categories. The majority provide no more than head-and-shoulder sketches of the major actors in the trial, such as the defendant, lawyers, victims, key witnesses, and judges. A second category show lawyers, judges, and defendants in the inner well of the court where one would not expect to find women unless in the dock or witness-stand. The third category was made up of full or partial depictions of the public areas of the court. This final category contained 96 illustrations over 26 years and forms the focus of discussion here.[58]

While far from being sophisticated, the illustrations in *The Illustrated Police News* were often surprisingly detailed and there is much for socio-legal scholars to glean from their content. Firstly, the illustrations suggest that large numbers of people were attending trials as spectators across the court systems until the end of the nineteenth century. It could be argued that coverage of trials in the popular press are only able to gives us insights into attendance at trials that are deemed worthy of press coverage. However, the 96 sketches show spectators in the Central Criminal Court, police courts, county courts, coroners' courts, and quarter sessions. Secondly, the drawings indicate that both middle-class and working-class women participated in the trial as spectators alongside men. The general focus of illustrations on parties, lawyers, judge, and jury means that it is not always possible to make detailed observations about the representation of spectators, though the images regularly contain tantalizing glimpses of bonnets and feathers which suggest that public galleries were frequently composed of both sexes. Moreover, they show that women spectators were not always confined to the galleries of the court but also appeared on the bench at the invitation of judges up to the 1880s. Sketches are often too crude to accurately determine the class of the women shown from their dress but one way to gauge their social standing is to examine where they were positioned in the court, as the middle and working classes were generally segregated in courts of this era.[59] By way of example, Figure 1 shows the Assize court at Maidstone where the working classes were left

---

57 These were accessed using the British Library's Nineteenth-century Newspaper Collection. The newspaper ran until the 1930s but only nineteenth-century issues are available through the database.
58 llustrations of coroner's inquests have been excluded from this figure.
59 Mulcahy, op. cit., n. 25; Graham, op. cit, n. 23.

Figure 1. *The Illustrated Police News*, Saturday, 12 November 1881

© The British Library Board, *The Illustrated Police News,* 12 November 1881, p. 1

standing behind a spiked fence which sliced the court in two and the middle classes watched from the balcony.

The regular presence of middle-class and working-class women as spectators in courts, even if only in sensational trials, suggests that a more nuanced account of the role of women in the Victorian and Edwardian public sphere might be necessary. Analysis of *The Illustrated Police News* indicates that women appeared as spectators in a number of trials in which it might be argued that they would be expected to have a special interest, such as cases involving child-trafficking, or baby-farming.[60] But they also regularly featured in the public gallery in trials for murder, abduction, libel, and inquests, as well as in the crowds that attempted to get into courts or awaited the exit or entry of key protagonists. Perhaps most significantly, women are depicted as behaving in exactly the same way as men. This includes depictions of them as engaged, bored, and animated. It also includes sketches of women misbehaving. The content analysis undertaken for this study revealed numerous examples, including the one in Figure 2, of women engaging in verbal and physical outbursts by throwing objects, shouting out and protesting against aspects of the proceedings.[61]

---

60 'Trafficking in Children' *Illustrated Police News*, Saturday 10 June 1893; 'The Tranmere Baby-Farming Case' *Illustrated Police News etc.* (issue 817), Saturday 11 October 1879.

61 'Outrage in Court' *Illustrated Police News* (issue 1056), Saturday 10 May 1884; 'Violent Scenes in Court' *Illustrated Police News* (issue 1635), Saturday 15 June

Figure 2. *The Illustrated Police News*, **Saturday, 9 March 1889**

1895; 'The Wimbledon Mystery' *Illustrated Police News* (issue 932), Saturday 31 December 1881; 'Scenes in Court – Stratford' *Illustrated Police News* (issue 963), Saturday 29 July 1882.

The high circulation rates of the *Illustrated Police News* and fact that characterizations of women as active participants in the trial appear so regularly suggests that the working-class audiences who consumed this newspaper were not unduly concerned by representations of women behaving in the same way as men. Contrary to the separate-spheres thesis which has dominated much analysis of nineteenth century behaviour, these illustrations make clear that the era may well be best represented by a troubling mix of phenomena rather than notions of homogeneity within groups based on class and gender. Contrary to the many orthodoxies of modernity such as the suggestion that it is only the male flaneur who is free to observe and wander at will, these images present us with women who are comfortable in the public sphere and are confident performers within it.

THE IDEAL SPECTATOR AS THE ABSENT SPECTATOR

In direct contrast to the impressions conveyed by these images, it is apparent that other discourses emerged during this era that appeared to encourage women to confine their interest in legal proceedings and engagement with the public sphere. Commentators have suggested that female spectators of trials across European society began to arouse suspicion within middle-class circles and were increasingly characterized as being capable of, and displaying, more extreme behaviour than men. The masculine domain of the courthouse began to be seen as one which needed protecting from the corrupting influence of the feminine which thrived on morbid curiosity, the courting of attention by flamboyant dress, and a tendency to heighten the theatrical elements of the trial by excessive responses to evidence.[62] In a French context, Fischer-Taylor has described how commentators on demeanour in the nineteenth-century courtroom became increasingly taxed by what she has labelled the irresistible impulse of the female spectator towards disorder and irrationality in the environs of the court.[63] Nead's work on the reporting of criminal trials in England also argues that in the early decades of the twentieth century, women were often described as having an inappropriate and voracious appetite for murder which called into question the very nature of modern femininity. In her analysis of press coverage of celebrated trials, she reports how the press became anxious about the ways in which women waiting to get into the public galleries of courthouses spilled over into the public highway and got in the way.[64] Simpson has also drawn attention to the moral panic caused by the Fadda trial in 1879 in which the political elite in Italy were stunned by the 'swarming masses' that sought

62 Fischer-Taylor, op. cit., n. 27.
63 id.
64 Nead, op. cit, n. 5.

68

entry into the specially constructed public gallery, most of whom were well-dressed women.[65] He argues that for some commentators the presence of mothers, wives and unmarried women at the trial seemed to betoken the collapse of the Italian family and marked them out as '... destroyers of nationhood, their venal appetites eternally in search of vicarious thrills, and aroused by talk of transgressive sex'.[66] These characterizations serve to reveal the fragility of law's relationship with the feminine in which the realms of emotion and imagination provide a sharp relief to law's masculine domain of control, discipline, and sobriety.[67] What emerges from these works is a strong sense of anxiety about women who were conceived of as being out of place in the courthouse.

The suggestion that women should be treated as a distinct type of spectator is clearly reflected in Abraham Solomon's iconic treatment of the subject, produced less than a decade before the first issue of *The Illustrated Police News*. I argue that this is significant not because of what it might tell us about the reality of practice but, rather, because of what it tells us about the contribution that art has made to the realization of certain codes of behaviour within the legal arena. In common with other paintings of the time, Solomon appears to pay considerable attention to the social protocols to which the wealthy second- and third-generation industrialists of the time were aspiring. The newly-emerged middle classes of the industrial era were far from having a coherent identity, but shared notions of morality and respectability together with the clear demarcation of their standards from the working classes, became essential to their success as a group. Viewed from this perspective, Solomon's work has a lot to tell us about how some members of the Victorian bourgeoisie *wanted* women to behave in the environs of the court.

There are numerous examples of how these social codes, which attempted to consign women to separate and private spheres, manifested themselves in the treatment of women in the legal system during this period. The assumption that women who attended courts should be treated differently took physical form when architects of Victorian law courts segregated women from men in the court and its environs.[68] Concerns about the debasing influences of the trial on the female mind were also reflected in contemporary legal reasoning which justified judges clearing the court of women when their innocence was likely to be compromised. After the creation of secular divorce courts in 1858, judges regularly ordered women and children out of the court or heard cases involving 'unnatural practices' in camera. Indeed, it was only after women became jurors in the 1920s that judges

---

65 T. Simpson, *Murder and Media in the New Rome* (2010) 1.
66 id., p. 207.
67 C. Douzinas, 'The Legality of the Image' (2000) 63 *Modern Law Rev.* 813–30.
68 Mulcahy, op. cit., n. 25; Graham, op. cit., n. 23.

Figure 3. Abraham Solomon, *Waiting for the Verdict* (1857) Tate Britain

© Tate, London 2014

stopped clearing female spectators from criminal courtrooms when evidence of even a mildly sexual nature was submitted.[69]

Waiting for the Verdict and *Not Guilty*, shown as Figures 3 and 4, provide a direct response to contemporary concerns about the incontrollable impulse of the feminine. In contrast to the sketches in the *Illustrated Police News* which admit of the possibility of women being engaged, entertained or disgusted by legal proceedings, Solomon's art suggest that there is no place at all for women in law courts. The courtroom remains remote in both paintings and can only be glimpsed through open doors and corridors. Both paintings portray the predominantly female members of the defendant's family as recipients of justice rather than participants in the trial. Whilst it may be plausible that a family might wait outside the court while the jury is deliberating in the first painting, the complete lack of female agency is emphasized in *Not Guilty* when the news of the acquittal which has just been pronounced in their absence is communicated to the family outside the courtroom.

---

69 C. Graham, 'The History of Law Court Architecture in England and Wales; The Institutionalization of the Law' in SAVE Britain's Heritage, *Silence in Court: The Future of the UK's Historic Law Courts* (2004) 36–47.

Figure 4. Abraham Solomon, *Not Guilty, The Acquittal* **(1857) Tate Britain**

The idea that the private sphere of the feminine and the public sphere of the court are distinct domains is further indicated by the division of *Waiting for the Verdict* into two distinct sections. The first, which stands to the right of the vertical line marked by the left edge of the door frame and space between the floor tiles, depicts the masculine domain of the remote and busy court full of male barristers, with a male judge in his scarlet robes of office at their apex. The second, which stands to the left of the line, could be said to represent the feminine domain of family and dependency. While the masculine sphere is full of people busily going about their work, the feminine is populated by people in a state of misery who are dependent on the outcome of deliberations in the masculine sphere of the painting. Only a straying petticoat and the wistful over-the-shoulder look of the young female relative suggests any connection between the two. Significantly, Abraham Solomon did not come from a conventional family and his sister enjoyed some success as an artist in her own right,[70] but, consciously or subconsciously, he has produced a highly conventional account of the role of women in the public sphere which expects women to aspire to confine their activities to the

70 P. Gerrish-Nunn, 'Rebecca Solomon' in Geffrye Museum, op. cit., n. 51, p. 19.

private and domestic sphere. Whilst they do not carry the critical weight of Solomon's work, the separation of the masculine legal sphere from the feminine private sphere is also reflected in subsequent depictions of the trial in nineteenth-century fine art. Many of the same themes can, for instance, be discerned in George Elgar Hicks's *Before the Magistrates* (1882), or Edward Rippingille's much poorer reworking of the same theme in *The Paternity Suit*.

These images can be seen as an important part of socially constructed protocols about how women should behave in the legal arena. Commentary on *Waiting for the Verdict* and *Not Guilty* confirm prevalent expectations. A journalist for the *Illustrated London News* suggested that the beauty of the sister in *Waiting for the Verdict* might well require the protection of her brother who stood trial[71] and a writer for the *Times* referred to the 'feminine fortitude' of the older mother.[72] Historians would no doubt remind us that for many middle-class women these images would not have been understood as repressive. Indeed, the secret of their popularity might well have been the incentives they provided to acquire the moral strength and status accorded to participation in the private and emotional sphere. It is in this way that artistic discourse regulated sexuality not by denying it, but by enabling one type of behaviour over another.[73] Denied the same opportunities to enter art academies, work as artists, display their work or write about it, women of the time had fewer opportunities to challenge these patriarchal codes, with the result that fine-art depictions of the trial were able to view subjects almost exclusively through the male gaze.

CONCLUSION

This article has attempted to provide a revisionist history of the socio-legal dynamics of the trial in the latter part of the nineteenth century by examining the agency of women consigned to the public gallery for want of permission to occupy the inner sanctum of the court. It has been argued that the quest to marginalize the role of women in the trial, which also found expression in the prohibition on women jurors, lawyers, and judges, found vivid expression in the behavioural codes reflected in the paintings of Abraham Solomon. His popular paintings may not always have reflected practice but they undoubtedly contributed to the construction of the exemplar of the passive female spectator. By way of contrast, the images of women contained in the *Illustrated Police News* present a much more varied and complex account of the role of both middle-class and working-class spectators which does not rely on the idea of the public gallery as an essentially male

71 'Waiting for the Verdict', op. cit., n. 53.
72 *Times*, 18 May 1857, 9.
73 L. Nead, *Myths of Sexuality: Representations of Women in Victorian Britain* (1988).

72

province. The content analysis of almost forty years of this paper suggests that not only did women attend trials but that, contrary to common expectations of the gaze in modernity, women watched men perform. Moreover, it implies that while some went to trials alongside men to be titillated, others may well have been interested in striving to scrutinize and evaluate what they saw. What is not in doubt is that women spectators did attend trials and were keen to claim the space as their own just as they would soon after stake their claim to be admitted to the inner bar of the court and solicitors bench.

The work described here has also attempted to contribute to ongoing debates about methodology in socio-legal studies. Rather than seeing art and visual culture as conduits through which prevalent norms can be represented outside of the system, it has been argued that the relationship is much more complex and symbiotic. It is tentatively suggested that images of law might even be viewed as a site for the production of legal meanings. In the very least, it is contended that visual culture has played a critical role in the construction and constant reconstruction of legal norms. These claims are made with a view to encouraging socio-legal scholars to move beyond the narrow confines of text and lived experiences of law to a broader interrogation of the what art can tell law about itself. While there is now a considerable body of work which looks at law and the moving image or law in popular culture, the relevance of fine art and still images continues to be much neglected. Moreover, the role of the image has only gained in importance since the images discussed here were produced as new forms of spectatorship and spectacle have been rendered possible by photojournalism, televised trials, live streaming of proceedings, and citizen journalism. If the physical presence of spectators in everyday trials is now rare, the possibilities for socio-legal accounts of the contemporary spectators have only just begun.

JOURNAL OF LAW AND SOCIETY
VOLUME 42, NUMBER 1, MARCH 2015
ISSN: 0263-323X, pp. 74–101

Judicial Pictures as Legal Life-writing Data and a Research Method

LESLIE J. MORAN*

This article examines the use of pictures as a source of data and tools for researching the lives of the judiciary, both the life of the judiciary as an institution as well as the life of individual judges. The point of departure is that image making and image management is of particular importance for the judiciary – an elite in positions of power. The images produced can tell us much about how those who occupy judicial positions shape and represent the nature of the judicial institution and their position within it to themselves, fellow judges, and outsiders. The focus here is judicial visual images, a neglected, sometimes poorly understood and underused source of data. The article explores how 'found' and 'researcher-made' pictures can be used to write the life of the judiciary. It considers the challenges that need to be acknowledged and addressed when using visual data.

The objective of this article is to examine the use of pictures as a source of data and a tool for undertaking research into the lives of the judiciary. I use the phrase 'lives of the judiciary' to refer to both the life of the judiciary as an institution as well as the life of individual judges. The point of departure is the insights offered by scholarship that focuses on elites in society who occupy positions of authority. Image making and image management is of particular importance for those in positions of power. This image work has two aspects. One is a concern with the outward, public face, of legitimate authority. The other is self-regarding, for the audience of peers: legitimating their position and the power they possess to themselves and their immediate circle.[1] Barker calls this 'endogenous legitimation', of the self-justification

* School of Law, Birkbeck College, University of London, Malet Street, London WC1E 7HX, England
l.moran@bbk.ac.uk

1 R. Barker, *Legitimating Identities: The Self-Presentations of Rulers and Subjects* (2001) 31.

74

of rulers by the formation and display of their identity as rulers.[2] The judiciary, Baum argues, are one group of elites preoccupied with image making and image management.[3] Judicial image work uses a range of media, takes a variety of forms, and engages a variety of audiences.[4] The images produced can tell us much about how those who occupy judicial positions shape and represent the nature of the judicial institution and their position within it to themselves, their fellow judges, and to outsiders.

The central argument of this article is that those who engage in writing the lives of the judiciary not only need to pay more critical attention to the image preoccupations of the judiciary but also have regard to the rich diversity of images made and their various uses. The focus here is on judicial visual images. It is not proposed that pictures should supersede other sources of data but, rather, that pictures are a neglected, sometimes poorly understood and underused source of data. They offer much potential for those under-taking research into the lives of the judiciary. This article explores how visual images might be used to research and write the life of the judiciary as an institution. The images considered here fall into two broad categories: 'found pictures', being pictures produced by others, and researcher generated pictures or 'made pictures'. In examining the potential of the two types, the article also explores the many challenges facing a researcher engaging with visual images. Consideration will be given to the many assumptions and expectations about the nature of the visual objects that need to be addressed when working with pictures. What significance needs to be given to the materiality of these visual objects? How important is an awareness of the rich cultural traditions they draw upon in order for a researcher to make sense of pictures as sources of data and as devices for generating data?

Throughout, the article draws on my experiences of working with pictures to undertake research on the judiciary.[5] I have used a variety of 'found pictures' as data, including painted and photographic portraits, sketches, sculpture (in particular, funerary monuments), film, and television.[6] They

---

2 id., p. 3.

3 L. Baum, *Judges and Their Audiences: A Perspective on Judicial Behavior* (2006).

4 For an introductory survey of the variety of forms and relevant judicial and scholarly literatures, see L.J. Moran, 'Some reflections on the aesthetics of contemporary judicial ceremony: making the ordinary extraordinary' in *The Political Aesthetics of Power and Protest*, ed. A. Virmani (2015).

5 I leave to others the task of working on visual images of other branches of the legal profession. For an example of a photographic project that covers the whole range of legal professions in England and Wales. see J.F. Hunkin, *Faces of the Law* (2008). Legal academics are notable by their absence from this project. In 1989 the United States National Portrait Gallery staged the exhibition, 'Portrait of the American Law'. The exhibition crossed a wide spectrum of legal professionals including academics: see F.S. Voss, *Portraits of the American Law* (1989).

6 Work exploring film and television representations will not be referred to here. See L.J. Moran, B. Skeggs, and R. Herz, 'Ruth Herz Judge playing Judge Ruth Herz: reflections on the performance of judicial authority' (2010) 14 *Law, Text, Culture*

come from a variety of collections and archives including national portrait galleries, collections of legal professional organizations, court buildings, law schools, newspaper collections, and online sources. I have also made pictures of the judiciary as part of the research process. To date, these are digital photographic images made with a single-lens reflex digital camera, a mobile-phone camera, and a computer. The article also draws upon examples taken from my research practice of using pictures as part of the process of generating data through interviews. Throughout, insights from disciplines across the humanities and social sciences that have shaped my research practice will be drawn upon.[7]

The article begins with a brief survey of research that explores the lives of the judiciary. The purpose is to search for evidence of the use of pictures in judicial life writing. What follows is an exploration of a range of issues connected to the use of pictures as a source of data. It begins with some general matters that every researcher who plans to engage with visual materials in general and pictures in particular needs to be aware of and sensitive to. The central theme is 'the materiality of pictures'. This phrase calls attention to pictures as three-dimensional objects and the importance of a wide array of social and cultural factors that impact on their production and their capacity to generate meaning. This is followed by an examination of the potential of the two broad categories of judicial pictures referred to above, 'found pictures' and 'made pictures', to provide data. In this article, the former is made up of painted and photographic portraits of the judiciary. The 'made pictures' are images I have made as part of my research on judicial ritual. A number of challenges associated with making pictures will briefly be considered before we turn to the potential of this practice to generate new data. The final section turns to the use of pictures as a method of undertaking research; as a device for facilitating interview dialogue.

USING PICTURES TO WRITE THE LIVES OF THE JUDICIARY: A BRIEF SURVEY

What evidence is there in published work on the lives of the judiciary about the role pictures play in this area of research? Beginning with work on the life of the judiciary as an institution, this brief survey then turns to work that explores the lives of individual judges.

Pictures are most notable by their absence from projects that examine the life of the judiciary as an institution. In Alan Paterson's classic empirical

198; L.J. Moran 'Projecting the judge: a case study in the cultural lives of the judiciary' (2008) 46 *Studies in Law, Politics and Society* 93.
7 C. Mitchell, *Doing Visual Research* (2011); S. Pink, *Doing Visual Ethnography* (2001); J. Prosser, *Image-based Research* (1998); G. Rose, *Visual Methodologies* (2001); P. Tinkler, *Using Photographs in Social and Historical Research* (2013).

study of the highest United Kingdom court, 'the primary research subjects' as the title of the book suggests were the Law Lords.[8] The list of sources used ranges from official law reports and papers relating to those cases to extra-judicial writings, judicial biographies, interviews (ranging from thirty minutes to two and a half hours long, using open-ended questions), and observation.[9] There is no reference to pictures of these judicial subjects as a source of data and no pictures are used in the published results of this research. Paterson has returned to this topic in a study of the transition of the United Kingdom's final court of appeal from the Appellate Committee of the House of Lords to the Supreme Court. In a reflection on methodology, Paterson notes that there is an increasing amount of visual material, including live television broadcasts of courtroom proceedings and documentaries about the new Supreme Court and its judges. Although the author acknowledges that video recordings of the courtroom are an important new source of data about the judiciary and, more specifically, about their interaction with counsel, there is little evidence that they have been used for that purpose in the study and no images of these exchanges are incorporated into the publication.[10] The resulting monograph includes one photographic image: a colour picture of part of the architectural detail on the outside face of the Houses of Parliament, the building that housed the Appellate Committee.[11] Similarly you will find no visual images of the judiciary in Penny Darbyshire's important study of the working lives of the judiciary of England, despite the fact that one of the drivers of her research is 'the public image of judges'.[12] There is no reference to 'found' pictures as a source of data or any indication that the she made pictures of her judicial subjects as part of the research. Nor is there any evidence that pictures were used to facilitate dialogue with her research subjects in this ethnographic study. The only picture appears on the monograph's dust jacket, spanning the front and back cover. It is a close-up of the royal crest sitting on top of a pediment over an entrance flanked by the titles 'Crown Court' and 'County Court'.

The absence of visual images in research on the life of judicial institutions is by no means a peculiarly British phenomenon. Pierce's study of the High Court of Australia contains no pictures though you will find visual representations in the form of graphs and tables presenting quantitative data.[13] Nor will you find pictures in the historical study of British colonial judges by Canadian scholar John McLaren.[14] Lawrence Baum's study, *Judges and*

---

8 A. Paterson, *The Law Lords* (1982) 5.
9 id., pp. 4–6.
10 id., p. 3.
11 A. Paterson, *Final Judgment: The Last Law Lords and the Supreme Court* (2013).
12 P. Darbyshire, *Sitting in Judgment: The Working Lives of Judges* (2011) ch. 2.
13 J.L. Pierce, *Inside the Mason Court Revolution: The High Court of Australia Transformed* (2006).
14 J. McLaren, *Dewigged, Bothered, & Bewildered: British Colonial Judges on Trial, 1800–1900* (2011).

Their Audiences, is an example of American scholarship that makes no use of visual images in general or pictures in particular.[15] Their absence from Baum's study is more surprising. The main insight offered by this study is that judicial self-presentation is a notable dimension of judicial behaviour. Relations between the judiciary and their audiences, 'people whose esteem they care about', play a key role in the judicial preoccupation with image making.[16] While this may take many forms, including the style and content of written judgments, it also has many visual dimensions. Some are to be found in practices of staging judicial performances in the courtroom.[17] Painted and photographic portraits, sketches, and sculptures are other objects through which judicial image making takes place with a variety of audiences in mind.[18] If the visual dimensions of the judicial image are hinted at in Baum's study, there is little evidence that they were the direct object of inquiry.

While this sample of work is small it exemplifies key characteristics of the data sets and methods most commonly used in researching the life of the judiciary as an institution. These ranges from national depositories of state papers, published judicial decisions, papers relating to litigation, newspaper and other mass media reports, and personal papers of individual members of the judiciary. The transcripts of interviews are another key source of data. Textual analysis of these writings is the dominant method.[19] Pictures are confined to the margins, as a thin outer skin provided by publishers as part of their marketing strategy rather than a valuable source of data or research tool.

Pictures appear to be more commonly used when writing the lives of individual judges. Portraits of the subject frequently grace the front covers of judicial biographies and autobiographies. They span a range of images. For example, books by Lord Denning and about Lord Denning use formal painted and photographic portraits where the subject is depicted in full judicial regalia as well as informal photographic portraits,[20] such as one that

---

15 Baum, op. cit., n. 3. The United States Supreme Court has attracted much scholarly and journalistic attention resulting in many books. As a general rule, with the exception of the book's cover, little use is made of visual images in these studies.

16 id., p. 21.

17 Examples of scholarship in this field include J.J. Baker, 'A History of English Judges' Robes' (1978) 12 *Costume* 27; L. Barshack, 'The Totemic Authority of the Court' (2000) 11 *Law and Critique* 301; P.D. Blanck et al., 'The Appearance of Justice: Judges' Verbal and Nonverbal Behavior in Criminal Jury Trials' (1985) 38 *Stanford Law Rev.* 89; P. Carlen, 'The Staging of Magistrates' Justice' (1976) 16 *Brit. J. of Criminology* 48.

18 L.J. Moran, 'Judging pictures: a case study of portraits of the Chief Justices, Supreme Court of New South Wales' (2009) 5(3) *International J. of Law in Context* 61.

19 L. Epstein and J. Knight, 'Courts and Judges' in *The Blackwell Companion to Law and Society*, ed. A. Sarat (2004) 170. See, also, L.J Moran, 'Studying the judiciary after the cultural turn' in *Social Research after the Cultural Turn*, ed. S. Roseneil and S. Frosh (2012) 124.

20 I. Freeman, *Lord Denning: A Life* (1993) uses a painted portrait. A formal photographic portrait graces the cover of A. Denning, *The Due Process of Law* (1980).

78

shows Lord Denning wearing a panama hat.[21] Another uses a caricature sketch.[22]

The biography of Rose Heilbron is an example of a work that uses pictures not only on the covers but also in the body of the book.[23] A photographic image of Heilbron's carefully made-up face, with perfect arched eyebrows and precisely painted gently smiling lips, framed by a full-bottom wig and a lace stock (scarf) worn by Queen's Counsel, appears on the front cover. It is an edited picture. Most of the detail of the original is blacked out. This gives the face a luminous quality. On the back cover is a full colour reproduction of a three-quarter body portrait of Heilbron wearing the red robes of a High Court judge. Standing without the wig and red white-fur-lined mantle, both of which sit on a table to her right, the composition allows the artist to portray Heilbron's hourglass figure. The backdrop shows light cascading through a window on her right, illuminating a room, a private space rather than a courtroom, dominated by three gothic arches. These two pictures portray Heilbron's two pioneering achievements referred to in the subtitle of the book: '. . . England's first Woman Queen's Counsel and Judge.'

There are over eighty photographs inside the book. They fall into two groups. Forty five are photographic reproductions of newspaper headlines and reports about Heilbron's career, some of which also contain formal photographs of her as Queen's Counsel and judge, dressed in the respective wigs and robes.[24] The captions that accompany each of the other photographs give a flavour of their range and content. 'Stylized photograph of Rose soon after her marriage 1945' is attached to what appears to be a carefully staged head-and-shoulder studio portrait produced for private use. 'Family holiday in Llandudno' is an example of one of many family snapshots that depict aspects of the subject's private and domestic life. 'As Treasurer of Gray's Inn calling a student to the bar, 1985' is a professionally produced photograph made to record particular (sometimes less formal) institutional events depicting Heilbron's various roles and activities. Printed on glossy paper and segregated into clusters of pictures interspersed through the book, the photographs are free-standing rather than illustrations that accompany specific parts of the text; a reader can either skip over them or contemplate them as distinctive visual data relatively free from an accompanying text that might confine their meaning.

How important is this visual data for the author, Heilbron's daughter, also a Queen's Counsel? What role did the visual data play in her production of the biography? The author has little to say directly on the sources and

---

21 E. Heward, *Lord Denning: A Biography* (1997).
22 J.L. Jowell and J.P.W.B. McAuslan, *Lord Denning: The Judge and the Law* (2008).
23 H. Heilbron, *Rose Heilbron* (2012).
24 On photographs of the judiciary in newspaper reports, see L.J. Moran, 'Every picture speaks a thousand words: visualising judicial authority in the press' in *Intersections of Law and Culture*, eds. P. Gisler et al. (2012) 31.

methods used. There is one brief comment about the data she used in her preface:

> I have been lucky to have been able to tap into many valuable written sources. My Mother was a hoarder. She left me a vast assortment of material including diaries, press cuttings, letters and speeches as well as her own contemporaneous notes from which, together with my own knowledge and that of my late Father, I have been able to draw upon.[25]

There is no explicit reference to visual data here. The archive used by the author is brought under the heading 'written sources'. The inclusion of 'press cuttings' under the title 'written sources' follows a well-established tradition of paying little attention to the visual dimensions of press reports.[26] The inclusion of photographic reproductions of press cuttings, many of which include photographic images, and the presence of other photographs in the book is some evidence that visual data was a valuable, if poorly acknowledged, source. While conversations, particularly with her father, are identified as another source, as are the author's own memories, there is no evidence of how – if at all – the author used photographs to facilitate these conversations and generate memories. In contrast, the book is littered with references to Heilbron's image in general and her visual image in particular. Her performances of femininity and their representation in a variety of media is a recurring theme of the study. At an early point in her professional career, Heilbron engaged a professional press-cuttings service to collect newspaper reports of her activities. There is much in this biography to suggest she was acutely aware of the importance of image making and image management.[27]

Again, while this is far from being a systematic study[28] of the use of pictures in life writing individual judicial subjects, it offers a number of insights. One is that pictures may well be found in public, professional, and private archives and used in life-writing projects. Details about who

---

25 Heilbron, op. cit., n. 23, p. xi.
26 The visual aspects of newspaper reports, the layout, the use of different fonts, the role of pictures all tend to be ignored when researchers make use of newspaper reports: see Moran, op. cit., n. 24.
27 Heilbron, op. cit., n. 23, p. 104.
28 The United States has a particularly rich tradition of judicial biography and autobiography: for an introduction, see, on autobiography, L.K. Ray, 'Autobiography and opinion: the romantic jurisprudence of Justice William O. Douglas' (1998) 60 *University of Pittsburgh Law Rev.* 707; L.K. Ray, 'Lives of the Justices: Supreme Court Autobiographies' (2004) 37 *Connecticut Law Rev.* 233. On biography, see P.B. Purland, 'Judicial biography: history, myth, literature, fiction, potpourri' (1995) 70 *New York University Law Rev.* 489; R.A. Posner, 'Judicial Biography' (1995) 70 *New York University Law Rev.* 502. On life-writing traditions, or the lack thereof, in other jurisdictions, see, for example, C.L. Pannam, 'Judicial biography – a preliminary obstacle' (1964) 4 *University of Queensland Law J.* 57 and J.A. Thomson, 'Judicial biography: some tentative observations on the Australian experience' (1985) 8 *University of New South Wales Law J.* 380.

commissioned them, where they appeared, how they were used, and how they were collected can all shed light on the judicial subjects at the heart of life-writing projects. The appearance of pictures in the body of these studies also suggests that pictures currently play a more prominent role in writing individual judicial lives than is currently the case when writing the lives of the judiciary as an institution.

TAKING ACCOUNT OF THE MATERIALITY OF JUDICIAL PICTURES

Before considering judicial pictures as sources of data and their use as a research tool, brief consideration will be given to the 'the materiality of pictures'.[29] This is a phrase that calls attention to pictures as three-dimensional objects. It is important to consider the materiality of pictures as the particular nature of and, more specifically, the physical properties of pictures may all impact on the meaning-making potential of the visual object. For example, the use of oil paints rather than a mobile phone camera, a matte finish rather than a glossy one in the making of pictures, the use of gilded frames rather than framed by the edge of a computer screen when displaying pictures, may all contribute to a viewer's perception about the object and thereby the subject depicted. It may be perceived as precious, unique, of enduring significance, generating perceptions of the picture, and its subject as something to be contemplated and revered. In the alternative, the picture's materiality may suggest frivolity, superficiality, being of the moment, to be briefly glanced at then disposed of.

Picture formats tend to fall into two categories, landscape and portrait. The landscape format is wider than it is tall while the portrait format is taller than it is wide. The very shape of the picture tells the viewer something about its subject matter. As the latter category suggests, this is the common format used in making portraits, both painted and photographic. Portraits made using a landscape format are exceptional. They tend to represent the sitter through the depiction of particular events that tell a story that captures the character of the sitter.[30]

Size also has significance. Three-quarter and full-body portraits tend to be large in scale. It is a form and scale associated with the depiction of subjects of exceptional status. They assume and call for grand and imposing locations that allow audiences to view the subject at a distance and from below. In

29 Tinkler, op. cit., n. 7, ch. 1. Much attention has been paid in scholarship on the materiality of visual images to shifting analysis away from sole reliance on image content. But the literature on visual research suggests that that the impact of materiality on meaning is a contested one.

30 An example of this in the context of judicial portraiture is a portrait of Michael Kirby by artist Ralf Heimans in the Australian National Portrait Gallery, Canberra. See L.J. Moran, 'Judicial bodies as sexual bodies: A tale of two portraits' (2008) 29 *Australian Feminist Law J.* 91.

contrast to this, head-and-shoulders compositions tend to be smaller in scale. It is a style of portraiture associated with informality, intimacy, familiarity, and closeness between the sitter and the viewer. The small scale of the head-and-shoulders composition is associated with domestic spaces and functions, not with public affairs or matters of state.[31] The head-and-shoulders portrait is also a pose associated with the sitter's individual character and personality rather than their official or institutional role. In good part, this is expressed in the importance given to the face. The emphasis upon the face brings together identification with character, personality, and truth.

The technology used to make pictures is another important dimension of their materiality that impacts on the meaning-making capacity of the visual object: the veracity of that represented within the frame of the picture. The epistemological status of pictures is debated most frequently with regard to photographic images. Painted portraits tend to include marks on the surface of the image that evidence the labour and choices that go into making the picture. The technologies associated with photography appear to mechanically record in great detail the objects placed in front of the camera with little or no evidence of human manipulation. This is described as the 'naive realist' position.[32] Priority is given to the picture as an accurate unmediated record of what is seen in the frame of the picture. The multiple manipulations that go into making a photographic image, choosing and arranging the objects, including humans, in front of the camera, organizing the lighting, aperture, depth of focus, and so on may go unacknowledged or unconsidered in the act of viewing. It is now commonplace to caution against the dangers of the naive realist position. However, the 'temptations of realism' still exist and need to be constantly identified and resisted.[33]

At the other extreme is a position that doubts the capacity of the photographic image to act as a record of anything other than the traces of the mechanical and human processes that went into making the representation. Neither extreme is particularly useful. The exceptional recording capacity of camera technologies can be acknowledged while, at the same time, maintaining an awareness of and sensitivity to the processes used and choices taken in the making of the picture.

Another aspect of a picture's materiality, its location, impacts on its meaning.[34] A framed photograph of a judge in full robes displayed in London's National Portrait Gallery may generate different meanings when displayed on a bookcase in the judge's own home. The 'acquisition and disposal policy' of the National Portrait Gallery in London explains that portraits in that collection are of 'the most eminent persons in British history

---

31 D. Piper, *The English Face* (1957) 161.
32 Tinkler, op. cit., n. 7, pp. 3–10.
33 P. Burke, *Eyewitnessing: The Uses of Images as Historical Evidence* (2001) 21.
34 See M. Pointon, *Hanging the Head: Portraiture and Social Formation in Eighteenth-century England* (1993).

82

...'.[35] So the incorporation of a judicial portrait on the walls of that institution prompts an audience to read the portrait in very particular ways. In the BBC Four television documentary, 'The Highest Court in the Land: Justice Makers', produced and directed by Nicola Stockley, Lord Hope, a Justice of the Supreme Court from 2009–2012, walks towards the camera holding up a small framed photograph of himself in full-bottomed wig and judicial robes to the off-camera interviewer in his home in Edinburgh. He explains that it is a picture that depicts him as Lord Justice General, Scotland's most senior judge with responsibility for criminal courts. He describes the pose: '... this is me looking very grim as I thought was probably suitable for me as a judge in charge of the criminal process in Scotland.'[36] If the composition and quality of the picture suggests it was made by a professional photographer and is an official picture of the sitter, its location in the family home set amongst other photographs of Lord Hope suggests it is a photograph of particular domestic significance. In that setting, its audience is Lord Hope and his immediate family and friends whereas in its 'original location' in a courthouse, official building or judicial website, the intended audience for the same picture, an official image of Lord Hope as a judge, is more likely to be fellow judges, members of the legal profession, court staff, and members of the public. In the home, the picture has a personal meaning. Lord Hope explains it is on display as a personal record of an important legal career milestone of which he is particularly proud. His comment to camera suggests that when displayed in the home it offers an opportunity for distance from his official persona; looking 'grim' loses some of its authenticity and effectiveness, revealing a rather different aspect to his character. The appearance of this 'family photo' in the BBC Four documentary also draws attention to the power of television to relocate the picture. It turns that family picture and the intimate moment it generates into a new type of public picture that is now located in the homes of the TV viewers. In the context of a documentary about the Supreme Court, Lord Hope's private and family object is now made public as part of the persona of the Supreme Court that is being made and made visible to the public through television.

The complex web of social relations that shape the process of making pictures and influences what gets represented in the frame of the picture is another dimension of every picture's materiality. Data about these relations can be found in a variety of sources such as diaries, art historical scholarship, and interviews with those that make images, commission images, and are the subject of images. I have used interviews with painters and photographers who have been commissioned to make portraits of the judiciary to explore

35 At <http://www.npg.org.uk/about/corporate/gallery-policies/acquisition-and-disposal-policy.php>.
36 The documentary can be viewed at <http://www.youtube.com/watch?v=PZtYENfNa7k>.

83

these matters. Some of the insights generated by these interviews will be used in the following discussion of pictures as sources of data as well as in the section that examines pictures as a research tool.

JUDICIAL PICTURES AS VISUAL DATA: FOUND PICTURES

Painted and photographic portraits of individual members of the judiciary considered in this section generate particular challenges. Many fit a pattern identified by art historian Charlotte Townsend-Gault. They appear to be bland, predictable, and vacuous, and indifferent art.[37] But it would be wrong to dismiss them for those reasons. Pictures that put the judge at the centre of the image have been made from the sixteenth century.[38] They are potentially a valuable resource and worthy of detailed consideration.

Fine art scholarship on portraiture offers a number of insights relevant to using judicial portraits as research data. As a general rule portraiture is strongly associated with the empirical.[39] The portrait offers a likeness of the sitter based on direct observation. Portraiture is a type of image associated with the truth of the subject of the picture. The portrait not only represents the physical appearance of the sitter but also the truth of the sitter's character and personality.

A portrait of Australian judge Michael Kirby, a gay man, for several years a judge in the High Court of Australia, painted by Sydney-based artist Josonia Palaitis, provides a vehicle through which these points may be illustrated. Josonia Palaitis is noted for her 'photo realist' approach to portraiture:

> The visual representation on the canvas is what you would expect most people who were seeing the subject would see in real life . . . It is a very technical style of painting.[40]

It is a style of portraiture that draws attention to the veracity of the representation. Michael Kirby described the resulting overall empirical effect: 'Every vein and wrinkle and hair and blemish [is] recorded for all to see.' The truth of the portrait is not confined to these surface details. Kirby suggests it '. . . burrows deep under my blemished skin. It detects and reveals

---

37 C. Townsend-Gault, 'Symbolic Façades: Official Portraits in British Institutions since 1920' (1988) 11 *Art History* 511, at 511–12.
38 R. Tittler, *The Face of the City* (2007) and L.J. Moran, 'Imagining the judge: fragments of a study of judicial portraiture' in *Legal Staging: Visualisation – Mediatisation – Ritualisation: Legal Communication through Language, Literature, Media, Art and Architecture*, eds. K. Modéer and M. Sunnqvist (2012) 205.
39 J. Pope-Hennessy, *The Portrait in the Renaissance* (1966).
40 An interview with Josonia Palaitis in Sydney, Australia, 9 March 2007, transcript on file with the author.

© 2015 The Author. Journal of Law and Society © 2015 Cardiff University Law School

moods and emotions that are part of my inner self.'[41] Likeness represents depth, his inner life, even to the extent that it can reveal something to the subject he or she may not always be aware of; something otherwise hidden, unrecognized, unspoken. Kirby reported the portrait shows him '... more angry than I feel inside.' He continued:

> Yet perhaps the artist recognises, better than I do, the feelings of the inner heart. Maybe the many injustices in the law and in life, witnessed over thirty years as an Australian judge, take a toll that the professional office holder learns to suppress. Obedience to the law obliges the limits of the judicial function. Yet being a party to apparent injustices can sometimes make even a judge angry.[42]

Josonia Palaitis's particular style of portraiture plays with empirical associations attached to photographic images to achieve this effect. It uses a very particular aesthetic to engage the viewer and to invite a range of reactions to the sitter.

Other artists use different approaches to representation and as a result use a very different visual language to portray the subject. These will impact on the way data about the sitter is represented. They need to be considered by a researcher who is using portraits as a source of data. The point was vividly expressed during the course of an interview with another artist who has painted a portrait of Michael Kirby, Judy Cassab. When I asked her to comment on the portrait reproduced in a book of her work that I brought to the interview, she took the book, turned it upside down and placed her hand over Kirby's painted face.[43] As she did so she talked about the importance of the 'abstract' aspects of the painted image: the colours used and the marks made by the artist's brush. She explained these are a vital part of the portrait, '... his personality came out through all the colours.'[44]

Other sources of data in judicial portraits are the subject's body, its posture, the clothing that covers its surface, and the props and background against which it is set.[45] A photographic portrait of James Jacob Spigelman,

---

41 M. Kirby, 'Hanging Judges and the Archibald Prize, 2006', at <www.michaelkirby.com.au/images/stories/.../2088-Hanging_Judge.pdf> 6. This echoes a common conceit. See R. Rushton, 'What Can a Face Do? On Deleuze and Faces' (2002) *Cultural Critique* 219, at 219.

42 Kirby, id., p. 5.

43 L. Kelpac, *Judy Cassab: Portraits of Artists and Friends* (1998).

44 Interview with Judy Cassab, Double Bay, Sydney, 14 February 2007, on file with the author. The importance of colour also came up in relation to the portrait of Michael Kirby by Palaitis. Black is a dominant colour. Kirby explained:
   > I knew from Jo Palaitis's other works that she is usually happiest with light, colour and bright objects. I warned her that 'lawyers love black'. 'Put more black into it', I repeatedly urged. Eventually, the portrait emerged: dark and sombre with a Goya-like luminous blackness.
   See M. Kirby 'On the presentation of a portrait by Josonia Palaitis' (2007), 11, at <www.michaelkirby.com.au/.../2227-PORTRAIT_HANGING_NOV_200...>.

45 On portraiture, see R. Brilliant, *Portraiture* (1991); Piper, op. cit., n. 31; S. West, *Portraiture* (2004); J. Woodall (ed.), *Portraiture: Facing the Subject* (1997).

Chief Justice of New South Wales from 1998 to 2011, can be used to illustrate the point.[46] The portrait is distinctive because of the way it makes use of props more diverse than are to be found in any of the other official portraits of the Chief Justices of the NSW Supreme Court on display in the Chief Justice's court, the Banco Court.[47]

The judge is at the centre of the picture, dressed in red robes of office and wearing a full-bottom wig. His body is slightly turned to his left. His face is turned to the right so that the viewer sees almost his full face. He looks directly out of the picture. His eyes engage the viewer, drawing them in. On his right, on top of a low bookcase filled with substantial bound volumes organized according to their binding, is a small set of scales. On his left is a carved figure of a bird. Dominating the background is a large painting. It is of an interior with two Chinese porcelain pieces. At the centre of the painting is a shaped opening (a window?) that frames an oriental garden scene: a cascading willow, lakeside, bridge, and an oriental building. The opening forms a halo around the head and shoulders of the Chief Justice. The vase, with a Chinese dragon design, is over his right shoulder. The figure of a horse is over his left. The appearance of the objects and the painting as the backdrop certainly tell us something about James Spigelman. He has a passion for the arts. He was Chairman of the Australian Film Finance Corporation Board 1990–1992, Deputy Chairman of the Art Gallery of New South Wales 1983–1988, and President of the Museum of Applied Arts and Sciences 1995–1998. He also has a long-standing interest in things Chinese.[48] But these objects do not merely refer to the individual judge's interests. Art historical studies of two particular types of portraiture – portraits of members of professions and state and official portraits – offer important insights into the nature of the data that is be found in portraits such as this.

Using scientific and medical portraits as her case study, Ludmilla Jordanova demonstrates that portraits of members of elite professions are a particular form of self-fashioning and represention. The picture of a specific individual has a double function and offers two types of data.[49] One is

---

46 The portrait of The Honourable James Jacob Spigelman, AC, Sixteenth Chief Justice of the Supreme Court of NSW, 25 May 1998 – 31 May 2011 can be viewed at <http://www.supremecourt.lawlink.nsw.gov.au/supremecourt/honourable_james_jacob_spigelman.html>.

47 id.

48 During the course of his swearing-in ceremony, reference was made of his involvement (while still at school) in establishing an Asian Society to promote dialogue between Chinese and non-Chinese students. See The Honourable J.W. Shaw QC MLC Attorney General Of New South Wales, 'Swearing in ceremony of the Honourable J.J. Spigelman QC as Chief Justice of The Supreme Court of New South Wales' 25 May 1998, at <http://www.agd.nsw.gov.au/lawlink/supreme_court/ll_sc.nsf/pages/SCO_speech_spigelman_25059>.

49 L. Jordanova, *Defining Features: Scientific and Medical Portraits 1660–2000* (2000). See, also, Brilliant, op. cit., n. 45 and J. Ingamells, *The English Episcopal Portrait 1559–1835* (1982).

evidence of the identity of the individual sitter. The other is of the ideas, values, and virtues associated with the collective: the institutional identity.[50] The portrait makes the character of the institution visible, public, and accessible.[51] The sitter is represented as its living embodiment. But the application of Jordanova's insights to portraits of judges needs to be treated with some caution, as judges are not merely elite figures associated with the legal profession. They occupy a very particular position as officers of state. So what can work on 'state' and 'official' portraits add to Jordanova's insights?

Jenkins defines state portraits as 'representations of rulers or their deputies'.[52] Judges, by way of their historical connection with the sovereign as their organ of justice, as the third branch of government, fall within the parameters of the phrase 'rulers or their deputies'. Jenkins argues that state portraits have a specific purpose, foregrounding the qualities and characteristics of the office rather than the personality and character of the individual office holder. The individual is represented in such a way as to evoke through the image, 'those abstract principles for which he [sic] stands.'[53] It is, she suggests, a form of portraiture that resorts to special methods of handling the sitter, using distinctive aesthetic codes designed to give visual form to a particular set of institutional attributes, characteristics, qualities, particularly concerned with social and political rank. For example, it is common for state portraits to be large in scale. Full- and three-quarter-body poses dominate. The face takes up a relatively small area of the painted or photographic surface; the body dominates. The background is monotone or loosely figured, thereby causing the viewer's eye to focus on the sitter's body.

These insights into the characteristics of judicial portraits as state portraits highlight the importance of pictures as depictions of institutional values and virtues. In judicial portraiture, the pose of the body, background, costume, props, and so on are all signs through which the values and characteristics of the judicial institution are represented. I have argued elsewhere that in judicial portraits these include independence, integrity, impartiality, and majesty.[54] The judge's body, standardized and rendered nondescript by the voluminous judicial robes, symbolizes the judicial virtues of individual self-effacement through dedication to justice and the word of the law, usually represented as a book. Having an appearance that is bland and predictable, making it almost impossible to differentiate one judge from another, is also a part of the visual code that makes and makes public the judicial subject's

50 Jordanova, id., pp. 14–15.
51 id., p. 73.
52 M. Jenkins, *The State Portrait: Its origins and evolution* (1947). See, also, E.H. Kantorowicz, *The King's Two Bodies* (1957).
53 Jenkins, id., p. 1.
54 Moran, op. cit., n. 18.

embodiment of the key judicial virtues of sameness, repetition, endurance, continuity, and consistency.

With all that in mind, I want briefly to return to the portrait of James Jacob Spigelman. The books and scales are familiar props; symbols that characterize the sitter's selfless attachment to justice and devotion to the letter of the law. The Chinese symbols are exceptional. What attributes of the office of Chief Justice embodied by Spiegelman do they stand for? A passion for the arts may signify refinement and taste as virtues of high judicial office. The Chinese-inflected props and background make and make public the judicial virtues of an interest in and knowledge of other cultures and cultural awareness. Yes, this photographic portrait is an empirical record of the unique facts of that individual.[55] But it is also a portrait of a state official, a Chief Justice, and so the props and background tell us something about the qualities and the virtues of the office that the individual embodies. Burke suggests that a data set made up of a series of portraits made over a period of time provides opportunities not only to study the features that the pictures have in common but also creates the possibility of identifying and examining differences between them. Changes, even minor changes in the style of representation, Burke suggests, may be indicative of significant social and institutional change.[56] When put in the context of other portraits of Chief Justices of the same court, the appearance of a painting of a Chinese garden may indicate institutional change.[57]

A visual change I want to consider next is a change in the style of portraiture. Two contemporary examples of this trend are portraits of the first President of the Supreme Court of the United Kingdom, Lord Phillips, who held that office from 2009 to 2012, and the Court's current President, Lord Neuberger (Figures 1 and 2). They are part of a larger collection of portraits of all the judges, past and present, of the Supreme Court of the United Kingdom commissioned by the Court and made by a professional photographer. The portraits accompany short biographical notes of the judges on the court's website. They are also put to other uses. Sian Lewis, the court's first Head of Communications explained:

> They are more for identification purposes as much as anything ... we have a picture of each of them on the back of one of the leaflets that explains how we operate. It is so that when people come in they can see who is sitting ...[58]

55 R. Rosenblum, 'Portraiture: Facts versus fiction' in *Citizens and Kings: Portraits in the Age of Revolution 1760–1830*, eds. S. Allard and R. Rosenblum (2006) 14, at 22.
56 Burke, op. cit., n. 33, p. 28.
57 The official portrait of Spiegelman that hangs with all the other Chief Justice portraits in the Banco Court contains no Chinese symbolism and follows the tradition of depicting the sitter against a blank background.
58 Interview with Sian Lewis, Head of Communications, Supreme Court of the United Kingdom, 24 November 2009, on file with the author.

Figure 1. Lord Phillips, President of the United Kingdom Supreme Court 2009–2012

Reproduced with the permission of the Supreme Court © Supreme Court

These are examples of a style of judicial portraiture that is now common-place: a small-scale, close-cropped, head-and-shoulders composition. The face, in a full-face pose, dominates, taking up about half of the picture. Little of the sitter's body is visible. The subject's gaze is direct into the camera lens, engaging the viewer, inviting scrutiny. Each sitter is shown in ordinary business wear. Judicial robes and props are noticeable by their absence. The background is devoid of detail and characteristically uniform in colour and texture. It is in sharp contrast to the generally larger-scale three-quarter and full-body official judicial portrait considered above.

The reference to 'identification' in Sian Lewis's comment draws attention to the way this style of portraiture is associated with recording the distinctive features of the sitter through a preoccupation with the face. Other common uses of this style of portrait are passport photographs and police identification 'mug shots'. Common to all is the standardized compositional format seen in the Supreme Court portraits. Historians of photography have explored how this style of photographic portraiture was used to both exploit the camera's capacity to capture an abundance of detail and manage that detail by means of standardization. Making subjects look similar allows for easy comparisons that enable one subject to be differentiated from another: to be identified.[59]

59 Moran, op. cit., n. 18.

89

Figure 2. Lord Neuberger, President of the United Kingdom Supreme Court since 2012
(The original half-body composition was cut as indicated to make the portrait that accompanies his biographical note on the court's website.)

Reproduced with the permission of the Supreme Court © Supreme Court

But their use by the Court for official purposes draws attention to the fact that they are now a form of state portraiture and, as such, they present the sitter as the embodiment of the qualities and virtues of the institution. Allard, commenting upon the emergence in the nineteenth century of this intimate and informal style of portraiture in the context of images of important political figures, suggests that the emphasis upon the individuality of the sitter rather than the symbols of office expresses 'democratic and bourgeois principles'.[60] The qualities and characteristics of the institution and the social status attached to the post and the post holders are not, he suggests, missing but are now coded in a different way.

60 S. Allard, 'The status portrait' in Allard and Rosenblum, op. cit., n. 55, p. 82.

Status now has to be represented using a certain discretion. Status is now '... not so much [what] is shown as the manner in which it is shown that betokens dignity and exemplarity of the illustrious man ...'.[61] The lack of background, costume, and props emphasizes the importance of the face. The face of the judicial sitter now carries much of the burden of representing the judicial institution.

So, while this particular type of portraiture may help identify each individual judge, it also provides data about the virtues and values of the Justices as the embodiment of a contemporary judicial institution: the Supreme Court. Sian Lewis associated the pictures with a new 'accessibility' and institutional change. She explained:

> It was much more about accessibility and so on. People are very surprised that they don't sit in wigs and gowns. I think the pictures are a quite a good way of showing that it isn't like other courts. It is different. They wanted to keep that. They didn't want to sit there in their robes.[62]

When we look at the cropped photo portraits of the first two Presidents of the Supreme Court, what we see is two judicial subjects whose individual features are free from the obscuring effects of the symbolic regalia of judicial office. Their faces are clear, open, and engaging. The gaze of the sitter places them at the same level as the viewer. It draws the viewer in, inviting inspection. The symbolism found in these pictures represents the judicial subject as the embodiment of openness, visibility, transparency, and proximity, all of which are virtues of this judicial institution. The 'temptations of realism' makes the truth of these institutional values easy on the eye.

JUDICIAL PICTURES AS VISUAL DATA: MADE PICTURES

I turn now to consider the role of pictures made by the researcher. My own research on the judiciary has involved making visual images of the judiciary, particularly photographic images. In this section of the article I want to consider some of the challenges of making these pictures. I also want to explore what researcher-made pictures can add to research on the judiciary.

There are limited opportunities for a researcher to make photographs of the judiciary undertaking routine judicial activity.[63] In certain jurisdictions such as England and Wales, the law continues to limit making pictures in the

---

61 id., p. 83.
62 id. There is some continuity here between the two judicial institutions, old and new. When sitting as the Appellate Committee of the House of Lords, judges did not wear judicial robes.
63 Other ways of making pictures include painting, drawing, manipulating found images, for example, by making collages and composite pictures with or without digital manipulation.

91

courtroom and its precincts.[64] Another factor is that much judicial work, such as discussions about a case with fellow judges and writing judgments, takes place in locations that are 'backstage' and 'offstage'. Access to these locations is strictly controlled. Even when these restraints are not applicable, physical proximity remains a problem. In public, judges are often physically remote, protected by police and physical security barriers designed to keep all but authorized persons, or individuals with a strong telephoto lens, at a distance. Another challenge is the subject matter. Many aspects of judicial work are difficult to photograph; they involve activities, such as thought processes, that have little visibility. Ethical issues, taking pictures without consent, may also act as a check on making pictures. But making pictures of the judiciary is not impossible.

The first occasion on which I made photographic images of the judiciary was 1 October 2009. On that date the Supreme Court of the United Kingdom opened for business. It was also the date of the annual 'Judges' Service' marking the beginning of the legal year in Westminster Abbey,[65] followed by a 'breakfast' hosted by the Lord Chancellor in Westminster Hall.[66] All the judges of the higher courts, the High Court, the Court of Appeal, and the Supreme Court are invited to attend the service and breakfast on an annual basis. The judges who sit in courts below the High Court are invited on the basis of a rota or by nomination.[67] Judges and Queen's Counsel are required to wear full court dress. Approximately 600 people attend the 'private' Abbey service and an additional 300 join them for the following breakfast.[68] I have returned on several occasions: 3 October 2011, 1 October 2012 and, most recently, 1 October 2013. On each occasion I have taken photographs outside the Supreme Court and around the entrance and rear exit of Westminster Abbey. On 1 October 2012, I also made a number of short films using my iPhone: one of the route that the judges follow from the Supreme Court entrance to the perimeter gates of the Abbey, the others, taken in the

---

64 Section 41 of the Criminal Justice Act 1925 prohibits cameras in courts in England and Wales; s. 47 of the Constitutional Reform Act 2005 provides an exception applicable to the Supreme Court; s. 32 of the Crime and Courts Act 2013 makes provision for the Lord Chancellor in concurrence with the Lord Chief Justice to allow cameras in courts in England and Wales.

65 Westminster Cathedral hosts an alternative service for judges who are Catholics.

66 The breakfast originated as a response to the religious requirement that receiving the sacrament required prior fasting.

67 I. Denyer, 'Letter to John V.C. Butcher from the Head of the Crown Office, Ministry of Justice, 1 October 2013', at <http://lawyerssecularsociety.files.wordpress.com/2013/09/letter-from-crown-office-1-oct-2013.pdf>. The letter was in response to a letter from two members of the Lawyers Secular Society, see <http://lawyerssecularsociety.wordpress.com/2013/09/26/the-church-of-england-and-the-judiciary/>.

68 'Lord Chancellor's breakfast', at <http://www.parliament.uk/about/how/occasions/lcbreakfast/>.

92

Abbey itself, showing judges leaving after the service.[69] Pictures made on 1 October 2013 also included images of activities relating to a swearing-in ceremony at the Royal Courts of Justice that took place prior to the 'Judges' Service'.

The pictures in this visual research archive illustrate a number of uses of researcher-made pictures. One is to act as an additional visual record of events. 'Additional' refers to the fact that there are 'found pictures' of these events. They exist on the Abbey website and the websites of various media outlets that reported the events. The pictures in these archives will usually have been subject to a process of selection. It is unlikely there will be information about what has been left out or deleted. A researcher's photographs are potentially an important supplement to these archives of 'found' pictures providing a different visual record of an event. For example, my research archive provides a visual record of the route taken by the judges as they process from the Court to the Abbey. A Google-image search generates a variety of images of the judges processing along this route taken by media photographers. But my pictures document aspects of the procession that are not to be found in other archives. The pictures made during the course of my first visit record the judges using the pedestrian crossing to process from the Court to the Abbey. As the judges left the pavement outside the Court on 1 October 2009 to cross to the Abbey, they had to negotiate their way across the under-construction central isle of the pedestrian crossing. It was dotted with roadwork paraphernalia, a vibrant yellow, temporarily silent air-compressor encased in a wire-mesh cage, a jumble of red-orange plastic barriers, some police officers, court staff, and the odd professional photographer (Figure 3). A photograph of judges dressed in their gilded ceremonial robes negotiating roadworks is probably not an image that has value for the Supreme Court or the Abbey. Nor is it particularly newsworthy so as to attract the interest of the media. The picture of this particular feature of one of the processions supplements what exists in these other archives, providing data that would otherwise have been lost.

In terms of my own research, the data contained in the picture has a particular value. This otherwise 'missing data' has proved to be invaluable for my own exploration of the nature and significance of judicial ceremony and judicial ritual in contemporary society. The pictures of the judiciary on the pedestrian crossing record a juxtaposition of the extraordinary, judges in their gilded ceremonial robes marching in a formal procession, with the ordinary, the crossing. This juxtaposition begs a question about the nature and meaning of judicial ceremony and ritual. The pictures in my archive have facilitated an analysis of the many aesthetic choices relating to timing, location, gestures, costume, and props that go into making this particular

69 October 2012 was the only occasion I obtained an invitation to attend the service. I am grateful for Sir Igor Judge, who was then Lord Chief Justice for facilitating this invitation.

Figure 3. Justices of the Supreme Court of the United Kingdom negotiate their way across the under-construction central isle of the pedestrian crossing on their way to Westminster Abbey, 1 October 2009

© Leslie J. Moran

judicial event. They draw attention to the particular challenges of staging judicial spectacles on the street. As a 'theatre of justice', the street lacks the centripetal dynamics of the courtroom that concentrate attention on the judicial spectacle. My pictures capture the centrifugal and heterogeneous dynamic of the street that potentially diminishes the live judicial performance and makes its extraordinary qualities appear insignificant and out of place.[70]

Taking pictures of these events year after year draws attention to another use of researcher-made pictures: to act as a visual record that enables changes in these events to be documented and reflected upon. For example, repeated visual documentation has produced a record not only of the shifting composition of the Supreme Court bench but also of the presence and absence of particular members of the Bench at each annual event. My visual archive also records the changing audience for the judicial procession. In 2009 media workers, journalists, still and video camera crew, and their assistants made up a significant proportion of a large audience that crowded in front of the entrance of the Supreme Court. In 2010 my photographs record a rather different state of affairs: just one news crew recording the

70 L.J. Moran, 'Pedestrian crossings; some reflections on the occasion of a contemporary judicial spectacle' (2013) 25 *Dance Theatre J.* 30 and Moran, op. cit., n. 4.

94

judicial procession as it left the Court. The visual record of these changes offers some evidence of a variety of things: a change in the newsworthy status of the event, of its popular visibility and of its changing, declining, mass audience and, thereby, the shifting potential for public scrutiny of judicial activity.

Merely to highlight the way photographs can be used by researchers to record events underplays an important aspect of photography. Camera technology has a capacity to aid a researcher in recording an event in great detail with great speed. It can capture detail in two ways. It can record details in line with the researcher's avowed intention. For example, one purpose in taking pictures outside the Supreme Court in October 2009 was to make a visual record of media workers assembled in front of the Supreme Court on that day. They do achieve that goal and in more detail than I could possibly have captured by way of a contemporaneous written note in my research diary.

My pictures exhibit another important quality. They record more detail than I had in mind when I made the pictures. For example, on later viewing the pictures recording the presence of the media on my computer screen, I discovered things I was not aware of at the time I made the pictures. One picture shows a camera operator holding a printout of the identification pictures of the Justices of the Supreme Court referred to earlier. This unexpected detail is invaluable data relevant to my study of how pictures of the judiciary are used and made. Digital and screen technology enables a researcher to scrutinize the fine detail of the researcher-made picture, thereby further enhancing the capacity of these pictures to capture data.

Before leaving this topic, it is important to note that the research diary continues to have a role in this context. While the pictures themselves function as an aide-memoire, facilitating recollection and reflection, written notes made shortly after taking the pictures about the process of making the pictures can be of significance when later considering the meaning of what is captured in the frame. This is one way of attempting to ensure that the researcher has relevant notes that help to ensure that data about the materiality of the process of picture making is not lost. Also in terms of my own research, concerned with the process of making judicial images, the notes are a valuable source of data about my own experiences of the picture-making process.

JUDICIAL PICTURES AS RESEARCH METHOD:
PICTURE INTERVIEWS

Last but by no means least, I want briefly to consider the use of pictures as a method. There is evidence that photographs are an increasingly popular method in sociological and historical research.[71] However, there is little

71 For examples, see Tinkler, op. cit., n. 7.

evidence that similar developments have taken place in research on the lives of the judiciary, especially that concerned with the life of the judiciary as an institution. In contrast to this, the deliberate incorporation of pictures, primarily found pictures, as a method of generating data has become a common feature of my research practice. In most cases the pictures are a fundamental dimension of interview questions, shown to interviewees in a digital format via a PowerPoint file on a laptop computer. They have been used for a variety of reasons. I first used them in interviews during a research project on the sexual diversity of the judiciary.[72] Formal portraits of members of the judiciary who identified as 'gay' were used in interviews with artists who had painted them.[73] Their purpose was to prompt discussion and reflection about what the artist produced, and in particular about how, if at all, the sitter's sexuality was represented in the portrait. The pictures also prompted reflections and recollections about the experience of meeting the sitter and of the process of making the portraits. The use of pictures to facilitate dialogue in an interview has also been a part of subsequent work on judicial images. The pictures, sometimes showing the judge who is being interviewed and sometimes other members of the judiciary, give immediacy and familiarity to the topic. Using a picture of the interviewee early in the interview may also help the interviewee overcome any resistance to the topic in general or questions about visual images of the judiciary in particular. Pictures also offer a common focus for interviewer and interviewee to engage in a dialogue. They can help to foster a more relaxed atmosphere for both interviewee and interviewer, drawing attention away from the context of the interview. The ability of pictures to generate a conversation may also help to foster trust and, as a result, encourage communication.[74] With these preliminary points in mind, I want to turn to two examples where pictures of the judiciary have been used in interviews to generate data. The first, an extract from an interview with an artist, focuses on a discussion about the representation of the sexuality of the judicial sitter. The second is from an interview with a member of the judiciary and relates to responses to a picture of the judge that was attached to his biographical note on the judiciary website.[75]

The extract from the interview with the artist, Josonia Palaitis, is an example of the incorporation of a picture into an interview provided by the interviewee. It was the result of a happy accident. When I arrived at

72 L.J. Moran, 'Judicial diversity and the challenge of sexuality' (2006) 28 *Sydney Law Rev.* 566; L.J. Moran, 'Sexual diversity in the judiciary in England and Wales; research on barriers to judicial careers' (2013) 2 *Laws* 512.
73 L.J. Moran, 'Judicial legitimacy, diversity and the representation of judicial authority' (2010) 4 *Public Law* 662; L.J. Moran, 'Researching the irrelevant and the invisible: sexual diversity in the judiciary' (2009) 10(3) *Feminist Theory* 1.
74 Tinkler, op. cit., n. 7, pp. 174–5.
75 The website of the judiciary was changed sometime during 2009 when all photographs of the judges were removed from the website.

96

her studio to undertake the interview about her portrait of Michael Kirby, she told me that the portrait had recently been returned to her for varnishing and was in her studio. Next to it was a second portrait of a judge: a new, almost complete portrait of James Spigelman, then Chief Justice of New South Wales.[76] During the interview the artist also mentioned a third, earlier portrait she had made of Michael Kirby while he was the Law Reform Commissioner for New South Wales. The location of the interview was arranged so that we could both look at the portraits of Michael Kirby and James Spigelman. As we did so I asked, 'Do you ever think about the sexual identity or the sexual character of the sitters?' She responded:

> It is interesting to talk about this. When I did the first portrait [of Michael Kirby], my friend John Dowd suggested it and he lined up my introduction to meet him and so on. I didn't know who Michael Kirby was really. I didn't know what the Law Reform Commission was really. I just went in and met him. It wasn't until afterwards that a friend of mine asked me, 'Do you think he is homosexual?' And I thought what a strange thing for someone to talk about. Not only did I not realise, as most people wouldn't but obviously the word was out there, as this person suggested that to me, but it made me actually realise that it is probably one of the last things I think about ... That is something that doesn't occur to me. But as you say, a few years ago he made it public so when we met to paint his portrait last year we talked about that aspect of his life, not in any great detail but as part of the conversation. That was good. But it didn't actually make any difference to painting his portrait.
>
> I'm not quite sure, but I suppose all the other portraits I have painted, I guess, people are married or that they are not gay. I'm just trying to think of the people I have painted. I've painted a lot of portraits in my time.
>
> But with the Kirby portrait, when I was painting it last year, I guess I thought about it from time to time when I was painting the portrait. But I can't imagine that it particularly influenced what I painted or how I painted it.
>
> Maybe, I'm just trying to think and I'm just looking at it now and wondering. Yes, maybe there were times, painting the face. It is hard to remember, I just go into a zone when it is such close work and I'm doing the final details and stuff. Yes, maybe it was in my mind; but just there in my mind. I must say that doing Michael Kirby, certainly not with the first one that I did which is a long time ago, but doing the one I did last year, I would have to say that the sexuality thing was an aspect, a dimension of him that is there for me. Just like his being a judge. I had to read up about what high court judges do. It is all part of the input that I have, but certainly when we were in our meetings it was not a topic we dwelt on. There were a lot of other things that we talked about.[77]

The portrait of Michael Kirby prompts a series of interviewee reflections framed by the interviewer's question. Some of these relate to another picture and the artist's experience of painting that earlier portrait. Some reflections

76 Both completed portraits can be viewed on the artist's website, at <http://www.jpstudio.com.au/site/gallery.php?cat=2>.
77 Palaitis, op. cit., n. 40.

are contemporary with the picture that is before the interviewee and interviewer. The phrase 'I'm just trying to think and I'm just looking at it now' is of particular interest. It is a moment where looking again provides opportunities for new reflections and, in this case, different recollections that take the information being generated in new directions.

The second example is an extract from an interview with the then President of the Supreme Court of the United Kingdom, Lord Phillips. Overall the interview incorporated twenty-five 'found' photographs. Some, for example, twelve head-and-shoulder photographs of the Justice of the Supreme Court, including the one of Lord Phillips referred to earlier, were grouped together on a single PowerPoint slide. Others were shown individually. Eight of the photographs show Lord Phillips in a variety of formal and informal settings. In some he is wearing the ceremonial judicial robes and regalia of the Lord Chief Justice, a post he held between 2005 and 2009. In others he is informally dressed. The pictures came from a variety of official and news sources. The following extract is a response to one particular picture. It is a small, square-format close-up showing Lord Phillips holding a young child. Both he and the child are wearing matching open-necked casual patterned shirts. I put this image on the screen of the laptop accompanied by the following verbal prompt, 'This is an image of you that appeared on the Court of Appeal website when you were Lord Chief Justice.' The response was as follows:

> Lord Phillips (LP): Yes, we were each invited to provide a photograph for the website. So I thought I would choose a photograph that would show me as an ordinary person and not one of someone wearing a wig.
> Leslie Moran (LM): And what was the reaction of your colleagues to this image?
> LP: I have no idea. No, no idea.
> LM: It seems a radical departure from the full-bottom wig.
> LP: But you should see the images other colleagues provided.
> LM: I did.
> LP: I bet there were not many wearing full-bottom wigs.
> LM: It was very interesting to see how diverse the pictures of the judiciary were.
> LP: Yes. I would be surprised if almost anyone wanted to be seen in a full-bottom wig for the court website.
> LM: Why is that?
> LP: Most judges, if their photograph is to be seen by a member of the public, would prefer to be seen in their ordinary costume and not in some sort of disguise.
> LM: I see. You don't think that the symbols of the wig, the robe, the ermine trim, have significance for people now?
> LP: Well they probably do. But it depends on what message you want to get across. Most judges would not want to get across a message, 'How grand I am', but to get across a more personal impression.
> LM: And you don't think judges are nervous about presenting themselves as 'a person'?
> LP: We discussed whether we were going to do this and there were one or two of the judges not in favour of this, who thought that judges should be ciphers

98

and not seen at all. But by far the majority were in favour of having the public see what they look like.[78]

The data generated by this picture is of interest for a variety of reasons. It provides insights about the background to the use of the picture and the reasons for the choice of that picture. The latter sheds some light on the interviewee's approach to judicial institutional identity and changing perceptions relating to the representation of that identity. The reference to the photograph as a depiction of Lord Phillips as 'an ordinary person' at this point in the interview echoed a comment made earlier. Early in the interview, I introduced a slide with six official pictures showing two judges, one male and one female, in a variety of poses, dressed in the red robes and full-bottom wig. I asked Lord Phillips for his '. . . thoughts on these particular representations of the judiciary.' His response was:

> Well, they are wearing full robes and full-bottom wigs. The judiciary never wear these things, except on very rare formal occasions. It gives a fairly false impression of the judge as being something out of the ordinary whereas judges are in fact ordinary, albeit intelligent members of society doing a job without quite as much fancy dress as that.[79]

The interviewee's response to the picture found on the judicial website return to the idea of representations of the judge as an 'ordinary, albeit intelligent'. The picture that prompted the dialogue extracted above also provides data on Lord Phillips's perception of the attitudes of his fellow judges, some of which he suggests are in sympathy with his own and some of which stand in sharp contrast.

Before leaving this topic I want to draw attention to some of the challenges of using pictures in interviews. Not all interviewees will respond in the same way to the use of pictures. The contrast in these two extracts between the first interviewee's longer and more effusive recollections and reflections and the clipped responses of the second interviewee may be indicative of different perceptions about pictures. Pictures may not make all interviewees comfortable or more responsive. The researcher also needs to be prepared for a picture's failure to generate memories. In response to another picture of Lord Phillips with four other judges in full ceremonial robes, one a High Court judge and the others from the Court of Appeal, Lord Phillips said '. . . I can't quite remember what we were all dressed up for. It must have been some formal occasion.' There may be a variety of reasons for this. For example, Lord Phillips mentioned at another point in the interview that as Lord Chief Justice, he was repeatedly having his photograph taken. The particular picture I selected may have been a picture with no particular significance for Lord Phillips. In this instance I followed his

---

78 Interview with Lord Phillips, President of the Supreme Court of the United Kingdom, 22 November 2011, on file with the author.
79 id.

response with a prompt that offered some information about the context: 'I think they may be members of the judiciary who have a similar educational background.' This promoted a recollection:

> Oh, wait a minute. You are quite right. They were all at my school, I think. Yes. There must have been an occasion when we were all preparing to parade or something and I thought it would be a good idea to get the five members of my old school together.[80]

The context and possible reason for the picture was that all had been educated at the same public school, Bryanston. Care needs to be taken to ensure that researcher's prompt does not impose a meaning on the picture and thereby become the sum total of the interviewee's recollection.

The examples used in this section offer a number of illustrations of the use of judicial pictures in interview settings. They highlight the potential of picture interviews to generate useful data in the context of legal research. They also draw attention to their potential to facilitate interaction, and focus attention on aspects of law and, in this case, the judiciary that may be more difficult to achieve by other means. Last but not least, my experiences draw attention to some of the challenges of using pictures in this way.

CONCLUSION

The argument of this article is not that pictures should supersede other sources of data. It is that pictures are a neglected, sometimes poorly understood and underused, source of data. They offer much potential for those undertaking research into the lives of the judiciary. While current usage suggests that pictures have more of a role to play in researching and writing the lives of individual judges, one of the goals of this article has been to offer some evidence of how they might also be used to research and write the life of the judiciary as an institution. If 'found pictures' are likely to be the first port of call for researchers, they are not the only sort of visual data. There is scope for researchers to engage also in making pictures of the judiciary, thereby creating new and different visual data. Last but not least, one of the goals of this article is to encourage the use of pictures as part of a researcher's method. Pictures are useful devices for encouraging dialogue with interviewees, generating new data. Engaging with visual images offers many challenges. Every researcher will bring many assumptions and expectations about the nature of the visual objects through which representations of the research subjects are made and circulated. Awareness of the materiality of these objects, as well as the rich cultural traditions they draw upon, will enhance a researcher's ability to make sense of these objects and to work with them as sources of data and a tool of research. A rich

80 id.

100

multidisciplinary resource is available to help the researcher understand and respond to the challenges generated by the incorporation of pictures into research projects that focus on law, legal institutions, and individuals that work in the law. Using pictures to undertake research into law provides opportunities to engage with sources of data previously overlooked. It also provides new opportunities to enrich the toolbox of methods for undertaking legal research.

JOURNAL OF LAW AND SOCIETY
VOLUME 42, NUMBER 1, MARCH 2015
ISSN: 0263-323X, pp. 102–26

Ivor Jennings's Constitutional Legacy beyond the Occidental-Oriental Divide

MARA MALAGODI*

Sir W. Ivor Jennings (1903–1965) was one of Britain's most prominent constitutional law scholars of the twentieth century. He is mostly famed for his work in the 1930s on English Public Law. In 1941, Jennings, however, moved to Sri Lanka, progressively becoming involved in both an academic and professional capacity with constitutional processes across the decolonizing world in the early stages of the Cold War. This article provides an alternative account of Jennings's constitutional legacy to those of existing scholars by combining orthodox accounts of the 'Occidental Jennings' with an analysis of the neglected 'Oriental' experiences of this influential intellectual. It examines the ambiguous relationship between constitutionalism and democracy in Jennings's constitutional work overseas, and the impact of his postcolonial work on his views on constitutionalism.

INTRODUCTION

This article provides an alternative account of the constitutional legacy of the noted British constitutionalist Sir W. Ivor Jennings (1903–1965) to those that can be found in the existing literature. It does so by investigating a neglected aspect of Jennings's life and work, that is, his extensive constitutional engagement in former British colonies. Jennings is mostly famed for his work in the 1930s on English public law, referred to here as the 'Occidental Jennings' to denote the ensemble of orthodox accounts portraying the constitutionalist's life story, work, and legacy. However, in 1941, Jennings

* *Department of Law, London School of Economics, Houghton Street, London WC2A 2AE, England*
M.Malagodi@lse.ac.uk

I would like to thank the editors, Linda Mulcahy and David Sugarman, together with Harshan Kumarasingham, Peter Leyland, Martin Loughlin, Tom Poole, David Taylor, Grégoire Webber, and Asanga Welikala for their helpful comments on this article.

moved to Sri Lanka – where he resided until his appointment in 1954 as Master of Trinity Hall in Cambridge – and became progressively involved in constitution-making processes in decolonizing countries. I cumulatively refer to this period of Jennings's life, his academic outputs on the post-colonial world, and advisory work overseas as the 'Oriental Jennings'. Particularly in British scholarship, the 'Oriental Jennings' has remained almost completely absent from accounts of his life and work, with the result that Jennings's attitudes and legacy have been conflated with the 'Occidental Jennings'. A number of scholarly works have explored instances of Jennings's postcolonial constitutional involvement, but these outputs have tended to result in a piecemeal examination and fragmented picture of the 'Oriental Jennings'.[1] Significantly, no systematic study of Jennings's constitutional legacy overseas has been produced to date.[2]

This article analyses Jennings's constitutional legacy in South Asia where he was involved, both academically and professionally, with most of the region's jurisdictions.[3] Jennings played a direct role in the constitutional frameworks of Sri Lanka (1941–1955), the Maldives (1952–1953), Pakistan (1954–1955), and Nepal (1958), and had a long-term indirect engagement with India. It is argued that South Asia represents the core of the 'Oriental Jennings's experience and work. In this respect, it is important to highlight that Jennings was involved with postcolonial constitutional processes primarily in a professional capacity. He was one of the leading Western experts in the early stages of the Cold War, instructed either by the British government or local political leaders to dispense constitutional advice to decolonizing nations.[4] It is in this historical context that the embattled relationship between democracy and constitutionalism in Jennings's academic and advisory work takes centre stage in the assessment of his constitutional legacy. In fact, the different ways in which Jennings articulated the relationship between democracy and constitutionalism in Britain and in South Asia illuminate the contrast between his normative stance on British constitutionalism and his work as a practitioner overseas. Ultimately,

---

1 A. McGrath, *The Destruction of Pakistan's Democracy* (1996); J. Fernando, 'Sir Ivor Jennings and the Malayan Constitution' (2006) 34 *J. of Imperial and Commonwealth History* 577; and K.M. De Silva, 'Ivor Jennings and Sri Lanka's Passage to Independence' (2005) 13 *Asia Pacific Law Rev.* 1.

2 At the time of writing, the Institute of Commonwealth Studies (ICS) and the LSE Legal Biography Project are running a joint initiative to digitize and publish online the most significant documents in the Sir Ivor Jennings Papers held at ICS. See, also: H. Kumarasingham, *Constitution Maker – Selected Writings of Sir Ivor Jennings* (2015) and H. Kumarasingham (ed.), *Constitution Making in Asia – Decolonisation and State-Building in the Aftermath of the British Empire* (2015).

3 The expression 'South Asia' indicates: Afghanistan, Bangladesh, Bhutan, India, Maldives, Nepal, Pakistan, and Sri Lanka. During Jennings's life, Pakistan still comprised the East Wing, which then seceded and became the independent Republic of Bangladesh in 1971.

4 C. Parkinson, *Bills of Rights and Decolonization* (2007) 14–15.

the article illuminates Jennings's progressive metamorphosis from leftist, outsider, and democrat in his portrayals as the 'Occidental Jennings', to the conservative, pro-establishment, and authoritarian 'Oriental Jennings' in the postcolonial legacy of the Cold War era.

This article seeks to fill this void in the academic literature by drawing on an in-depth analysis of Jennings's private papers held at the Institute of Commonwealth Studies of the University of London and his correspondence with the British Foreign Office (FO) held at the National Archives, alongside his published work. A deeper exploration of the 'Oriental Jennings' merits attention because it illustrates the ways in which early Cold War political events prompted him to abandon the implementation of some of the constitutional ideas and models he held so dear in his writings, and for which he is well known in the English-speaking world. It also adds to our understanding of the man and the transportability of his theories by revealing how at times he adhered rigidly to aspects of his constitutional positions when they were unlikely to work outside of Westminster. It is hoped that these new and alternative accounts of Jennings the man and Jennings the constitutionalist will add nuance to our understanding of the interface of theory and practice, and colonial and postcolonial constitutional realities.

THE 'OCCIDENTAL JENNINGS'

Jennings was born in 1903 in Bristol from a family of modest means; he was an outstanding student, and succeeded in obtaining a scholarship from the University of Cambridge, where he was awarded a degree in law from St Catherine's College.[5] In 1925, Jennings was appointed a lecturer in law at the University of Leeds. In the same year, he joined Gray's Inn as a Holt Scholar – then a Barstow Scholar in 1926 – and commenced his professional legal training.[6] Jennings described himself as 'a scholarship boy', but as recorded in his memoirs, his 'relative penury' helped to motivate him.[7] In 1928, Jennings was called to the Bar of England and Wales and his practice as a barrister, while confined to opinion-writing work rather than advocacy,[8] acquired particular relevance to his work in Pakistan.

In 1929, Jennings was appointed lecturer in law at the London School of Economics and Political Science (LSE), where he remained until his move to Sri Lanka in 1941. At the LSE, Jennings authored his most famous works on English public law: *Principles of Local Government Law* ,[9] *The Law and the*

---

5 A. Bradley, 'Sir William Ivor Jennings: A Centennial Paper' (2004) 67 *Modern Law Rev.* 719.
6 C.J. Hamson, 'In Memoriam: Master Sir Ivor Jennings' (1965) 63 *Graya* 17–20.
7 Bradley, op. cit., n. 5, p. 719.
8 id., p. 723.
9 I. Jennings, *Principles of Local Government Law* (1931).

Constitution,[10] *Cabinet Government,*[11] *Parliament,*[12] and *The British Constitution.*[13] During this period Jennings established himself as a radical critic of A.V. Dicey's concepts of parliamentary sovereignty and the rule of law, together with his positivist method.[14] Loughlin describes Jennings's functionalist approach as based on an empirical orientation, a historical method, a scientific temperament, and a progressive outlook.[15] A reviewer of the first edition of *The Law and the Constitution* described the political orientation of the book as 'very distinctly left wing'.[16] Jennings was affiliated to the Labour Party, but by 1936–37 he had resigned his party membership.[17] In his autobiography, he wrote that political activity was not suited to an academic public lawyer, because 'it required too much simplification of the issues and too many compromises with one's conscience'.[18] As we shall see, Jennings adopted a different approach in his advisory work overseas, where he displayed more pragmatic, policy-oriented, and pro-establishment political attitudes towards postcolonial constitutional issues.

Jennings's political orientation and affiliation to the Labour Party are clearly reflected in the specific relationship between constitutional law and democratic politics he saw as being centred on the principle of popular sovereignty:

> For Jennings the main purpose of the constitution was to facilitate the efficient working of a democratic system. The 'efficient working of the democratic system' as the term was used in the 1930s is a synonym for the idea that 'the will of the people, as expressed through their elected representatives in the House of Commons, shall prevail, without undue delay'.[19]

In short, he argued that 'it is the people who are the guardians of the constitution' and that this safeguard is manifest in free and fair elections and the people's consent to government: 'Parliament is the legal sovereign and the electors the political sovereign.'[20]

According to Jennings, the British constitutional framework is ultimately guaranteed, in Lockean terms, by the people's right to rebel against tyranny. Thus, the key British constitutional tenet of parliamentary supremacy, while

---

10 I. Jennings, *The Law and the Constitution* (1933, 1st edn.).
11 I. Jennings, *Cabinet Government* (1936).
12 I. Jennings, *Parliament* (1939).
13 I. Jennings, *The British Constitution* (1941, 1st edn.).
14 I. Jennings, *The Law and the Constitution* (1959, 5th edn.) v–vi.
15 M. Loughlin, *Public Law and Political Theory* (1992) 167–76.
16 K.D. Ewing, 'The Law and the Constitution: Manifesto of the Progressive Party' (2004) 67 *Modern Law Rev.* 734.
17 Bradley, op. cit., n. 5, p. 724.
18 id.
19 Ewing, op. cit., n. 16, p. 735.
20 Jennings, op. cit., n. 10, p. 118.

a recognized principle of the common law, was not established in Britain by judicial decision; it was, instead, settled by conflict during the English Revolution and the Glorious Revolution.[21] His interest in democracy and liberty led him to argue that the latter in Britain is grounded in the spirit of a free people, who took up arms and fought for 'freedom for a reformed Church, freedom from royal absolutism, parliamentary freedom'.[22] The first edition of *The British Constitution* (1941) was published against the backdrop of the Second World War and informed by the stark contraposition between liberal Britain and Nazi Germany.[23] Jennings clarified that the essence of British democracy does not lie simply in a wide franchise, but in regular general elections where electors can effectively exercise a free and secret choice between rival candidates advocating rival policies: 'the symbol of liberty is His Majesty's Opposition'.[24] These factors 'differentiate British democracy from the so-called democracy of the Soviet Union and from the autocratic systems of Germany and Italy.'[25]

In the fifth edition of *The British Constitution* (1966), there was a shift in the countries Britain is compared to, which was consistent with the Cold War context and Jennings's post-1941 experiences overseas. British democracy was contrasted with 'the so-called "people's democracy" of communist countries and the autocratic systems of other authoritarian states'.[26] Similarly, Jennings's argument that written constitutions do not necessarily provide better safeguards against autocracy than the unwritten British constitution is illustrated in the first edition with reference to the ill-fated Weimar Republic,[27] but it is exemplified in the fifth edition by a generic reference to 'many dictators'.[28] This line of argument inevitably confronted Jennings with the burning questions of what kept Britain free, and what role constitutional structures played in safeguarding democracy. Jennings's answer seems to veer towards a degree of historical and cultural determinism as he argued that 'liberty is an attitude of the mind'.[29] Jennings did not attribute the success and endurance of democratic regimes solely to the genius of particular people; he argued that certain institutions – such as an independent judiciary, impartial laws, an efficient civil service, effective local government, and most importantly, a freely elected, active Parliament – are clearly necessary to protect liberty.[30] Jennings, however, remained

21 id., pp. 34–36.
22 Jennings, op. cit., n. 13, p. 226.
23 id.
24 id.
25 id., pp. 10–11.
26 I. Jennings, *The British Constitution* (1966, 5th edn.) 9.
27 Jennings, op. cit., n. 13, p. 13.
28 Jennings, op. cit., n. 26, p. 11.
29 id., p. 203.
30 id., pp. 206–8.

steadfast in his assertion that 'the source of our liberty is not in laws or institutions, but in the spirit of a free people'.[31]

Jennings's pioneering acknowledgement of the contingent character of constitutions and emphasis on cultural attitudes prefigured current preoccupations with culture in comparative law and socio-legal studies.[32] However, his belief that cultural attitudes were both the foundation and the 'black box' of a constitution limited his faith in the exportability of constitutional democracy overseas. In fact, even with regard to Britain, the tension in Jennings's writings between the democratic nature of the constitution and an anxiety about democratic politics remained unresolved throughout the five editions of *The Law and the Constitution* (1933; 1938; 1943; 1952; 1959) as expounded by Ewing:

> The fourth and fifth editions were written during the cold war, and there is a sense that much of what is related is by way of comparison with beliefs in some quarters about how government was conducted in the USSR, to which there is a brief mention.[33]

In the fourth and fifth editions of *The Law and the Constitution*, published in 1952 and 1959 respectively, at the peak of Jennings's Cold War engagement with constitutional politics overseas, his preoccupations with the democratic potential of the British constitution became more acute.[34] His concerns with abuses of power were reflected in his defence of 'manner and form' restraints to parliamentary sovereignty,[35] in the even more central role accorded to constitutional conventions and their binding nature,[36] in greater faith in the judiciary as the guardian of the constitution,[37] and in his diluted critique of entrenched charters of fundamental rights.[38] I maintain that Jennings's concerns with the functioning of constitutional democracy more likely resulted from his direct experiences in the postcolonial world than from an implicit comparison with the Soviet constitution as suggested by Ewing.[39] In fact, what transpires from Jennings's published and unpublished work is that he never visited the USSR nor wrote anything about its legal system.

In Jennings's view, the proper functioning of a constitution in a democratic country rests upon the acquiescence of the governed[40] and their

---

31 id., p. 209.
32 Ironically, Jennings's *bête noire*, A.V. Dicey, adopted the same 'cultural' approach to the limits of the law in his so-called 'lost lectures' on *Comparative Constitutionalism*, ed. J.W.F. Allison (2013).
33 Ewing, op. cit., n. 16, p. 751.
34 id., pp. 742–3.
35 Jennings, op. cit., n. 14, p. 153. 'Manner and form' restraints bind Parliament as to the procedure for passing future legislation.
36 id., p. 92.
37 id., p. 161.
38 Ewing, op. cit., n. 16, p. 749.
39 id., p. 751.
40 Jennings, op. cit., n. 14, p. 346.

recognition of political authority.[41] That is to say that constitutional government is based upon popular consent, and legitimate political authority is grounded in the historical, social, and political circumstances of a nation.[42] As a result, for Jennings 'constitutional lawyers or political scientists could not be satisfied with an Austinian-type theory based on authority because their business was to explain and justify that authority'.[43] Thus, his public law scholarship combined a focus on history with the study of institutions to explain the nature, powers, and working of political authorities.[44] It also featured a profound engagement with political theory and the philosophy of law to justify the authority that underpins the constitution and governmental institutions.[45] In 1938–39, Jennings spent a year as Visiting Professor of Political Science at the University of British Columbia, where his interest in the laws and politics of the British colonies[46] further developed from his days at the LSE.[47] He developed a keen interest in the study of institutions and concluded that to be a good lawyer, one had to be also a good political scientist.[48] The importance placed by Jennings on the political history, socio-cultural traditions, and institutional landscape of the constitutions that he studied is pivotal to his 'law in context' approach. When Jennings turned to look at South Asian jurisdiction, with which he was less familiar, he adapted his intellectual orientations and theories to the new political context of the Cold War.

THE 'ORIENTAL JENNINGS'

The 'Oriental Jennings' came into being because of a series of opportunities offered to him to influence the constitutional developments of a number of South Asian countries. In 1940, he was appointed Principal of the University College of Ceylon. The move to Sri Lanka in early 1941 inaugurated a new phase of prolific academic writing on the laws of the British Empire and then of the new Commonwealth, which represents a watershed in his writing and intellectual engagement.[49] It also led to a more practical engagement with

41 id., p. 335.
42 I. Jennings, *Democracy in Africa* (1963) 71–3.
43 J.A.G. Griffith, 'A Pilgrim's Progress: Law and the Constitution by Ivor Jennings' (1995) 22 *J. of Law and Society* 414.
44 I. Jennings, 'The Institutional Theory' in *Modern Theories of Law*, ed. A.L. Goodheart (1933) 69.
45 Jennings, op. cit., n. 14, pp. 331–2.
46 I. Jennings, *Constitutional Laws of the British Empire* (1938).
47 ICS 125/D/3.
48 Bradley, op. cit., n. 5, pp. 725–6.
49 I. Jennings, *The Constitution of Ceylon* (1953a, 3rd edn.); I. Jennings, *The Economy of Ceylon* (1950); I. Jennings, *The Commonwealth in Asia* (1951); I. Jennings (with H.W. Tambiah), *The Dominion of Ceylon – Development of its Laws and Constitution* (1952); I. Jennings, *Some Characteristics of the Indian Constitution*

decolonizing nations as Jennings served as constitutional advisor in many Asian and African jurisdictions – and even acted as legal advisor for Pakistan's Governor General in the infamous litigation over the dissolution of the country's first constituent assembly. This section begins to explore the deepening tensions between democracy and constitutionalism in Jennings's academic and advisory work overseas that emerged in this period.

This article concentrates solely on Jennings's scholarly and professional engagement in South Asia amongst his postcolonial experiences. It is argued that his work in South Asia represents the core of the academic production and advisory work of the 'Oriental Jennings'. In fact, Sri Lanka, India, and Pakistan are the only countries – alongside Britain – to whom Jennings dedicated entire monographs, three in the case of Sri Lanka. Moreover, in the Preface to *The Approach to Self-Government* (1956), Jennings wrote:

> I believe strongly in the importance of local knowledge and experience [...] In the main I have relied upon my own experience in Ceylon, Pakistan, and the Maldive Islands, and in seeking to draw lessons from the experience of India.[50]

Similarly, *The Commonwealth in Asia* (1951) examines India, Pakistan, and Ceylon;[51] and in *Problems of the New Commonwealth* (1958), the analysis concentrates on India, Pakistan, Ceylon, and Malaya as, in Jennings's view, it was India's accession to the Commonwealth that radically changed the nature of the Commonwealth.[52] The works of the 'Oriental Jennings' together with his constitutional legacy overseas have, however, remained almost virtually unexplored in academic writing.[53] In the special issue of *The Modern Law Review* to mark Jennings's centenary in 2003,[54] Martin Loughlin acknowledges that Jennings's post-war work on the drafting of Commonwealth constitutions represents one of the most conspicuous gaps in the collection.[55] The present article seeks to address this scholarly silence and concentrates in particular on his published work and archival material pertaining to South Asia in the papers of Sir Ivor Jennings.[56]

The Cold War context is of crucial importance in identifying the constitutional legacy of the 'Oriental Jennings' and understanding the political

(1953b); I. Jennings, *The Approach to Self-Government* (1956); I. Jennings, *Constitutional Problems in Pakistan* (1957); I. Jennings, *Problems of the New Commonwealth* (1958); I. Jennings, *Democracy in Africa* (1963); I. Jennings, *Magna Carta and Its Influence around the World Today* (1965).
50 Jennings, id. (1956), pp. vii–viii.
51 Jennings, op. cit. (1951), n. 49, pp. x–xi.
52 Jennings, op. cit. (1958), n. 49, p. 4.
53 See nn. 1 and 2 above.
54 (2004) 67:5 *Modern Law Rev.* 715–86.
55 M. Loughlin, 'Sir Ivor Jennings and the Development of Public Law' (2004) 67 *Modern Law Rev.*715.
56 The Ivor Jennings Papers were purchased by ICS from Jennings's widow in 1983. Access to the papers is open, subject to the usual conditions: <http://archives.ulrls.lon.ac.uk/resources/ICS125.pdf>.

considerations and constraints informing his constitutional vision and advisory work overseas.[57] After Sri Lanka, Jennings was instructed as constitutional advisor in former British colonies not simply for his legal expertise, but also for the trust the British government had placed in him not to offend British national interests and foreign policy.[58] In fact, Jennings deployed a 'modified' Westminster model overseas, ostensibly in order to better suit local circumstances, but also to strengthen particular pro-West local political actors. This proved especially important in the early years of the Cold War when Asia became a critical battleground for the two superpowers.[59] The tensions and discrepancies between Jennings's normative stance and his work as a practitioner overseas that emerge from a study of the 'Oriental Jennings' become more apparent when we return to two of the fundamental pillars, which underpin his approach to constitutional law dealing with democracy and constitutionalism.

The theories developed by Jennings in the early 1960s made little reference to his experiences in South Asia and were founded on two key arguments. First, Jennings's approach to constitutional issues reflected his belief that law and politics are inextricably intertwined. Jennings emphasized the importance of understanding country-specific local circumstances for successfully crafting a constitution, but also acknowledged that the work of the draftsman is constrained by the political will of those instructing him or her:

> The drafting of a constitution is a technical job, which, like many other technical jobs, is best done by those with experience of it. [...] A draftsman must however have instructions, for the essential principles of a constitution require political decisions.[60]

For Jennings, the details of constitutional drafting follow key political decisions regarding the organization of the polity. Thus, the relationship between law and politics in constitution-making moments is framed through a sequential argument:

> The framing of a constitution for an independent country is really only the latest step in constitutional development, and before that step is taken some aspects of the development become clear.[61]

He contended that constitution making requires political decisions to be made regarding essential constitutional principles before promulgation.[62] Jennings argued that these political decisions ought to relate to the country's specific historical, social, cultural, and economic conditions. In Jennings's

---

57 R.J. McMahon, *The Cold War: A Very Short Introduction* (2003).
58 Parkinson, op. cit., n. 4, pp. 13–14.
59 McMahon, op. cit., n. 57, pp. 35–77.
60 Jennings, op. cit., n. 42, p. 70.
61 id., p. 73.
62 id., pp. 75–81.

view, constitutional architecture reflects the political compromise and balance of power between the various political actors.

Second, Jennings's ideal constitutional formula for aspiring democratic regimes was centred on the legislature.[63] Thus, in his account, the key to successful democratization by constitutional means lies in the engineering of governmental structures informed by the principle of popular sovereignty. In particular, he placed central importance on the design, powers, and role of the legislature, as the institution most directly representative of 'the people', who are made the 'popular sovereign' by regular free and fair elections.[64] To sketch this normative formula in the early 1960s, Jennings appears to have drawn on his analysis of parliamentary supremacy in the British constitution, rather than on his professional authority overseas. But it is also possible to argue that Jennings's advisory work was driven by his reading of the specific socio-political circumstances of the countries where he was employed and by the political objectives of those instructing him in the Cold War context. In fact, the political considerations informing Jennings's constitutional advice often led to the marginalization of directly elected legislative bodies, which formed the core of his second pillar, in favour of powerful, but unaccountable executives to foster the stability of the various regimes vis-à-vis external 'threats'.

With regard to representative law-making bodies, there is a conspicuous gap in Jennings's constitutional engineering formula: he disregarded the importance of constitution-making processes and the composition of representative bodies in crafting democratic documents. Jennings underestimated the significance of 'constitutional moments', such as those that had occurred in the United States and India, in laying the foundations of constitutional democracy and legitimacy.[65] He seemingly took for granted the successful historical process that established British constitutional democracy through centuries of political adjustments and legal sedimentation.[66] Significantly, Jennings operated almost exclusively in countries directly under British colonial rule or heavily influenced by Britain in both their legal systems and governmental frameworks.[67] Thus, a key issue that the present article seeks to address is to what extent and in which areas Jennings departed from the British constitutional model in his work in South Asia – and ultimately why. This point is crucial to investigate the legacy of Jennings's constitutional work in South Asia.

63 id., pp. 71–2.
64 Jennings, op. cit., n. 10, p. 118.
65 B. Ackerman, *We the People* (1993).
66 P. Leyland, *The Constitution of the United Kingdom* (2007) 6.
67 Jennings, op. cit. (1956), n. 49, p. 21.

111

In order to better explore the claims that Jennings's work in South Asia had a larger influence on his writing than has been acknowledged to date, it is important to look at the historical context in which his constitutional work in South Asia took place and the specific features of his academic and professional inputs to the region's jurisdictions. The analysis here concentrates on the way in which Jennings's work has articulated the relationship between constitutionalism and democracy by exploring two issues across the various South Asian jurisdictions: the nature and powers of the executive and the position of fundamental rights vis-à-vis the institutional treatment of socio-cultural diversity.

In January 1941, Jennings moved to Sri Lanka where he resided for fourteen years. The island provided him with an ideal observatory on South Asia in a phase of critical political transformations across the region. In 1947, India and Pakistan gained independence from Britain and, in 1948, so did Sri Lanka. In 1951, the success of the anti-Rana revolution in Nepal allowed for the first bout of democratization in the country, while throughout the 1950s the British protectorate of the Maldives was affected by political turmoil. Jennings became involved, both academically and professionally, with all of these jurisdictions to different degrees. The wave of decolonization that swept the Indian subcontinent after the Second World War inaugurated an era of state and nation building across the region. As a result, all the newly independent states of South Asia sought to institutionalize radical political transformations through constitution-making endeavours. The drafting of postcolonial constitutions proved a difficult task,[68] not least because all the South Asian states featured clear-cut religious majorities: Hindu in India and Nepal, Muslim in Pakistan and the Maldives, Buddhist in Sri Lanka and Bhutan. With the exception of India, the majority religion played a key role across the region in state and nation building through constitutional politics. The Herculean task of postcolonial constitution making and forging 'unity in diversity' in South Asia was further complicated by the Cold War context. Pakistan was a close ally of Western powers, while India was loosely in the orbit of the Soviet Union. Thus, in the aftermath of the proclamation of the People's Republic of China in 1949, the Indian subcontinent became a battleground for both blocs throughout the 1950s.[69]

Jennings's work in South Asia took place in a formative phase of the region's constitutional development, and his legacy in the region must be understood in this context. In the remainder of the article I explore this dynamic by reference to four important case studies: Sri Lanka, India,

68 B. Metcalf and T. Metcalf, *A Concise History of India* (2001) 218–19.
69 P.M. McGarr, *The Cold War in South Asia* (2013) 21.

Pakistan, and Nepal, from which two hypotheses emerge. On the one hand, it is argued that Jennings developed a particular constitutional model for decolonizing nations. This was informed by the Cold War imperative of delivering political stability and regime continuity to 'Third World' countries and countering the 'threat' posed by the Soviet bloc, rather than a political commitment to promote constitutional democracy worldwide. In this respect, Jennings's constitutional work in South Asia built on his experiences in the region in an incremental way and reflected his view that law and politics are inextricably intertwined. On the other hand, Jennings was a constitutional lawyer trained in the British tradition. His understanding of the Westminster model, and belief in the supremacy of the legislature, inclined him to the imposition of certain aspects of this model whatever the political context. This makes it clear that the 'Occidental' and 'Oriental Jennings' can not, and should not, be viewed as distinct in his intellectual development. As we shall discover, Jennings's confidence in certain aspects of the British constitution was to profoundly shape his work, and failures, in South Asia.

1. *Ivor Jennings as constitutional advisor in South Asia*

Jennings was directly involved in the constitutional politics of Sri Lanka, Pakistan, and Nepal, but was only an observer to India's constitutional developments. Focusing on the context of his instructions and the constitutional outcome that resulted from his advisory work, the specific modalities in which Jennings articulated the relationship between constitutionalism and democracy become clear.

In Sri Lanka, Jennings's involvement with constitution making began two years after his arrival in the country. In 1943, the independentist political leader D.S. Senanayake unofficially enrolled him as his 'honorary constitutional adviser' until independence from Britain was obtained in 1948 in the form of dominion status.[70] Jennings's involvement in Sri Lanka initially displeased the British establishment as demands for constitutional reform were sidelined by wartime preoccupations,[71] but by the end of the war British foreign policy had transformed in line with the American policy[72] and entailed a programme of peaceful decolonization and devolution of political power to pro-West local elites.[73] As a result, Jennings's work in Sri

---

70 Jennings, op. cit. (1953a), n. 49, p. viii.
71 In his autobiography, Jennings wrote:
   I was at this stage very unpopular with the Colonial Office [...] It was said that I
   had been sent to Ceylon to start a University and had allowed myself to 'get mixed
   up in politics' [...] I had of course kept entirely clear of politics. What I had done
   was to give technical advice to the leader of the State Council when he asked for it.
   ICS125/C/xiv/1.
72 McMahon, op. cit., n. 57, p. 46.
73 ICS125/C/xiv/1.

Lanka came to be recognized as valuable by the British government: the 1946 Constitution drafted by Jennings on Senanayake's instructions had facilitated a constitutional, bloodless transition to independence.[74] The document reflected Sri Lanka's intention to function politically in the same way as the metropolis. It featured a Westminster-style parliamentary democracy, no Indian-style Bill of Rights, and a constitutional monarchy operating under the aegis of the Commonwealth.[75]

As a result of his assistance to Sri Lanka in constitutional matters, on 1 June 1948, Jennings was knighted by King George VI,[76] on the recommendation of Senanayake.[77] Then, in 1949, he was awarded the title of King's Counsel, presumably for his work in Sri Lanka.[78] Jennings resided on the island until 1955 and shared with the British and Sri Lankan political establishments the initial optimism about the Soulbury Constitution as a vehicle for democratization. However, with the 1956 general elections, Sri Lanka became increasingly polarized along ethno-linguistic lines, leading to brutal anti-Tamil riots in 1956 and 1958. Progressively, the Sri Lankan state was captured by the ethno-nationalist Sinhala Buddhist majority – a process which Jennings readily admitted the constitutional structures established in 1946 proved incapable of resisting.[79]

Jennings's avid interest in South Asia is further evidenced by the notice he paid to India. He never lived or worked in the country, but was an attentive observer of Indian constitutional politics.[80] In 1949, the Indian constituent assembly adopted the new constitution and proclaimed India an independent republic. The Constitution of India remains to this day the country's fundamental law. It is a long, entrenched, written document committed to constitutional democracy and secularism, which features a republican form of state, parliamentary form of government, and federal structure. The constitution enshrines the principles of constitutional supremacy and secularism and contains extensive sections of justiciable fundamental rights and non-justiciable directive principles of state policy. Writing in 1952, Jennings's assessment of the Indian document was rather critical:

> The Constitution is far too large and therefore far too rigid. [...] The Constituent Assembly was neither content to state general principles like a Constitution in the Latin tradition, nor to establish a set of institutions in the

---

74 Jennings, op. cit. (1953a), n. 49, p. viii.
75 H. Kumarasingham, *A Political Legacy of the British Empire* (2013) 120–3.
76 *London Gazette*, 1 June 1948, 3253.
77 A. Jeyeratnam Wilson, 'Sri Lanka: A Tale of Four Constitutions' (1998–1999), at <http://www.dlib.pdn.ac.lk:8080/jspui/bitstream/123456789/2997/1/Alfred%20Jeyaratnam%20Wilson%20Vol.XXIV%20%26%20XXV%201998-1999%20No.1%262.pdf>.
78 *London Gazette*, 26 April 1949, 2051.
79 Jennings, op. cit., n. 42, p. 66.
80 Jennings, op. cit. (1953b), n. 49.

English traditions. To the complications of federalism it has added the complications of a Bill of Rights.[81]

However, a decade after independence, Jennings changed his mind and commented that India had been the region's most successful constitutional experiment. In his view, India's constitutional achievements derived from the ability of its parliamentary institutions and uninterrupted rule by Congress to avoid a Balkanization of the country, which had seemed the likely outcome at independence.[82]

Jennings was also involved in constitutional reform in Pakistan. Like India, Pakistan had acquired independence from the United Kingdom through legislation passed in Westminster in 1947. When the constituent assembly began drafting a new constitution in July 1954, Jennings visited Karachi at the invitation of the assembly to review the draft to which he made only minor changes.[83] However, the growing tension between the Governor General, Ghulam Mohammad, and the constituent assembly, which was actively attempting to curb the Governor General's powers and establish parliamentary supremacy by codifying constitutional conventions into statute,[84] culminated in the dissolution of the assembly on 24 October of that year. In response, on 8 November, the constituent assembly's President Tamizuddin Khan filed a petition in the Chief Court of Sindh claiming that the Governor's dissolution was unconstitutional. The assembly instructed British barrister Denis Nowell Pritt QC to represent them,[85] while the Governor General engaged Jennings, who was also hired to prepare a draft of the constitution at the same time. Jennings's instruction in the case is significant:

> While Jennings was considered an outstanding constitutional expert of the day, particularly on Commonwealth matters, he was not being retained as a scholar but as an advocate. This meant that he would not be falling back on his vast store of constitutional law and history to reach an objective conclusion on constitutional questions. Instead, he had a client, Ghulam Mohammad, and Jennings was hired to prove that Ghulam Mohammad's dissolution of the Constituent Assembly was justified under the dominion constitution and the principles of English and Commonwealth law.[86]

81 id., p. 85.
82 I. Jennings, 'India After Ten Years' (1957) 28 *Political Q.* 236–42.
83 A. McGrath, *The Destruction of Pakistan's Democracy* (1996) 121–4.
84 id., p. 123.
85 D.N. Pritt (1887–1972) was a British barrister and left-wing politician; he was the MP for the constituency of Hammersmith North from 1935 to 1950. After his first visit to the Soviet Union in 1932 with the New Fabian Research Bureau, Pritt became – in the words of George Orwell –'perhaps the most effective pro-Soviet publicist in this country'. Expelled from the Labour Party in 1940, he eventually lost his seat in Parliament in 1950 due to the political changes brought by the Cold War. Between 1950 and 1960, he dedicated himself to legal work for the labour and anti-colonial movements. See: K. Morgan, 'Pritt, Denis Nowell (1887–1972) Lawyer and Political Activist' in *Oxford Dictionary of National Biography* (2004), at <http://www.oxforddnb.com/view/article/31570>.
86 McGrath, op. cit., n. 83, p. 120.

After losing at first instance,[87] Ghulam Mohammad appealed to the Federal Court and brought in Kenneth Diplock QC alongside Jennings QC, while the constituent assembly did not even have sufficient funds to agree to Pritt's offer to act pro bono upon the reimbursement of his living expenses.[88]

In March 1955, the Federal Court reversed the decision of the Chief Court and found in favour of the government.[89] For his services, Jennings received a salary seven times that of the Pakistani Chief Justice and a generous living allowance.[90] Moreover, on 9 June 1955, Jennings was awarded the honour of Ordinary Knight Commander of the Civil Division of the Most Excellent Order of the British Empire (KBE) in his capacity as constitutional adviser to the government by Queen Elizabeth II on the advice of Her Majesty's Pakistan Ministers.[91] Jennings's services were greatly appreciated by the British government during the Cold War. Pakistan had become a key strategic American ally in Asia through the South East Asia Treaty Organization (SEATO) against Communist China and the non-aligned movement of Third World countries in which India played a key role.[92]

Six days after the judgment of the Federal Court, Pakistan's Governor General declared a state of emergency.[93] A string of constitutional cases ensued, shaking the legal and political foundations of Pakistani democracy. Eventually, on 10 May 1955, a second, indirectly elected, constituent assembly was summoned by the Governor General and, in June, Jennings returned to Karachi to finalize the drafting.[94] Pakistan's first constitution, featuring a parliamentary form of government and a federal structure was adopted in 1956, but in 1958 the military coup by General Ayub Khan put an end to this fragile experiment in constitutional democracy and began the first of the many recurring cycles of praetorian rule in Pakistan, paving the way to a progressive Islamization of the state.[95]

Jenning's influence also extended to Nepal. In 1958, he was instructed by the British FO, upon the request of Nepal's King Mahendra Shah, to visit Kathmandu to assist a small commission in preparing a new constitution. The interest of the British government in Nepal during the Cold War was prompted by the Himalayan country's strategic location between India and the People's Republic of China, whose invasion of Tibet had begun in 1950.[96]

---

87 *Maulvi Tamizuddin Khan* v. *Federation of Pakistan* PLD 1955 Sindh 96.
88 McGrath, op. cit., n. 83, p. 175.
89 *Federation of Pakistan and Others* v. *Maulvi Tamizuddin Khan* PLD 1955 Federal Court 240.
90 McGrath, op. cit., n. 83, p. 160.
91 *London Gazette*, 9 June 1955, Supplement, 3308.
92 R. McMahon, *The Cold War on the Periphery* (1994) 6.
93 H. Khan, *Constitutional and Political History of Pakistan* (2001) 143.
94 For a detailed scheme of Jennings's suggestions on drafting in Pakistan, see: ICS 125/B/xv/7/1.
95 I. Talbot, *Pakistan: A Modern History* (1998).
96 J.K. Knaus, *Orphans of the Cold War* (1999) 100.

116

Jennings's mandate from the FO was clear: produce a constitution strengthening political stability in Nepal.[97] The design of the constitution was based on Jennings's reading of Nepal's socio-political situation after the revolution of 1951 rather than the principles he argued underpinned a functioning constitutional democracy like in Britain. He identified the Shah Hindu monarchy as Nepal's only stable political institution and drafted the new document around the King. Jennings's official mandate was to craft a document within the framework of constitutional monarchy and parliamentary democracy. However, in line with the importance he had articulated in his scholarly work of placing constitutional structures within local political contexts and his Cold War political expediency, Jennings's constitution established a framework completely tilted in favour of the 'hereditary executive' element of government – the monarchy – with a very limited scope for the 'representative executive'. On the basis of the so-called 'Pakistan formula', Jennings's political pragmatism, rather than reliance on British constitutional forms, ensured that executive powers were vested exclusively in the King and not in the cabinet, while the King was also granted extensive emergency powers enabling him to suspend the constitution. Unsurprisingly, King Mahendra suspended the constitution less than two years after its promulgation and ushered in the 'Panchayat regime' – a modern monarchical autocracy cloaked in the legitimizing traditional guise of the world's only 'Hindu kingdom' that would last for thirty years. Thus, by the late 1950s all South Asian countries, except India, had embarked on the treacherous path of autocratic government and ethno-nationalist politics. In this sense, history suggests that Jennings's reliance on political expediency rather than political principle was to have negative long-term effects for democracy in the region.

2. *Jennings's constitutional legacy in South Asia*

In the analysis of Jennings's constitutional legacy in South Asia, it is important to start with the recognition that none of the constitutions that he helped to draft survived in Sri Lanka, Maldives, Pakistan, and Nepal. Apart from in Sri Lanka, none lasted longer than two years. Moreover, Jennings's professional constitutional endeavours in Pakistan, Nepal, and Maldives were followed by bouts of authoritarian rule, mostly by the actors whose status he had upheld in his constitutional advisory work, while in Sri Lanka communal violence ensued. This suggests that despite his high status in British academic and political circles, his work to implant constitutional democracy in South Asia was unsuccessful. This section seeks to investigate Jennings's and other commentators' understanding of the reasons for such constitutional failures.

97 FO 371/135966.

Upon his move to Cambridge, Jennings clearly needed to take stock of the situation and sought to provide an explanation for the failed overseas constitutional developments he was involved in.[98] David Taylor recalls organizing a talk by Jennings for the Trinity Hall History Society on the failure of the many postcolonial constitutions he had drafted in the early months of 1965. The argument advanced by Jennings returned to his contention that an expert could draft a constitution to order, but that the document would only work if based on social and political realities.[99] His argument could partly explain the Sri Lankan experience, but it certainly does not apply to Nepal, where the text of the constitution significantly departed from key constitutional and democratic tenets. While sound constitutional design is not in itself sufficient to prevent constitutional failure, it remains a necessary condition for constitutional democracy to take root, develop, and function. In this respect, it seems that the legacy of Jennings's constitutional advisory work overseas was problematic for a number of reasons. First, Jennings interpreted, in an unquestioning manner, the legacy of colonial governmental institutions as tools of democratization rather than transporters of imperial hegemony. He downplayed the importance of an inclusive and legitimate political process supporting the drafting process. Second, while Jennings sought to translate British constitutional principles to local circumstances, he had a rather limited understanding of postcolonial realities beyond the small English-speaking elite circles he moved in, as he had no training in Asian history and languages. Lastly, Jennings faced the political constraints of his instructions in the Cold War context, which determined that the primary aim of his work should be to deliver political stability at all costs, even at the expense of democracy.

In respect to the first point above, it could be argued that Jennings greatly overstated the significance of British origins of the constitutions of Sri Lanka, India, and Pakistan:

> All three countries have learned the principles of democracy under British tutelage. It is unconceivable that there should be any fundamental change in this generation.[100]

Jennings also assumed that British colonial institutions represented the foundations of constitutionalism in South Asia. He, however, fundamentally misinterpreted the *raison d'être* of British colonial constitutional law. As Baxi observes:

> Colonial/imperial power provides scripts only for governance; by definition, it is a stranger to the idea of fundamental rights of the people. [...] All this needs

---

98 For the records of the Cambridge History Forum, see <http://www.cambridge historyforum.co.uk/CAMBRIDGE%20HISTORY%20FORUM%20SPEAKERS %20COMPLETE.pdf>.
99 Personal Communication, Dr David Taylor, 21 August 2014.
100 Jennings, op. cit. (1951), n. 49, p. 59.

to be stated in order to cure the modern superstition, which suggests that constitutional forms and ideals constitute a legacy of colonialism. The reality is otherwise. Colonialism and constitutionalism were always strangers. And the very act of enunciating a constitution marks a historic rupture.[101]

The proclamation of a new constitution entails two aspects: the political process through which a constitution is made, and the legal contents of the document. It is argued that the successful institutionalization of constitutional democracy is dependent on both aspects. From a procedural perspective, the processes of constitution making across South Asia in which Jennings was directly involved entailed an elitist approach to constitutional engineering. Small handpicked and unaccountable commissions prepared the constitutions of Sri Lanka, Nepal, and Maldives, while the courts and the executive outside of the legislature settled Pakistan's constitutional controversies.[102] Significantly, Jennings's failures in South Asia lie in stark contrast with the successful constitution-making process of India's constituent assembly, in which he was not involved. India capitalized on popular legitimacy as an inclusive legislative body representative of the Indian people. From a substantive perspective, this successful instance of postcolonial constitutional design and implementation radically departed from its colonial legacy in one fundamental aspect: Indian law makers engineered a constitutional edifice to make the people sovereign and guarantee equality before the law. Somewhat ironically, the problematic nature of Jennings's contribution to postcolonial South Asia is evident in both his stubborn adherence to British models regardless of the political context, and his outright subversion of British constitutional tenets. This can be seen in relation to his South Asian work as regards the nature of the executive together with the limitations to its powers, and the position of fundamental rights vis-à-vis the protection of minorities.

(a) Curbing the executive: the role of constitutional conventions

Two particular issues deserve to be analysed in more depth with regard to the treatment of executive powers because of what they reveal about the assumptions made by Jennings about the countries in which he wanted to import an English model. These are: the precarious position of constitutional conventions and the extensive nature of emergency powers. First, Jennings's legacy is detectable in the difficult translation of the informal parts of the British constitution. Royal prerogative powers and constitutional conven-

---

101 U. Baxi, 'Postcolonial Legality' in *A Companion to Postcolonial Studies*, eds. H. Schwarz and S. Ray (2000) 541.
102 A. Welikala, 'The Failure of Jennings' Constitutional Experiment in Ceylon' in *The Sri Lanka Republic at 40: Reflections on Constitutional History, Theory and Practice*, ed. A. Welikala (2012); also available at <http://republicat40.org/wp-content/uploads/2013/01/The-Failure-of-Jennings'-Constitutional-Experiment-in-Ceylon-How-'Procedural-Entrenchment'-led-to-Constitutional-Revolution.pdf>.

tions were incorporated into Westminster-style postcolonial constitutions. However, these informal parts of the ancient constitution were either drafted on the basis of the assumption that they would work in the exact same fashion as in Britain as was the case in Sri Lanka, or frozen in a seventeenth-century interpretation without including the substantive democratic transformations that had occurred in the metropolis after 1688 as happened in Pakistan and Nepal.

In Sri Lanka, the Soulbury Constitution established a constitutional monarchy, in which the Governor General was head of state as direct representative of the Crown in the dominion, and cabinet government. Thus, governance heavily relied on British constitutional conventions, some of which had been drafted into the constitutional text by Jennings. However, conventions proved to be the most difficult area of the constitution to interpret and apply.[103] For instance, in 1952 upon D.S. Senanayake's death, his son Dudley replaced him as prime minister without observing the Westminster litmus test of demonstrating he retained the confidence of the Lower House and passed over his cousin who was senior to him in the cabinet and the leader of the party.[104] Jennings's expectation that the British colonial legacy could ensure that constitutional conventions worked in Sri Lanka in the same way as in Britain proved mistaken. The difficult translation of the customary, unwritten, and non-justiciable parts of the British constitution, together with the uncertainty surrounding their enforcement, progressively undermined both the country's rule of law and democratic process. Harding illustrates the difficulty in exporting British constitutional conventions:

> Conventions have to be not only written into the constitution but also drafted very clearly to avoid confusion in the minds of actors who would naturally look to the wording of the constitution rather than the extensive and sometimes debatable constitutional history and understanding that led to it.[105]

In this respect, Jennings's constitutional legacy in Pakistan is most clearly identifiable in the litigation over the dissolution of the first constituent assembly in 1955. In September 1954, the first assembly had passed the fifth amendment to the Government of India Act to restrict the wide and ambiguous powers of the Governor General by codifying a number of constitutional conventions relating to governmental formation and working in a parliamentary system, to which the Governor responded with a dissolution order. In court, Jennings advanced the argument that since Pakistan was a dominion, the Amendment Acts were invalid because they

103 Kumarasingham, op. cit., n. 75, p. 146.
104 H. Kumarasingham, 'The Jewel of the East yet has its Flaws' (2013), at <http://archiv.ub.uni-heidelberg.de/volltextserver/15148/1/Heidelberg%20Papers_72_Kumarasingham.pdf>.
105 A. Harding, 'The Westminster Model Constitution Overseas' (2004) 4 *Oxford University Commonwealth Law J.* 156.

did not receive the assent of the Governor and the dissolution was lawful as a result. One of the key points raised by Jennings was that all legislation passed by the constituent assembly, not just ordinary legislation but also constitutional legislation, needed the Governor General's assent to be legally valid under English law as he represented the British monarch.[106] Jennings argued that Pakistan's dominion status required that the constitutional basis of the country, the Government of India Act and the India Independence Act, be interpreted in light of the English common law position on prerogative powers.[107]

The Federal Court's decision to accept Jennings's submissions did not engender political stability. Indeed, it undermined the sovereignty of Pakistan's constitution-making body, questioned the country's political basis of independence, and threw the nation into legal uncertainty by invalidating much of the legislation previously passed by the assembly. The Court's decision also gave a cloak of legality to what was effectively a coup d'état by the Governor General. In fact, he had intended to take control of the constitution-drafting process since the beginning of court proceedings, which he was in any case prepared to ignore had the Court ruled against him:

> One point that would have to be decided is whether a new Constituent Assembly should be summoned or whether a new constitution should be brought in operation by a Governor General's Ordinance.[108]

As Chief Justice Munir recalled later in his memoires, the President of Pakistan's first constituent assembly had lost his case even before entering the courtroom.[109]

Jennings's work in Nepal, like that in Pakistan, turned its back on the principles he had developed in his scholarly work when in Britain. In his confidential notes to the British FO, he commented that 'in Nepal [...] the only stable element is the monarchy'.[110] Unimpressed by Nepali political parties and politicians, he designed a constitution centred on the Crown. He stated that his draft was a compromise:

> It provided for Cabinet Government as long as it was practicable, but gave the King ample powers to suspend Cabinet Government; or even the whole Constitution, if it proved unworkable. To give the King a buffer against popular discontent, I invented a Council of State.[111]

As a result, the British constitutional convention by which the King shall only act on the advice and recommendation of the Prime Minister was completely diluted and distorted.[112] Similarly, the long-standing British

---

106 Section 6(3) India Independence Act 1947.
107 *Federation of Pakistan and Others*, op. cit., n. 89.
108 ICS 125/B/xv/7/1.
109 McGrath, op. cit., n. 83, pp. 216–17.
110 ICS 125/B/xiii/5/2.
111 id.
112 *Constitution of the Kingdom on Nepal*, 1959, Article 10.

convention that the monarch shall not withhold Royal Assent to a Bill passed by Parliament was overtly subverted in the Nepali document, which explicitly allowed the King to withhold Royal Assent at his discretion.[113] In the end, the Nepali monarch was vested with unusually wide powers in stark contrast with the British principles of parliamentary sovereignty, constitutional monarchy, and limited government Jennings had long espoused in his home jurisdiction.

Second, Jennings's strengthening of unconstrained and often unaccountable executives is also clearly identifiable in his treatment of the 'state of exception' at the constitutional level.[114] For instance, in Nepal Jennings devised a series of constitutional mechanisms to preserve a cloak of legality in emergency circumstances and concluded that his draft featured cabinet government as long as practicable.[115] Ample powers were vested in the King to suspend cabinet government on the basis of the so-called 'Pakistan formula', or even the entire constitution, and assume direct powers under the power to remove difficulties.[116] The subversion of key British constitutional principles in South Asia allowed for authoritarian political moves to go legally unchallenged.

(b) Courts, fundamental rights, and the protection of minorities

In other contexts, Jennings's insistence on the adoption of Westminster-style principles served to damage the enjoyment of political rights by the people of South Asia in ways that are now considered problematic. His dislike of Indian-style entrenched charters of fundamental rights patrolled by courts with extensive judicial review powers entailed severe limitations on formal constitutional guarantees across the South Asian jurisdictions he worked in. He disregarded the dangers of the ethno-nationalist propaganda of authoritarian regimes and the importance of a strong incorporation of fundamental rights for the protection of minorities.

In Sri Lanka, in line with the Westminster model, Jennings did not include an Indian-style Bill of Rights in the 1946 constitution. Only section 29 contained limitations on legislative activity on the basis of religious and communal freedom and non-discrimination on the basis of religion and community.[117] Moreover, the constitution set up a centralized system of government without the benefit of well-established party machinery.[118] In

---

113 id., Article 42.
114 Agamben had characterized emergency rule as a 'state of exception', drawing on Carl Schmitt's definition of the sovereign as 'he who decides on the exception'. It is an exceptional juridical measure because it entails the suspension of the law by legal means: G. Agamben, *State of Exception* (2005) 1.
115 ICS 125/B/xiii/5/2.
116 *Constitution*, op. cit., n. 112, Articles 55, 56, 77.
117 Welikala, op. cit., n. 102.
118 Kumarasingham, op. cit., n. 75, pp. 131–6.

this context, the rejection of substantive forms of recognition through communal representation and territorial devolution was further complicated by an overestimation of the political elites' nationalist appeal vis-à-vis emerging Sinhala-Buddhist nationalism. Ultimately, the urban-based nationalist parties failed to take root amongst the illiterate masses in the countryside, which rapidly fell under the control of communal political organizations.[119]

Jennings's insistence on the Westminster model in Sri Lanka was to lead to violence. In 1956, the Sri Lanka Freedom Party led by Bandaranaike won the general elections on the basis of a Sinhalese-Buddhist ethno-nationalist platform. The new government launched the divisive agitation for 'mother tongue' and passed the controversial Official Language Act 1956, which made Sinhala the only official language in a country where a sizeable segment of the population spoke Tamil as their mother tongue. The weakness of constitutional review mechanisms in the 1946 document made it difficult to mount a challenge to the legal validity of the Act in the courts, and the streets became the main theatre for identity politics. Sri Lankan society increasingly polarized along ethnic lines, leading to the vicious anti-Tamil pogroms of 1956. In the early 1960s, Jennings reflected on his work in Sri Lanka in light of the recent political developments and wrote:

> The policy of 'one citizen, one vote' has been adopted, though [...] some modifications were made in constituencies in order to achieve a balance of representation. [...] In Ceylon the devices used were only partially successful. Those of us who helped to frame the constitutional and electoral laws did not fully appreciate the strength of communalism between the illiterate and semi-literate electorate. We did provide for something like proportional representation of minorities, but we did not provide them with sufficient protection against communal legislation, and ambitious politicians made full use of their ability to appeal to the communal sentiments of the majority.[120]

It is important to emphasize that towards the end of his life, Jennings expressed regret for not having institutionalized in Sri Lanka stronger constitutional limitations to authoritarian government and to prevent discrimination against minorities – most likely in the form of an entrenched Bill of Rights. Jennings accepted that he had misread the socio-political circumstances of Sri Lanka and assumed that communalism was much more of a threat to India and Pakistan.[121] It is significant to compare the Sri Lankan constitution with the diametrically opposite approach taken by the Indian constitution in dealing with the protection of minorities through entrenched and justiciable fundamental rights. India's secular federal constitution, devoid of almost any explicit cultural reference except special provisions for Scheduled Castes, Scheduled Tribes, and Other Backward

119 Jennings, op. cit., n. 42, p. 66.
120 id.
121 Jennings, op. cit (1958), n. 49, pp. 17–18.

Classes, incorporated a strong notion of positive equality and successfully combined the principles of recognition and redistribution. In fact, India's constitution, imbued with the principles of civic nationalism and accommodation of diversity, has been at the core of India's statecraft.[122] It represented a sharp break with the British colonial legacy because it adopted the essential practice of the Westminster parliamentary model over the colonial mixed parliamentary-bureaucratic system, extensive justiciable fundamental rights, and universal suffrage.[123] It was because of this rupture with its colonial past through the establishment of democratic institutions that the constitution acquired such a central position in India's state and nation building.

With regard to Pakistan, in 1954 Jennings expressed his scepticism about entrenched fundamental rights; he stated that Bills of Rights ought be accompanied by wide emergency powers, because in times of crisis it is necessary to suspend liberties. To avoid this conundrum, he argued that it was preferable to avoid altogether including a Bill of Rights in a constitution: 'it is in time of emergency that fundamental liberties need protection. It is, therefore, far better to establish a tradition of liberty by firm and stable government and by impartial administration of the law.'[124] Similarly, Jennings stated that in Nepal the commission forced upon him a chapter on fundamental rights based on the Indian model. However, he made sure in his drafting that it would have been easy for the King (but not for politicians) to suspend them if they proved too restrictive.[125]

Jennings's focus on the imperative of 'political stability' can be read as a diktat of Cold War politics, where the interests of the British government overlapped with those of local elites. In 1964, Patrick McAuslan, reviewing Jennings's *Democracy in Africa*, commented:

> Sir Ivor Jennings is the Ramsay MacDonald of the academic world; in his youth a radical, debunking the myths and shibboleths of the preceding age; now in a position of great eminence, he has become a paternal conservative [...] and a cold war warrior to boot.[126]

In the Cold War context, where the role of the foreign constitutional expert in the delicate phase of decolonization was to deliver regime stability and counter Soviet influence, Jennings did perhaps help battle the Communist 'threat' in South Asia, but at the expenses of constitutional democracy.

122 Jennings, op. cit. (1953b), n. 49, p. 35.
123 P. Brass, *The Politics of India since Independence* (1994) 2–4.
124 ICS 125/B/xv/7/1.
125 ICS 125/B/xiii/5/2.
126 P. McAuslan, 'Sir Ivor Jennings' Democracy (for Africa)' 13 *Transitions* (1964) 13.

124

This article has sought to address the scholarly silence on the constitutional work and legacy of the 'Oriental Jennings', and bring it in conversation with the more orthodox accounts of the 'Occidental Jennings'. In particular, the analysis has concentrated on Jennings's deployment of the 'Westminster export model' overseas and the impact of the Cold War on his advisory work. Towards the end of his life, Jennings betrayed a degree of pessimism about the implantation of constitutionalism in the former British Empire, but remained steadfast in asserting his belief in the primacy of culture in determining constitutional developments:

> A constitution is a means to an end; and the end is good government. The quality of government depends upon the people who exercise it, not upon the constitution.[127]

This point, however, leaves unanswered the question about the role and responsibility of constitutional structures in the conduct of democratic politics. While Jennings convincingly interpreted constitutional frameworks as the product of the history and genius of a particular people, his analysis of the impact of constitutional structures on political conduct remained deeply unsatisfying, especially with regard to postcolonial constitutions. Jennings's functionalist approach produced a compelling analysis of the British constitution, but in its practical application to South Asian realities it led to substantive modifications of the Westminster model – often an outright subversion of its key tenets as in Pakistan and Nepal – that neither served the cause of constitutional democracy, nor explained the different constitutional trajectories of the region's jurisdictions.

Conversely, over two decades of direct experience of South Asian constitutional politics contributed to Jennings's rethinking of key issues pertaining to constitutionalism. First, with regard to constitutional entrenchment and the binding nature of constitutional conventions, especially those surrounding royal prerogative powers, the various South Asian experiences had exposed the frailty of conventions and the difficulty they pose for constitutional drafting and interpretation.[128] In particular, the Sri Lankan experience demonstrated how misguided was the expectation that constitutional conventions would function in Colombo just like in London. The Pakistani court cases revealed the inner ambiguity of their implantation overseas, and the Nepali constitution-making process exposed how easily they could be subverted.

Second, by the end of his career, Jennings developed a more positive attitude towards Bills of Rights and judicial review. It is argued that this shift in his views resulted from both the shift in the Colonial Office's position on

127 Jennings, op. cit., n. 42, p. 82.
128 Jennings, op. cit., n. 14, pp. 92–103.

Bills of Rights,[129] and the comparison of the outbreaks of communal violence in Sri Lanka with the relatively successful management of socio-cultural and religious diversity in India. India's radical departures from the Westminster model in terms of secularism, federal restructuring along linguistic lines, entrenched fundamental rights, and a strong notion of positive equality succeeded in rebuffing centripetal forces and creating a sense of national belonging. Most importantly, India exemplified a concrete and compelling institutional alternative to Westminster.

To conclude with a reflection on the scholarly silence over the 'Oriental Jennings', it seems that the implicit 'Occidental-Oriental' dichotomy prevalent in the analysis of Jennings's life and legacy can be framed through the concept of orientalism elaborated by Edward Said.[130] Orientalism is a way of making sense of the Orient, epistemologically based on the distinction between East and West, in which the Occident is in a structurally hegemonic position vis-à-vis the Orient. Thus, the long-standing academic silence about the 'Oriental Jennings' – in my view more unwitting than deliberate – reflects this epistemological asymmetry. The existing scholarly accounts of the 'Occidental Jennings' have never been conceived as partial, defective, or fundamentally incomplete – notwithstanding the fact that they did not analyse half of Jennings's academic writings and twenty years of his life. The 'Oriental Jennings' has been regarded as peripheral, disconnected, and marginal – just as the countries and constitutional experiences that the 'Oriental Jennings' encompasses. This conclusion mirrors Sujit Choudhry's broader assessment of the academic field of comparative constitutional law as 'narrow' with regard to the relatively limited set of standard Western jurisdictions that command central attention and from which South Asia has been largely excluded.[131] It is to be hoped that academic research and dialogue will lead to a less Eurocentric approach to this field of study.

---

129 Parkinson, op. cit., n. 4.
130 E. Said, *Orientalism* (1978).
131 S. Choudhry, 'Managing linguistic nationalism through constitutional design: Lessons from South Asia' (2009) 7 *ICON* 577.

JOURNAL OF LAW AND SOCIETY
VOLUME 42, NUMBER 1, MARCH 2015
ISSN: 0263-323X, pp. 127–49

The United Kingdom's First Woman Law Professor: An Archerian Analysis

FIONA COWNIE*

In 1970, at Queen's University Belfast, Claire Palley became the first woman to hold a Chair in Law at a United Kingdom university. However, little is known about the circumstances surrounding this event, or Claire Palley herself. This article (part of an extended project exploring her life history) seeks to address the question 'Was there something about Claire Palley herself that made it more likely she would become the United Kingdom's first female law professor?' Initially focusing on method, it seeks to answer that question by utilizing, for the first time in the context of legal education, the theoretical perspective provided by the work of the sociologist Margaret Archer. Reflecting upon Claire Palley's subjectivity, it focuses on those aspects of her personality which enabled her to pursue a successful career and become a pioneer in her chosen profession.

INTRODUCTION

Both at the time of her appointment and since, almost nothing has been said publicly about Professor Palley's pioneering role. At the time, there was no mention of her appointment in the *Times*, despite the fact that the paper took its role as a journal of record seriously then, and included a section on 'University News'. It was not until the appointment of Gillian White at Manchester in 1975 (the second woman to become a Law Professor in the United Kingdom) that Claire Palley's appointment was mentioned in the *Times*. Professor C.F. Parker, then President of the Society of Public

* *School of Law, Keele University, Staffordshire ST5 5BG, England*
f.cownie@keele.ac.uk

I would like to thank Claire Palley for participating in this research and for generously agreeing to share her life story. I would also like to thank Linda Mulcahy, David Sugarman, and Tony Bradney for their helpful comments on an earlier draft of this article. Any errors remain the responsibility of the author.

Teachers of Law (SPTL) wrote to the paper to point out that a statement released by Manchester University, talking about Gillian White as the first *English* woman to be appointed to a Chair in Law in the United Kingdom, was very carefully worded. He noted that Claire Palley (who had been born in South Africa) and Frances Moran (Professor of Law at Trinity College Dublin 1944–63) had both held chairs in law before Gillian White. (Professor Parker's reference to Frances Moran, the very distinguished holder of the Regius Chair in Law at Trinity College, is rather confusing, as she did not hold a United Kingdom Chair).[1] This discussion of Claire's appointment came not only several years after the event, but was also somewhat opaque. Similarly, when the history of Queen's University Belfast was published in 1994 no mention was made of Claire's achievement.[2] Thus the public record of the appointment of the first woman to hold a Chair in Law in the United Kingdom is extremely scant.

One of the most frequent questions I am asked about the appointment of Claire Palley is 'Why her?' 'What was it about her that made it likely she would be the first woman to occupy a Chair in Law in a United Kingdom university?' These questions, of course, are mainly focused on only half the story, what social scientists call 'agency', based on the characteristics of the individual involved. In the main, this article focuses on providing an answer to that question by analysing Claire Palley's subjectivity. But in thinking about an individual's subjectivity, we also have to take account of 'structure', which includes forces in society such as criteria for appointment and promotion.[3] And in thinking about structure, we also need to take account of 'culture', the attitudes, behaviours, and ways of doing things which reflect a shared understanding of the way the world works. As this project progresses, it is intended to take a holistic approach to Claire Palley's life, placing it in its social, economic, and political contexts. At this initial stage, however, the focus is firmly on Claire's subjectivity.

It is here that the theory put forward by Margaret Archer is particularly useful. Archer is a proponent of realist social theory, which sees structure and agency as 'distinct strata of reality, as the bearers of quite different properties and powers', and her work is often referred to as being that of a 'critical realist'.[4] Technically, talking about a critical-realist approach to the study of social life is incorrect, because critical realism is '... a philosophical approach that seeks to be an ontological "under-labourer" for a range of

---

1 C.F. Parker, 'Women Law Professors' *Times*, 28 June 1975, 13. Claire Palley remembers that she did not point out to Professor Parker that she was English by descent and a citizen of the United Kingdom at birth!

2 B.M. Walker and A. McCreary, *Degrees of Excellence: The Story of Queen's, Belfast 1845–1995* (1995).

3 K. Knorr-Cetina and A.V. Cicourel (eds.), *Advances in Social Theory and Methodology* (1981).

4 M.S. Archer, *Structure, Agency and the Internal Conversation* (2003) 2.

substantive theories in the natural and social sciences.'[5] 'Critical realism' is therefore used here as a convenient way of referring to theories, such as Archer's, which share a basic commitment to critical-realist tenets.

In *Structure, Agency and the Internal Conversation*, the most recent of a quartet of books which Archer has written exploring aspects of this topic, she analyses the ways in which structures influence agents, and vice versa.[6] Her basic point is that agents/actors have self-consciousness and structures do not, and her focus is on the mediating process between the two. To deal adequately with the interplay between structure and agency, we must specify *how* structural and cultural powers impinge upon agents, and *how* agents use their own personal powers to act 'so rather than otherwise'.[7] Structural properties impinge upon agents so as to condition their actions; this process involves both constraints and enablements, and they shape the situations in which we find ourselves, such that some courses of action are impeded and others facilitated.[8] The fundamental question is 'How do agents interact with structural constraints and enablements?' Archer argues that they do it through the 'internal conversation', which can be broadly understood as our innermost thoughts. In this article, I seek to show how the particular kind of 'internal conversation' in which Claire Palley engaged made her the sort of person who might be appointed to a pioneering role in a university law school.

LEGAL BIOGRAPHIES AND WRITING WOMEN'S HISTORY

The fact that we know so little about the appointment of Claire Palley to her Chair in Law is unsurprising. In the legal sphere, as with other professions, when biographies have been written, they have tended to be those of men. This is true of the numerous biographies of judges, and in general of the biographies of famous (and not so famous) legal practitioners. In a legal context it is evident that even when biographies of women have been written, they have generally concentrated on female legal practitioners or judges, rather than academics. Recent examples include Mary Jane Mossman's excellent comparative study of the first women to become legal practitioners in jurisdictions ranging from India to North America, and Hilary Heilbron's

---

5 A. Mutch, 'Constraints on the Internal Conversation: Margaret Archer and the Structural Shaping of Thought' (2004) 34 *J. for the Theory of Social Behaviour* 429, at 429. For a discussion of critical realism, see A.Sayer, *Method in Social Science: A Realist Approach* (1992); A. Sayer, *Realism and Social Science* (2000).
6 The other three books Archer has written on the relationship between structure and agency are: M.S. Archer, *Realist social theory: the morphogenetic approach* (1995); M.S. Archer, *Culture and agency: The place of culture in social theory* (1996); M.S. Archer, *Being Human: The Problem of Agency* (2000).
7 Archer, op. cit., n. 4, p. 3.
8 id., p. 4.

biography of her mother, Rose Heilbron, the first female judge in England.[9] Even when biographies of legal academics are written, they also tend to be about men, such as R. Gwynedd Parry's biography of Sir David Hughes Parry QC and Nicola Lacey's biography of Herbert Hart.[10] Of course, this is partly a reflection of the general position of women in society, and of the fact that women were denied leading roles in these spheres. Nevertheless, the result is that our knowledge of the (professional) lives of women legal academics and their contribution to the development of the discipline of law is particularly scant. Consequently, throwing light on the life of the United Kingdom's first woman law professor enables us to reconsider what personal qualities might assist women wishing to gain success in the (legal) academy. As Rosemary Auchmuty said of her biographical subject, Miss Bebb (of *Bebb* v. *The Law Society* fame), '... to the student of women's legal history she *is* important, because she was part of a struggle for equality that is still ongoing.'[11] That is equally true of the life of Claire Palley.

BIOGRAPHICAL METHOD

In considering the use of biography as a research tool, it is useful to bear in mind the distinction between 'life story' and 'life history'. As Goodson argues, 'life story' is the story we tell about our life. 'Life history' is a collaborative venture between the subject of biography and the researcher, which draws on a wide range of evidence so as to locate the life in a broader contextual analysis.[12] The life history is the life story located within its social, political, and historical context. In order to obtain the life *story* upon which this life *history* is based, I interviewed Claire Palley, in her own home, over a period of four days in November 2013. All the interviews were recorded and transcribed, and a document produced, which tells Claire's life story. Each interview lasted about two hours, some days for longer. In addition, notes were taken (with Claire's permission) of informal conversations during those four days, and these notes provided additional information which was incorporated into the life-story document (which ran to some 20,000 words). All Claire's words in this article are taken from that source (on file with the author) unless stated otherwise. The interviews were strongly informed by ethnographic method, viewed as 'social events in which the interviewer (and for that matter the interviewee) is a participant

---

9 M.J. Mossman, *The First Women Lawyers* (2006); H. Heilbron, *Rose Heilbron: The Story of England's First Woman Queen's Counsel and Judge* (2012).

10 R.G. Parry, *David Hughes Parry – a jurist in society* (2010); N. Lacey, *A Life of H.L.A. Hart: The Nightmare and the Noble Dream* (2006).

11 R. Auchmuty, 'Whatever happened to Miss Bebb? *Bebb v The Law Society* and women's legal history' (2010) 31 *Legal Studies* 199, at 199.

12 I. Goodson (ed.), *Studying Teachers' Lives* (1992) 6.

observer.'[13] Claire also provided copies of various documents, including CVs, articles, and speeches. The final life-story document was checked by Claire for factual accuracy; she made no changes to the analysis, although she commented upon it, and some of those comments are included in this article.

Clearly, the production of the life story on which this life history is based was a collaborative venture. It was also influenced by my previous experience of using an ethnographically informed approach to interviewing.[14] As a researcher, I drew up an interview schedule of topics I thought might ensure that we explored all aspects of Claire's life, but as we talked, I also gathered information about aspects of Claire's life which she introduced to the conversation.[15] The life story thus emerged as the consequence of a series of what Burgess would term 'conversations with a purpose'; Burgess describes '. . . a series of friendly exchanges in order to find out about peoples' lives.'[16]

Discussion of obtaining data by having 'conversations' inevitably leads to a consideration of the location of the self in the research process. As Measor and Sikes comment:

> The sociologist is in the action and a part of the context. Therefore there is an obligation on them to unpick, or at the very least document their own place in what happened. The sociologist is not a passive transcriber, nor a dispassionate observer.[17]

Feminist writing on methodology, in particular, has for some time stressed the importance of reflexivity in research.[18] In order to address these issues, I want to draw the reader's attention to the fact that like Claire Palley, I am a female law professor who has also undertaken substantial administrative roles in the institutions in which I have worked. During the preparations for this research I discovered that Claire and I shared a mutual friend (Professor William Twining, Emeritus Quain Professor of Jurisprudence at University College London) and she told me that she had consulted him before agreeing to participate in the research. Claire and I had never met before the interviews took place, but we met as academic colleagues and she invited me

---

13 M. Hammersley and P. Atkinson, *Ethnography: Principles in Practice* (2007, 3rd edn.) 120.

14 See F. Cownie, *Legal Academics: Culture and Identities* (2004) 20.

15 I am particularly grateful to Dvora Liebermann, PhD student at the London School of Economics, for her invaluable suggestions about topics to include in my interviews with Claire Palley.

16 R. Burgess, *In The Field* (1984) 102, 105.

17 L. Measor and P. Sikes, 'Visiting Lives: Ethics and Methodology in Life History' in Goodson, op. cit., n. 12, p. 212.

18 See, for example, L. Stanley and S. Wise, *Breaking out: Feminist consciousness and feminist research* (1983); S. Roseneil, 'Greenham Revisited: Researching Myself and My Sisters' in *Interpreting the Field: Accounts of Ethnography*, eds. D. Hobbs and T. May (1993); B. Skeggs, 'Techniques for Telling the Reflexive Self' in *Qualitative Research in Action*, ed. T. May (1992).

131

to stay with her in order to carry out the interviews. Whilst I was staying with her we discovered a mutual love of music and in between interviews listened to concerts on the television. Following Oakley's view that 'in research there should be no intimacy without reciprocity', I also shared aspects of my life with Claire – we talked about husbands and families, about teaching law and about food and music.[19] As Hammersley and Atkinson comment, 'The value of pure sociability should not be underestimated as a means of building trust.'[20] The process of self-disclosure is an important aspect of life-history research, as it reinforces the trust between researcher and researched. Hammersley and Atkinson point out that, for the researcher, this tends to involve presentation of those aspects of one's self and life that provide a bridge for building relationships with participants and the suppression of those which constitute a possible barrier.[21] Claire and I both adopted this approach, skirting round the subject of politics at first, until we had worked out where we were both 'coming from'. But, in general, Claire was very open about all aspects of her life; on just two occasions she said, 'We won't put this down, but I'll just tell you' when she thought that to say something publicly might hurt other people.

In drawing attention to these details of the research process, I am acknowledging my role as researcher in the construction of the life story, which was based around data elicited by establishing a relationship of trust which progressed as the research progressed, to the extent that it can be referred to as 'interactive' research. Clearly, this research could also be classed, in ethnographic terms, as 'insider research'. Insider research does not appear at all in Gold's classic categorization of field roles, and it is frequently not discussed in textbooks on methodology.[22] Some writers see insider research as problematic: methods texts tend to stress the need to maintain a sense of distance.[23] Frequently, alienation or distance has been seen as a positive analytical tool, and the consequent denial of self as an epistemological necessity.[24] Conventionally one is cautioned that familiarity may be a problem; Roseneil has described the potential difficulty of being too close 'to see the sociological significance of that which appears to be completely normal, or to form criticisms.'[25] However, Coffey argues that drawing a simple dichotomy between involvement and over-immersion is unhelpful and crude. In her view, the self is very much part of the research

19 A. Oakley, 'Interviewing women: a contradiction in terms' in *Doing Feminist Research*, ed. H. Roberts (1981) 49.
20 Hammersley and Atkinson, op. cit., n. 13, p. 70.
21 id., p. 109.
22 R. Gold, 'Roles in Sociological Field Observations' (1958) 36 *Social Forces* 217.
23 See, for example, Hammersley and Atkinson, op. cit., n. 13; S. Delamont, *Fieldwork in Educational Settings: Methods, Pitfalls and Perspectives* (2002, 2nd edn.).
24 A. Coffey, *The Ethnographic Self: Fieldwork and the representations of identity* (1999) 21.
25 Roseneil, op. cit., n. 18, ch. 7.

endeavour and researchers should not seek, by implication or otherwise, to deny that fact.[26]

Thus there is much debate among social scientists about the advantages and disadvantages of 'insider research'. Advantages include the researcher's understanding of the context in which the researched subject lived, the ability to speak a common language (including jargon and 'in-jokes'), and the likelihood of obtaining rich data from the research subject. I would certainly argue that, for this project, my position as an academic insider helped me to obtain some rich data. Equally, my previous experience of carrying out insider research over extended periods has given me experience of subjecting data gained in this way to academic critique.[27] However, there is a risk that some detachment may have been sacrificed in order to obtain this quality of data. Nevertheless, I have striven to achieve what Bourdieu termed 'participant objectification', seeking to avoid the false choice between the unreal intimacy of a subjectivist position and the equally misleading superiority of objectivism.[28]

Oral history also plays an important part in a project such as this. As Nelson argues:

> Numerous studies have shown that there is a gap between what we can discover when we rely on published accounts of some historical event and what we can discover when we ask questions of the on-site participants of those same events.[29]

However, oral history 'can lead us astray' because as a method it is notoriously bad for giving an overview or an accurate sequence of events.[30] It is important, therefore, to understand that while at this initial stage in the project the life history is generally presented uncritically, as the project progresses the focus will broaden as will the critique. At present, however, the focus is on Claire's subjectivity, and the interest lies in using the theory of Margaret Archer to analyse the life story in an attempt to uncover what it was about Claire Palley herself that made her a likely candidate to become the United Kingdom's first female law professor.

26 id., p. 36.
27 I have previously carried out insider research among Quakers: A. Bradney and F. Cownie, *Living Without Law: An ethnography of Quaker decision-making, dispute avoidance and dispute resolution* (2000), and also among contemporary legal academics: F. Cownie, *Legal Academics: Culture and Identities* (2004).
28 R. Jenkins, *Bourdieu* (1992) 47.
29 M.K. Nelson, 'Using Oral Histories to Reconstruct the Experiences of Women Teachers in Vermont 1900 – 1950' in Goodson, op. cit., n. 12, p. 168.
30 id., p. 185.

Margaret Archer's notion of the internal conversation involves three inter-related arguments. First, that our subjectivity is our own internal property, that it is real, and that it is influential. It is a personal interior property, with a first-person subjective ontology and with powers that can be causally efficacious in relation to ourselves and society. Secondly, we live in a social world that has powers and properties which can constrain (and enable) our actions. Thirdly, that we are capable of reflexively monitoring ourselves in relation to our circumstances, whilst the structural forces are incapable of doing the same towards us.[31]

Archer rejects the behaviourist argument that there is no difference in kind between a person's knowledge about herself and her knowledge about other people; she argues that we have inner lives, knowable only by our first-person selves. This she conceptualizes as 'the inner conversation'.[32] This private life of the mind is not simply:

> ... a passive matter of 'looking inward' to see what we found there, but an active process, in which we continuously *converse* with ourselves, precisely in order to define what we do believe, do desire and do intend to do.[33]

Archer goes on to argue that the 'internal conversation' is a process by which:

> ... agents reflexively deliberate upon the social circumstances that they confront ... the ongoing 'internal conversation' will mediate agents' reception of these structural and cultural influences. In other words, our personal powers are exercised through reflexive interior dialogue and are causally accountable for the delineation of our concerns, the definition of our projects, the diagnosis of our circumstances and, ultimately, the determination of our practices in society.[34]

In considering the internal conversation, Archer argues that humans are reflexive beings, who deliberate about their circumstances, and thus decide on their personal courses of action in society. However, we do not all exercise our reflexivity in the same way.[35] Through the empirical work she carried out in order to test her theory, she identifies humans as engaging in three kinds of internal conversation.[36] 'Communicative reflexives' initiate internal dialogues in their own minds, but seek to resolve issues by sharing their problems, discussing their decisions with others.[37] 'Autonomous reflexives' engage in an internal dialogue with themselves; they neither need

31 Archer, op. cit., n. 4, p. 14.
32 id., p. 22.
33 id., p. 34.
34 id., p. 130.
35 id., p. 167.
36 id., part II.
37 id., p. 167.

© 2015 The Author. Journal of Law and Society © 2015 Cardiff University Law School

nor wish to supplement this by external exchanges with other people.[38] 'Meta-reflexives' are reflexive about their own reflexivity; it is easiest to understand this concept through an example. A person thinks:

> I think X is pretty stupid; but they made a smart remark just now. Why do I think they're stupid? Because they're obese, and I'm prejudiced about fat people. I shouldn't be taken in by stereotypes.

This is an exercise in meta-reflexivity. Meta-reflexivity is something many people engage in occasionally, but Archer's 'meta-reflexives' engage in it frequently.[39]

It is because of the ability of Archer's theory to draw out, in a particularly clear way, the aspects of an individual's subjectivity which cause them to take certain decisions, and make it likely that they will have certain attitudes and hold to certain values, that it is particularly apposite as a means of identifying what it was about Claire Palley that made it unsurprising, in terms of her subjectivity, that she was the first female professor of law in the United Kingdom.

Archer's theoretical work is closely argued and persuasive and is well-regarded by her peers.[40] Her ideas provide a clear framework for considering how structural/cultural properties shape situations for agents. They constitute constraints and enablements which are responded to by agents using their own personal powers. This is a process of reflexive mediation, whereby agents mediate the influence of structural factors upon the courses of action they pursue. This reflexivity is practised through the 'internal conversation'. In the analysis which follows, I seek to demonstrate how Archer's theoretical framework gives us insights into Claire Palley's 'internal conversation', and by so doing, provides us with some indications of the aspects of Claire Palley's subjectivity which assisted her in becoming the United Kingdom's first female professor of law.

CLAIRE PALLEY AND AUTONOMOUS REFLEXIVITY

In the empirical work which she published in *Structure, Agency and the Internal Conversation*, Margaret Archer identified objective features in the social background of her interviewees which were propitious for the development of the three particular iterations of reflexivity which she identified. For 'autonomous reflexives' it was an early 'contextual dis-

---

38 id., p. 210.
39 id., pp. 255–6.
40 See, for example, N. Wiley, 'Structure, Agency and the Internal Conversation by Margaret S. Archer: Review by Norbert Wiley' (2005) 110 *Am. J. of Sociology* 1528; A. Mutch, 'Constraints on the Internal Conversation: Margaret Archer and the Structural Shaping of Thought' (2004) 34 *J. for the Theory of Social Behaviour* 429.

135

continuity' which deprived them of a durable group of interlocutors and thus threw them back upon their own internal mental resources for the purposes of deliberation.[41] As we shall see, Claire Palley generally falls into Archer's category of 'autonomous reflexive'.

Born in South Africa in 1931, her circumstances contrived to provide that 'contextual discontinuity' that Archer speaks of:

> My childhood was a little bit disrupted, really, because my parents separated (temporarily) when I was a small child, of about a year old, and I went to live with my grandparents. I sort of regarded my grandmother as my mother really, I suppose.

Her tendency to autonomy was developed by the fact that this was a house full of adults, which revolved around her grandfather, who was a judge. 'It was a very, sort of, quiet house ... [with a] huge library, I used to sit in the library and look at the books.' Some concessions were made for the small child, but mostly by Claire's grandmother:

> I had a very close relationship with my grandmother, she was wonderful, I used to come to her bed at about seven o'clock in the morning and then she'd have a new fairy-tale book and she used to read to me in bed. And the tea was brought and then we'd have tea and Marie biscuits. And then at eight o'clock my grandfather would come from his bedroom with his newspaper and I had to disappear.

Claire's only sibling was a younger sister, nearly eight years younger; the age difference, especially when they were young, did not aid a close relationship, and when they were older, the two sisters disagreed politically for a long time, so did not grow close.[42]

The contextual discontinuity in Claire's life continued as she went to boarding school, and then on to university, where she initially read microbiology. Her reasons for doing so are revealing:

> ... I didn't want to go back home when I left school, so I decided I would do Microbiology; there was a book called The Microbe Hunters by a man called Paul de Krieff and he wanted to discover microbes, but the great thing about this was you could only do Microbiology at Capetown University, which was why I wanted to do Microbiology.

Capetown was far away from Claire's home in Durban. So by the age of 18, she had moved between her grandparents' home and her own, then spent time at boarding school and finally moved away to Capetown to study. Archer notes that it is a feature of autonomous reflexives that their social context lacks stability, so that before a person has become familiar with it,

---

41 Archer, op. cit., n. 4, p. 257.
42 Claire commented that her sister '... became an MP and was on the Constitutional Commission for the new Constitution in South Africa, and was very active, and on the Human Rights Committee, and has moved progressively Left. We get on better now she has moved to the Left.'

136

they move on and are deposited in a new context.[43] Thus autonomous reflexives gather no enduring network of early friends with whom they build a lasting relationship anchored in a common context; instead, they are thrown back on their own resources. Claire acknowledges that this is true of herself. Speaking of her friendship with William and Penelope Twining she commented: 'But that's an exceptional friendship. I was very friendly too with Daphne Park until she died, but I've been quite a lonely person in my life.'

Claire's experience at university continued to reflect her tendency to autonomous reflexivity. Archer argues that autonomous reflexives tend to embark on projects whose realization will separate them from their initial context and frequently represent a socio-economic break from it.[44] Claire's decision to study at Capetown was made possible financially because she gained a scholarship, so she did not have to rely totally on her parents' support. She gained the scholarship because she performed extremely well in the South African Matriculation examination, which she describes as 'lucky', perhaps indicating the way she felt about its ability to facilitate her project of studying away from home. And in moving physically so far from home Claire's project entailed a social separation as well as an economic one.

Another indication of Claire Palley's autonomous reflexivity appeared when she discovered, very quickly, that microbiology was not for her:

> And then I found I was behind the rest of the class, because I'd never done advanced Mathematics at school, I'd never done Chemistry, I'd never done Physics, Zoology was a new subject and here I was doing all these subjects and the boys had done it all at school, and I was getting left behind; it was terrible ...

Claire's solution to this discovery was not to give up, or to run back home, but to deal with the situation herself: she decided to study law instead, and went to see the Dean of the Law Faculty:

> He was very nice; he knew my grandfather, and although it was five months into the first year, he allowed me to change at that stage to Law and three months later I passed the exams, which was sheer luck, because I should never have passed, because I could pass easily things like Latin and Constitutional Law, that very easy, but I had to fill up with psychology and economics. Economics was ok, but psychology ... awful, I couldn't stand it and never used to go, I never went to the practicals, and managed just to creep through; one of the demonstrators used to sign me in although I wasn't there, and I just got a Third (the only time in my life I got a Third!). And so from then I went on with Law.

This approach to resolving a serious setback in the project upon which she had embarked, of getting a good degree, by thinking what to do, then getting

---

43 Archer, op. cit., n. 4, p. 346.
44 id.

137

on with it, along the lines of 'I got myself into this mess, now I have to get myself out of it' displays precisely the characteristics of Archer's 'autonomous reflexives'. These are people, Archer argues, who know what they want in society and formulate clear projects to achieve it. If the project is subject to 'contraction' or 'constraint', it is scrutinized subjectively and lessons are learnt. Autonomous reflexives '... both know what they want and also know a good deal about how to go about getting it. They do so strategically, as agents who endorse the life-politics of the possible.'[45]

The second characteristic that Archer identifies in 'autonomous reflexives' is that a considerable amount of their internal conversation is about society '... about the means, the "costs" and the "benefits" of seeking to realise one's ultimate concerns within it.' Since this involves a two-way relationship between structure and agency, which can involve both 'elastication' and 'contraction' of their aspirations, autonomous reflexives tend to change over their lifetimes. In becoming detached from their original 'social moorings', the new contexts they confront present them with a different array of questions to answer.[46] This is certainly true of Claire Palley, who found herself moving from South Africa to Southern Rhodesia as a direct result of marrying her husband, Ahrn Palley. She had met him at university, when they were both studying law, although he was 17 years her senior, and was a qualified doctor, working as a pediatrician. (He had always wanted to be a barrister, and so studied law as a mature student.) Ahrn Palley became an MP in Southern Rhodesia, where the Palleys moved in the late 1950s because of their opposition to apartheid.[47] In fact, as they soon found out, the political situation in Rhodesia was not much better, in terms of racial tension, than South Africa. At that time, Rhodesia had one of the largest white-settler populations in Africa, and a political system which was very similar to the apartheid regime of its close neighbour, giving little voice to the black population of more than two million people.[48] Although he sat for the Democratic Party (which Claire described as 'a sort of right-wing Labour Party') for one year, in 1958–59, Ahrn Palley, being firmly opposed the unequal treatment of the black population, soon found it too right-wing, and sat as an independent MP for the predominantly black constituency of Highfield from 1962 to 1970.[49] Ian Smith, later notorious as the Prime Minister who made a unilateral declaration of independence from British rule in 1965, described Ahrn Palley as 'a one-man opposition party' and was said, despite their political differences, to hold him 'in the greatest respect'.[50] Claire too did not share the outlook of the majority of her white

45 id., p. 254.
46 id., p. 213.
47 Obituary, 'Ahrn Palley' *Times*, 15 May 1993, 17.
48 D. Sandbrook, *White Heat: A History of Britain in the Swingin' Sixties* (2007) 126.
49 Obituary, op. cit., n. 47.
50 id.; Sandbrook, op. cit., n. 48, p. 128.

compatriots. She recalls visiting Rhodesia shortly before going to live there: '... we went to see it and there were white women sitting in the hotel drinking at ten o'clock in the morning ... just the sort of society which I disapproved of.'

The Palleys' radical political views meant that they were not accepted by the ex-pat community in Rhodesia:

> In fact it is one of the things that made me finally decide that the future of the boys was in England. White society, because he was pro-African, boycotted us. My husband wanted the children brought up as Jews, and my youngest son went to a Jewish nursery school. When it was his fourth birthday, he invited everyone in his class, like all the other children did, and he had his twenty three invitations out but only two children came. I can remember him sitting waiting at the party, waiting, waiting (and his brother, who had a birthday the same day, but was two years older, and went to a different school, had all his classmates there) and I can remember it to this day. Eventually my son opened his two presents, and the ones that we had bought him. I will never forget that day.

The ostracism experienced by the Palleys while shocking in its cruelty to their young son, was unsurprising in the context of Southern Rhodesia. As Claire says, 'People thought that there was apartheid in South Africa, but that Southern Rhodesia was a British colony and it was fine. But it was not true in fact. There was enormous discrimination.'[51]

The new situation in which she found herself provided Claire with much to think about. She shared her husband's anti-racist views, but was not politically active when they first arrived in Rhodesia, as she had five sons in quick succession. However, she soon began to make her own contribution to the struggle against apartheid:

> I used to write articles in a magazine called the Central African Examiner, which was like the Economist for Central Africa. And also in women's magazines. So I'd write about women's rights and particularly black African women, and their lack of rights.

Claire's decision to publish these articles, focusing on gender and social inequality, reflects that aspect of her 'internal conversation' which is about society, and the means of realizing her concerns within it. She was bringing up five children, but nevertheless, finding injustice around her, wanted to do something about it, and journalism allowed her to do that.

Another feature which Archer identifies as characterizing autonomous reflexives is an unproblematic dovetailing of their concerns; their ultimate concern is work outside the home, and all other concerns (including inter-personal relations) tend to be subordinated to this concern. This does not mean such persons are inconsiderate, because they also try to elaborate what Archer calls 'an ethic of fairness', which gives other people their due, while protecting their own ultimate concern.[52] And the concern with work is not

---

51 See, for example, B. Pimlott, *Harold Wilson* (1992) 451.
52 Archer, op. cit., n. 4, p. 213.

with ambition, but with intrinsic satisfaction – autonomous reflexives seek an occupational context which meets this desire, while imposing the minimum of undesired requirements.[53]

The decisions that Claire Palley took about her life reflect this aspect of Archer's theory precisely. After her move to Southern Rhodesia she was bringing up her five sons while her husband worked as an MP, and was managing a household of thirteen people:

> I used to joke that I was running a boarding house, because I had eventually the five children and my husband and me, which was seven and my mother-in-law which was eight and my brother-in-law also lived with us, so that was nine and four African servants, so that was thirteen, and you had to buy food and shop and supervise; you'd be surprised how much organisation it took all the time.

However, it was not long before Claire was focusing on work outside the home as well, just as Archer would predict. She not only wrote journalism, as we have seen, but also began to act as a research assistant for her husband, providing him with the evidence he needed for the speeches he was making in parliament:

> I also acted as a research assistant to my husband, and did a lot of research for him. I remember spending about three weeks on research relating to the Law and Order Maintenance Bill, which the governing party wanted to introduce so it could ban meetings, have a mandatory death penalty for offences like arson. And I worked on the Civil Authorities (Special Powers) Act and the Offences Against the State Act. And I researched that and he must have spent two or three weeks on that Bill, virtually two or three weeks during all working hours talking about Law, which was all stuff that I wrote.

In December 1959 Claire was appointed to a lectureship at the University College of Rhodesia and Nyasaland. She describes it as 'a branch of London University':

> The University College of Rhodesia and Nyasaland taught London University degrees. And it had all sorts of benefits. All staff were required to do a London PhD, and you were allowed to do it full-time, even though you were teaching. You had to register for a PhD, but you were allowed to do it while you were teaching.

Archer argues that by accentuating 'work' as their prime concern, autonomous reflexives focus upon 'performative achievement' as that which they value most highly; but because they also have to accommodate subsidiary concerns, such as inter-personal relations, this involves elaborating an 'ethic of accommodation' to justify their ultimate concern with work in relation to their treatment of others. 'The ethic of accommodation offers a definition of "fairness" – a justified demarcation between the rights and responsibilities of the subject and the rightful expectations of others.'[54] This

---

53 id,. p. 350.
54 id., p. 217.

is not just a matter of convenience; Archer notes that autonomous reflexives tended to be morally very sensitive, and it is important to understand that inter-personal relations are *amongst* their concerns, causing them to ensure that they dovetailed this subordinate concern with their primary one of work.[55] Claire's concern for her family, even when she was heavily involved in her academic work, both in terms of teaching and in researching for her PhD, can be seen in the way she structured her life (with her husband's assistance) so as to be able to spend some 'quality time' with her children:

> And he was very good towards the end of my PhD, when I was trying to complete my PhD, doing full days lecturing. And he used to come home at five o'clock in the evening from Parliament, see that the children were bathed, see that they had their supper, then I could come and tell them a story before they went to bed. That way for 6 months he was absolutely wonderful when I was finishing my doctorate.

The next defining feature of communicative reflexives is their individualism. Archer comments: 'These are independent people, whose self-sufficiency makes them something of a "loner".'[56] This is true regardless of whether they are married or in a similar intimate relationship; quintessentially they are not dependent upon others; they are philosophical individualists, with a '... profound belief that they, and everyone else, must take personal responsibility for themselves.'[57] The autonomous, existential quality of Claire's philosophy of life has deep roots in her upbringing:

> I owe my character of being tough to my father. He said you must always stand up for the truth, you must be brave. He told the story of George Washington and the cherry tree. I don't know how many times I have heard that story![58]

Claire's father had a strong influence on her belief in personal autonomy:

> He joined up on the first day of World War 1, was decorated almost immediately because he rescued a wounded officer, and ended up as an officer. He was in the predecessor to the Royal Flying Corps, flying from naval vessels, and then the RFC was formed and he trained for the first bombing raids over Berlin ... My father joined up again in World War 2, and got his wings again. His attitude made me feel I must be courageous, and although I do like to be loved, I will stand up and say things even though it's painful.

Archer argues that every agent prioritizes their concerns, and crystallizes them into determinate projects. They also arrive at some orientation towards

---

55 id., p. 237.
56 id., p. 217.
57 id., p. 214.
58 As a little boy, George Washington damaged his father's favourite cherry tree with his new hatchet. The tree died. His father discovered the dead tree and was very angry, asking if anyone knew anything about it. George owned up, though he was very frightened. His father was not angry, but praised him for telling the truth. (This story is popular, but probably apocryphal.)

their encounters with constraints and enablements. It is the combination of these two deliberate outcomes which constitute their 'stance' towards society.[59] The importance of 'stance' is that fundamentally it represents a subjective judgment by the agent about the importance she attaches to her objective social context and its place in her life: '... according to their concerns, subjects determine how much of themselves they will invest in the social order.'[60] Thus 'stance' means that our personal powers are crucial in mediating the importance of society to us, and in the case of autonomous reflexives, means that they will be 'accommodative' towards the social, seeing their context as a means towards the realisation of a concern.[61] Adopting a stance:

> ... is not like holding an abstract point of view; it is rather a commitment to a distinctive course of practical action in society. It is a commitment which subjects make to themselves, within the internal conversation, and ... it is an acceptance of a particular way of being-in-the-world.[62]

In the case of autonomous reflexives, who invest themselves in performative concerns, this produces '... active agents, who are actively seeking a context which will prove compatible with that which they care about most.'[63] We can see this reflected in Claire's life when she makes the decision to leave Rhodesia. While her ultimate concern was to remain an academic, Claire also wanted to fulfil her duty to her children as well as wanting to be an activist.

> Meanwhile, Ahrn and I had decided to send the children to boarding school in England. His political views were making life increasingly difficult for them ... I wanted to move to the UK so that the children had somewhere to go in the holidays, and so that I could go regularly to visit them; not only me but my husband too. I wanted to visit them in term-time, and have them with me all vacations. My husband used to quote Kipling to me and say how terrible it was that children didn't see their parents for a year or couple of years, that they needed to see their parents regularly, and it was my duty to go to the UK and establish a home for the children ... He brought the adverts from The Times home, and pointed out to me the Aberystwyth appointment and eventually the Belfast appointment ... The whole of my life was around the children – I wasn't thinking of my career, the last thing I was thinking of was my career, or that I'd get promotion when I got there. I was thinking 'I've got to do things for the children'.

Although expressed in terms of the needs of the children, it was undoubtedly the case that when she successfully gained a lectureship at Queen's University Belfast, it enabled Claire to pursue her own career as well as providing her with a family home nearer to her children. By undertaking this

---

59 Archer, op. cit., n. 4, p. 349.
60 id., p. 351.
61 id., p. 353.
62 id., p. 354.
63 id., p. 353.

move, she thus achieved the 'dovetailing of concerns' which Archer identifies as a key feature of the lives of autonomous reflexives.[64]

There is one final characteristic that Archer notes about autonomous reflexives. They display a distinct preference for self-employment, or working as lone practitioners (in academic terms, we would refer to the 'lone scholar'):

> They neither need nor welcome supervision because they are their own task-masters and shun the conviviality of group-working as a distraction ... However, they also contribute to the development of any institution they belong to, because of their hard work and innovative contributions. Because they devote themselves single-mindedly to that which they care about most, they foster institutional growth and development ... Hence their effects are morphogenetic.[65]

The morphogenetic characteristics of Claire's character can be seen early in her life when she was working at the University College of Rhodesia and Nyasaland, where she became Secretary of the AUT and campaigned for equal rights for women:

> ... we got equal salary and we got equal travel rights so that when you were terminated or whatever you had the travel rights, so that was a very great help when I moved; my children's fares were paid for. The university fought it like mad, but they couldn't do anything about it, there it was, it was equal, the AUT had agreed and I had the same rights as any man who moved his family ...

The morphogenetic character of Claire's professional life was also clear after she had left Belfast. Claire visited the University of Kent in 1973 to act as external assessor for a Chair appointment; while she was there she was offered a Chair herself, which she decided to accept. As she explains:

> It had become increasingly difficult for the children in Belfast, and I was under some pressure from my husband to give up our house in Belfast (he said 'It's a waste, having a family home in Belfast when the children can't easily go there') so I moved to Kent.

At that time, Kent was a radical law school, with many young scholars who were disillusioned with black-letter law and were adopting alternative socio-legal or critical approaches instead. Claire remembers:

> There was a lot of fighting about what you could teach. To give you an idea of what it was like, the textbook for the first year English Legal System course was Berger and Luckman's *Social Construction of Reality*, which is very good, but a difficult book for first-year law students.

During the course of her first year at Kent, Claire was approached to become Master of Darwin College, a position which involved her being only part-time in the law school. As Chair of the Law Board, Claire's task was to try and mediate between a very radical law school, which had strong views

---

64 id., p. 213.
65 id., p. 359.

about the type of legal practitioners they wished to produce, and the university's more pragmatic desire to have employable law graduates who would go on to have conventional legal careers: '... my job was to get the Law Board on board, get it on a proper footing and not throw out the baby with the bath water':

> ... because there was very little law in the Kent degree, the result was disproportionate numbers of Kent graduates failed the professional exams, because they hadn't had the opportunity of doing standard Tort or Land Law or Contract or Criminal Law which had been done in the other universities. So other students could really sail through the exam, but these Kent people really had a hard time, which wasn't very good for the University, as you could imagine.

Claire was first helped and then succeeded in this morphogenetic project by Brian Simpson, who was appointed to a Chair at Kent soon after she arrived. One of the things Brian, as Dean of Social Sciences, had to do at Kent, together with Claire, was to build links with the legal profession. This brought its own challenges:

> Brian and I went and cultivated the local law profession. I remember going to one dinner and having artichokes, being taken to the local county hotel in Canterbury and being offered dinner by the local lawyers. It was the first time I'd had them, so it was a bit tricky! You know, you look at them on your plate and I thought to myself 'I'm not sure I know how to eat these!'

By the time she left Kent in 1984 to become Principal of St Anne's College Oxford, Claire felt that they had implemented some changes: 'Well, that was Kent, and we managed to pull it back from the edge.' In line with Archer's theory, Claire's tenure of administrative offices at Kent arguably reflected her ability to contribute to the institution to which she belonged.

While most of Claire Palley's internal conversation ties in neatly with that of an autonomous reflexive, it is important to acknowledge that her internal conversation did not develop entirely consistently during her life. In many ways, Claire's marriage did not contribute to her development as an autonomous reflexive. She notes that during her marriage, she was very much under her husband's influence (unsurprising in some ways, as he was much older and more experienced than she was, quite apart from the different social mores which then pertained). She commented:

> During my marriage, I was very much influenced by my husband; for 13 years I was very much under his influence. It wasn't really until I went to Belfast and lived on my own that I had an independent life of my own. I was 35 years old before I had a bank account – when I went to Queen's and wanted to buy a house, so I needed a bank account.

Thus, while during the course of her marriage Claire continued to exhibit characteristics of an autonomous reflexive, the development of her internal conversation should be seen in the overall context of her personal life at that time.

144

It is also the case that Claire showed some signs of meta-reflexivity as well. Indicative of this is her comment about the way in which her attitude to race changed around the time she went to university. She met an Indian advocate, '. . . and I had never seen an educated dark person in my life. He was the most charming gentleman. It made me think again . . .'. At university, studying economics, an African student asked a question in the middle of the lecture:

> And I thought to myself 'Hmm what a cheek!' And then I thought to myself 'Ha! What a brilliant question!' And the professor saw that it was a brilliant question and he stopped what he was doing and he spent the whole of the lecture going round that question. And I remember that very well and it changed my whole attitude towards African people.

These examples of 'thinking about thinking' suggest that while Claire Palley was generally an autonomous reflexive, she also engaged in meta-reflexivity. Similarly, reflecting on her academic success, Claire noted the role her husband had played in ensuring that, despite very bad morning sickness, she still attended classes:

> I did very well in my Finals, but it was because of him; he made me work. I would never have worked, I was lazy. I had a bad phenomenon – if you can do things very easily you just take it for granted that you can do it, you see, 'Look how clever I am, no hands' just like riding a bicycle with no hands. Our children do that. And I was a bit like that, until I met him.

So while autonomous reflexivity is the dominant mode of 'internal conversation' which Claire Palley engaged in, there is also evidence of some meta-reflexivity. And that conclusion is borne out by the comment Claire made on reading a first draft of this article. While regarding my interpretation of her as an autonomous reflexive as an accurate one, she added 'But I'm a meta-reflexive as well, you know'.[66] While Claire's autonomous reflexivity is strongly reflected in her life story, there are also clear signs of meta-reflexivity.

BECOMING THE FIRST FEMALE LAW PROFESSOR IN THE UNITED KINGDOM

When Claire moved to Belfast in 1966, she did so to take up a lectureship. But she was rapidly promoted, first to a Readership in 1967 and then to a Chair in Public Law in 1970. In some respects, her rapid promotion was unsurprising; she arrived at Belfast with a PhD and having already gained both teaching and administrative experience in Southern Rhodesia, where she had established a law school at the University College of Rhodesia and Nyasaland. Yet, despite her previous experience, and the fact that she had published a series of articles and a book, in other ways Claire's appointment

---

66 Telephone interview with Claire Palley, 8 August 2014, on file with the author.

was very surprising, since there were very few women legal academics at all at that time, and very few of them held promoted positions.[67]

The most comprehensive sources of information on universities and their staff at that time are the *Commonwealth Universities Yearbooks*. These gathered information from all Commonwealth universities annually; each edition is based on data gathered the previous academic year. In the 1970 edition (which contains data gathered in the 1969–70 academic year, the year of Claire's promotion) the *Yearbook* records 430 men holding full-time positions and 77 holding part-time positions in United Kingdom law schools. Women are recorded as holding 41 full-time positions and 3 part-time positions. Out of the 32 law schools recorded as offering 'full' law degrees (as opposed to service teaching for other disciplines) 10 had no female academics on the staff at all.

In the 1971 edition of the *Yearbook*, when Claire Palley's appointment to a Chair appears for the first time, only four other women are recorded as holding promoted positions in the United Kingdom: Olive Stone as a Reader at the LSE; Valentine Korah as a Reader at UCL, and Gabriele Ganz and Evelyn Gavin as Senior Lecturers at Southampton and Strathclyde respectively. This gives some indication of the historic importance of Claire's appointment.

At the time that Claire applied for her post, it appears that Queen's was one of the larger law schools, along with Leeds, Liverpool, and Manchester, which all had 300–350 undergraduates.[68] Only Birmingham, with 450–500 undergraduates, and Oxford and Cambridge, with over 600 each, were larger.[69] During the quinquennium 1968–73, Queen's underwent a period of expansion, appointing thirteen new Chairs (of which Claire was one).[70] It would seem likely that a strong research profile would have been required for a law school which was looking to make its mark and maintain its position among its competitors.[71]

Claire had a PhD, awarded by London University in 1965 (it was unusual at that time for legal academics to hold a PhD).[72] She immediately published

---

67 See the *Commonwealth University Yearbooks* for the 1960s and 70s. Discussion of the general position of female (legal) academics in the 1970s is outside the scope of this article, but see, for example, M. Tight, *The Development of Higher Education in the United Kingdom since 1945* (2009) 291–3 and M. Rendel, 'Women Academics in the Seventies' in *Is Higher Education Fair to Women?*, eds. S. Acker and D. Piper (1984) 163.

68 J.F. Wilson and S. Marsh, 'A Second Survey of Legal Education in the United Kingdom' (1975) 13 *J. of the Society of Public Teachers of Law* 241, at 250.

69 id.

70 Walker and McCreary, op. cit., n. 2, p. 138.

71 Professor William Twining, who worked at Queen's at that time recalls that: 'Queen's was a pretty strong Law School at the time.' Professor William Twining, telephone interview, on record with the author.

72 Society of Public Teachers of Law (SPTL), *Directory Of Members 1971* 5.

146

this with Clarendon Press (a prestigious publisher) as *The Constitutional History and Law of Southern Rhodesia 1888–1965*. By 1967, when she was promoted to Reader, she had also published an article in the *Modern Law Review* on 'The Judicial Process: UDI and the Southern Rhodesian Judiciary'.[73] In the next three years she published two articles in Zambian publications on 'rethinking the judicial role' and two in the *Northern Ireland Legal Quarterly* on 'Constitutional Devices in Multi-Racial and Multi-Religious Societies' and 'Wives, Creditors and the Matrimonial Home'.[74] These were closely followed by another four pieces in 1970, the year she was promoted to a Chair.[75] In addition to her academic publications, she also wrote a considerable amount of journalism. During her years in Belfast (1966–73) she authored or co-authored around ten articles in the *Times* on various aspects of human rights, both in Northern Ireland and in Rhodesia.[76] Claire also told me that she regularly appeared on BBC radio programmes, both domestically and on the World Service during these years. Consequently, Claire was not only productive academically, she could also contribute to raising the public profile of Queen's. In addition, her expertise lay in public law and Claire told me that the law degree at Queen's at that time included a lot of public law, so she could also contribute to the teaching needs of the law school. She also taught Roman law and family law, which were other areas in which the law school had teaching needs. Overall, Claire's agency, and her reflective autonomy, had put her into the position where she could be promoted to a Chair.

The system of appointment at Queen's at the time involved 'curators' who sat on the appointment panel; some of these were permanent curators, drawn from other departments and 'the great and the good', while two were 'special curators' from the department or faculty in which the post was established. If the special curators agreed on the outcome of the appointment exercise, it was very rare for the permanent curators to intervene. In Claire's case, the two special curators were Professor Lee Sheridan (then head of the law school) and Professor William Twining; since they agreed on the

---

73 C. Palley, 'The Judicial Process: UDI and the Southern Rhodesian Judiciary'(1967) 30 *Modern Law Rev.* 263.
74 C. Palley, *Rethinking the Judicial Role: The Judiciary and Good Government* (1969); C. Palley 'Rethinking the Judicial Role' (1968) 1 *Zambia Law J.*; C. Palley, 'Constitutional Devices in Multi-Racial and Multi-Religious Societies' (1968) 19 *Northern Ireland Law Q.* 377; C. Palley, 'Wives, Creditors and the Matrimonial Home' (1969) 20 *Northern Ireland Law Q.* 132.
75 C. Palley 'Law and the Unequal Society: Discriminatory Legislation in Rhodesia under the Rhodesian Front from 1963 to 1969 Part 1' (1970) 12 *Race* 15–47; C. Palley 'Law and the Unequal Society: Discriminatory Legislation in Rhodesia under the Rhodesian Front from 1963 to 1969 Part 2' (1970) 12 *Race* 139–67; C. Palley, 'Note on the Development of Legal Inequality in Rhodesia 1890–1962' (1970) 12 *Race* 87; C. Palley, 'Adoption Act (NI) 1967' (1970) 21 *Northern Ireland Law Q.* 304.
76 See the *Times* digital archive.

appointment, the permanent curators did not question the decision.[77] It would appear that Claire Palley possessed the overall profile which it is likely that a law school such as Queen's would have been looking for.[78]

When asked about making this ground-breaking appointment, Professor Twining recalls that he did not have a sense of history at the time: 'I just thought it was the right thing to do.' The Chair for which Claire applied was externally advertised, and there were both internal and external candidates who were shortlisted for the post. Professor Twining recalls that at the appointments panel, the focus, in terms of discrimination, was, in accordance with section 3 of the Irish Universities Act 1908, on the need to avoid any religious discrimination, rather than on the fact that a woman was being appointed to a Chair. He also recalls that there was at the time a concern that Queen's should not become too provincial, which to some extent favoured ex-pats like Claire, because they had teaching experience outside Northern Ireland.[79] Yet there were, Professor Twining recalls, some people not on the appointments committee who questioned whether a woman could hold a Chair of Law. His recollection is that members of the committee pointed to Frances Moran in Dublin as an example of a very successful female Professor of Law.[80]

CONCLUSION

Analysing Claire Palley's life history through the theoretical lens of Margaret Archer allows us to provide an answer to the question with which this article began: 'Was there something about Claire Palley herself that made it likely she would become the United Kingdom's first female law professor?' Archer's theory is very helpful in focusing attention on an individual's subjectivity, and providing a framework with which it can be logically analysed. Through the exploration of the 'internal conversation' of Claire Palley, it is possible to see, at various stages in her life, those aspects of her subjectivity which contributed to her eventual appointment as a Professor of Law in Belfast in 1970. I would suggest that Claire Palley's clear tendency to autonomous reflexivity made her well-equipped to pursue a successful academic career. By itself, this does not provide a complete explanation of how it was that she became the first woman to be appointed to a Chair in Law in the United Kingdom. But it provides strong evidence that as a scholar and thinker who took her career, as well as her private life, seriously, Claire Palley was certainly the type of person one might expect to play a pioneering role in the legal academy. Her personal qualities, high-

77 Twining inteview, op. cit, n. 71.
78 id.
79 id.
80 See text relating to n. 1 above.

148

lighted by the Archerian analysis, included a strong streak of determination and resilience, supported by an independence of mind which reflected an inner strength. Thus, she was well-equipped to succeed in the male world of legal academia in which she found herself.

In evaluating the contribution of Archer's theory to a legal biography, while acknowledging its utility in terms of its focus on the personal qualities of the individual, I think it is equally important to draw attention to that which it does not do. This is not a theory (at least as it is expressed in *Structure, Agency and the Internal Conversation*) which encourages a holistic analysis of the context in which the individual lived. Thus, it has been said that Archer's theory involves 'too much of an internal conversation'.[81] It is hard not to agree with this criticism, although it is certainly not fatal to the insights which can usefully be drawn as a result of the application of her theory to new data.

Application of Archer's theory has allowed us to highlight certain aspects of Claire Palley's subjectivity, to understand how they were developed by her circumstances and the people in her life. And, most importantly, it encourages us to consider why certain individuals succeed and the conditions of that possibility. Susan Bartie has argued recently that legal scholars have much to learn from their predecessors.[82] She does not limit her argument to the simplistic one that we can learn from the past, and indeed, warns against drawing '. . . crude connections between past lessons and future reform'.[83] Bartie's more subtle argument is that studying the lives of scholarly predecessors can be 'empowering'.[84] By this she means that studying the academic careers of individual scholars can reveal how academic lawyers have answered:

> . . . the most important questions that all legal scholars must face: what and how to write and teach. In so doing, they concentrate the reader's mind on what makes a successful legal scholar and who legal scholars should seek to emulate.[85]

This article is the beginning of an exploration of the biography of Claire Palley which, in due course, may lead us to consider what in her scholarly life we might wish to emulate as we contemplate the life history of the first woman professor of law in a United Kingdom university, informed by our knowledge of her 'internal conversation' and the ways in which that contributed to her success.

81 F. Vandenberghe, 'Structure, Agency and the Internal Conversation' in *Revue du MAUSS Permanente* (19 June 2008), at <http://www.journaldumauss.net/./?structure-agency-and-the-internal>.
82 S. Bartie, 'Histories of legal scholars: the power of possibility' (2014) 34 *Legal Studies* 305.
83 id.
84 id., p. 317.
85 id., p. 318.

149

JOURNAL OF LAW AND SOCIETY
VOLUME 42, NUMBER 1, MARCH 2015
ISSN: 0263-323X, pp. 150–72

Judah Benjamin: Marginalized Outsider or Admitted Insider?

CATHARINE MACMILLAN*

Judah Benjamin (1811–1884) was one of the greatest of nineteenth-century lawyers. This article analyses how a young man who might have been marginalized in society because of the circumstances of his birth, ethnic origin, and religious identity rose to prominence in law, politics, and business in the United Kingdom and the United States.

In June, 1883 an extraordinary dinner was held in the Inner Temple. Presided over by the Attorney General, Sir Henry James, two hundred members of the English bench and bar gathered to honour one they recognized as their leading barrister, Judah Benjamin. The event was extraordinary not only in the rarity of such tributes but because the subject of this tribute had arrived as an outsider eighteen years earlier. Benjamin had begun life in the West Indies, the son of an impecunious Jewish merchant with an often precarious and itinerant existence. By his retirement, Benjamin had dominated the legal professions of the United States and the United Kingdom, written a major English law treatise, acquired fame (or infamy) as a politician in mid-century America, and run a sugar plantation. His obituarist's statement that he had led a 'life [that] was as various as an Eastern tale'[1] acknowledged Benjamin's success yet hinted that he was something of an outsider.

* School of Law, University of Reading, Foxhill House, Whiteknights Road, Reading RG6 7BA, England
c.macmillan@reading.ac.uk

I would like to thank Georgia Chadwick for her help with the Louisiana cases, JoAnne Sweeny for her help with the United States Supreme Court cases, and Margaret Polk for her assistance with the New Orleans commercial court cases.

1 *Times*, 9 May 1884, 10.

This article examines aspects of Benjamin's remarkable life to determine how an outsider moved from the margins of society to acquire influence and the nature of the influence acquired. Benjamin was an outsider who became an insider at the top of his chosen professions. Benjamin remains an enigma to historians, an important character who defied attempts to produce critical biographies of himself. '[O]ne of the most secretive men who ever lived',[2] he was buried in Père Lachaise cemetery in Paris under his wife's family's name. He destroyed his papers to deliberately thwart prospective biographers fearing that his life would be construed according to their prejudices.[3] While biographies exist,[4] Benjamin succeeded in preventing a critical assessment of himself and his various roles. This success presents methodological challenges in critically reconstructing his life and assessing its significance.

A subject who leaves personal papers bequeaths biographers with the material from which a framework of the life can be constructed. In many instances these papers provide insight into the thoughts and emotions of the subject. They also provide links to the people and events of the subject's era, links that allow the biographer to set the life in context and assess the context of the subject's life. A subject without personal papers entirely deprives the biographer of significant internal insights into the subject and also hampers the contextualization and critical appraisal of the life in question. It is the case, though, that the subject who leaves personal papers often leaves to the future a particular view of herself and impedes a truly candid and critical perspective. Benjamin's biographers have been hampered by a lack of a corpus of personal papers that has, in turn, led to an unfortunate marginalization of his importance in the legal and political histories of the nineteenth-century trans-Atlantic world. Sources of information about Benjamin's life exist, although locating and assessing these sources is a time-consuming process.

As a lawyer, Benjamin's life is assessed from a number of surviving sources. He wrote two legal works: *Digest of the Reported Decisions of the Superior Court of the Late Territory of Orleans, and of the Supreme Court of*

---

2 R. Meade, *Judah P. Benjamin, Confederate Statesman* (1943/2001) xv.

3 The observation was made to Francis Lawley: P. Butler, *Judah P. Benjamin* (1907) 7–8.

4 The principal biographies are: Butler, id.; Meade, op. cit., n. 2; and E. Evans, *Judah P. Benjamin, The Jewish Confederate* (1989). Lesser biographies include: R. Osterweis, *Judah P. Benjamin, Statesman of the Lost Cause* (1933); L. Gruss, 'Judah Philip Benjamin' (1936) 19 *Louisiana Historical Q.* 964; M. Rywell, *Judah Benjamin: Unsung Rebel Prince* (1948); S.I. Neiman, *Judah Benjamin: Mystery Man of the Confederacy* (1963); A. Goodhart, 'Judah Philip Benjamin, 1811–84' in his *Five Jewish Lawyers of the Common Law* (1949); and S. Naresh, 'Judah Philip Benjamin at the English Bar'(1996) 70 *Tulane Law Rev.* 2487.

the State of Louisiana[5] and *A Treatise on the Law of Sale of Personal Property*.[6] To these publications, one must add the legal arguments he submitted to American and British courts. Detailed searches in private archives may well reveal some of his legal opinions. Law reports, journals, newspaper reports, and the occasional transcript provide an indication of his oral arguments. The use of his cases and writings offer an indication into his influence upon the development of the law. To these sources one must also add the observations of his legal contemporaries, often expressed in their memoirs. As a politician, several sources of information exist about Benjamin. One lies in the newspaper reports and the reports of the proceedings of the Senate. A second lies in the Confederate Records held in the Library of Congress,[7] including a few private papers. A third is in the correspondence of his contemporaries. Finally, while Benjamin did not keep a letter book, some of his correspondence survives in the personal papers of others. Some of his Confederate correspondence has been published.[8] The account that follows draws upon most of these documents. While sources allow a reconstruction of Benjamin's life and his enormous influences, they largely fail to provide insight into Benjamin's thoughts, perceptions, and motivations.

This failure is significant not only in the understanding of Benjamin's life but also in a greater understanding of one of the most prominent Jewish figures in the nineteenth-century English-speaking world. This prevents a greater understanding of the acceptance of Jewish people in America and the United Kingdom. Historians are divided as to the acceptance of Jews in both countries at this time. Neither country suffered the virulent anti-Semitism that resulted in the ghettos and pogroms of central and Eastern Europe. These English-speaking countries were also largely Protestant with the result that the Catholic minority 'were more intensely abhorred than Jews were'.[9] Jews thus suffered the effects of prejudice but this was neither as virulent as occurred elsewhere nor were Jews its greatest victims in either country. In America, Dinnerstein observed, Jews enjoyed full legal equality under the

5 J. Benjamin and T. Slidell, *Digest of the Reported Decisions of the Superior Court of the Late Territory of Orleans, and of the Supreme Court of the State of Louisiana* (1834).
6 J. Benjamin, *A Treatise on the Law of Sale of Personal Property* (1868). Benjamin wrote a second edition (1873) and supervised a third, by Arthur Beilby Pearson and Hugh Fenwick Boyd (1883).
7 Confederate States of America records, 1854–1889, Library of Congress MSS 16550.
8 The United States War Department, *The War of the Rebellion: a Compilation of the Official Record of the Union and Confederate Armies*, series I–IV (1880–1901); United States, Naval War Records Office, *Official Records of the Union and Confederate Navies in the War of the Rebellion* (1894–1922).
9 L. Dinnerstein, *Antisemitism in America* (1994) x. See, also, W.D. Rubinstein, *A History of the Jews in the English-Speaking World: Great Britain* (1996).

constitution, albeit an equality not fully manifested until after the Second World War.[10] Benjamin lived his American life at a time when Jews received a form of political acceptance but suffered considerable disadvantages. His last years in America, during the Civil War, a time of intense stress, were ones in which anti-Semitism 'positively exploded'[11] and Benjamin suffered a series of intense, anti-Semitic attacks that had not occurred earlier in his career.[12]

The historiography of the Anglo-Jewish community changed during the twentieth century. The initial Whig history of a successful advancement to political emancipation[13] gave way to a much more complex and nuanced view of a community in which British anti-Semitism played a much greater and more destructive role.[14] Anti-Semitism, it was argued, compelled Jews to conform with the practices of gentiles to gain acceptance.[15] It must be noted, though, that this later view is not without its critics: for Rubinstein, British anti-Semitism has always existed 'yet it has probably been more subtle, harder to find ... equivocal and contradictory than in any other country'.[16] An examination of Benjamin's life sheds light on how and why a Jew could be accepted within English society and become a leading professional. The argument advanced here is that Benjamin arrived in England at a point in which the role of Jews was in the midst of transition. There was a partial emancipation which allowed Jews increasing civic participation. In 1845 Jews had been declared eligible for important municipal offices and in 1858 Lionel de Rothschild, after long debate, was able to take his seat as the first Jewish MP in Parliament. It was not until 1871, though, that the Universities Tests Act removed the barriers preventing Jews from becoming scholars or fellows in English universities. England still awaited the fiercer anti-Semitism that attended the arrivals of Eastern European Jews fleeing the pogroms of the 1880s. Benjamin's life, it is also argued, demonstrates how some individuals can 'overcome' the initial marginalization which attends the circumstances of their birth to move within the mainstream of society.

10 Dinnerstein, id.
11 id., p. 27.
12 id., p. 33.
13 See, for example, C. Roth, *History of the Jews of England* (1941) and V.D. Lipman, *Social History of the Jews in England 1850–1950* (1954).
14 See, for example, G. Alderman, *Modern British Jewry* (1998, 2nd edn.) and D. Cesarani (ed.), *The Making of Modern Anglo-Jewry* (1990).
15 See, for example, T. Kushner, *The persistence of prejudice: Antisemitism in British society during the Second World War* (1989).
16 Rubinstein, op. cit., n. 9, p. 34. See, also, M.R. Marrus, 'European Jewry and the Politics of Assimilation: Assessment and Reassessment' (1977) 49 *J. of Modern History* 89 and A. Gilam, 'A Reconsideration of the Politics of Assimilation' (1978) 50 *J. of Modern History* 103.

Benjamin did not begin life as an American. Born in the Caribbean on St Croix in 1811 to Sephardic Jews, Philip Benjamin (probably from St Nevis) and his wife Rebecca (raised in England, possibly born in Holland).[17] The sketchy knowledge of his parents' origins indicates the migratory nature of their lives. St Croix was then a Danish possession under British occupation, which allowed Benjamin to later assert that he was a British subject. When he was two, his family left the West Indies and settled first in Wilmington, North Carolina, then Fayetteville, and finally Charleston. Young Judah thus began his existence as an outsider, a Jewish boy who spent his early years moving between communities. The Carolinas formed a part of a wider Caribbean world, dependent upon the waterborne trade of commodities largely produced by slave labour, and Benjamin's West Indian origins were unlikely to have marked him as different.[18] His later Confederate colleague, South Carolinian George Trenholm, viewed him as 'a Carolinian by birth'.[19] His father's naturalization in 1824 made him an American citizen. Precociously clever and hardworking, the young man was admitted to Yale at fourteen. Benjamin's Southern origins, his Judaism, his youth, and his parents' impecuniosity set him apart from his classmates at Yale. While his tutor acknowledged that 'he was highly distinguished as a scholar'[20] and popular with his classmates, he abandoned his studies and departed Yale in 1827. Although not expelled, his biographers have considered that his departure was occasioned by misdeeds connected with gambling.[21]

Penniless, disgraced, and only sixteen, Benjamin's letter to Samuel Stone indicates his determination in the face of adversity. Describing himself as both 'a gentleman' and 'a stranger', Benjamin cogently stated both his practical abilities as a clerk and academic abilities as a scholar seeking employment.[22] He returned, however, to his parents in Charleston and wrote to President Day at Yale to beg forgiveness for his 'improper conduct' and

---

17 Meade, op. cit., n. 2, pp. 4–6.
18 Benjamin demonstrates that the society of the Southern states, prior to the Civil War, were a part of a more cosmopolitan Caribbean world dependent upon and constructed around slavery: M. Guterl, *American Mediterranean: Southern Slaveholders in the Age of Emancipation* (2008) ch. 2.
19 Letter from George Trenholm to Charles Prioleau, 5 July 1866, Business Records of Fraser, Trenholm & Company, Merseyside Maritime Museum, Liverpool B/FT Box 1/134.
20 Letter from Simeon North to Mr Brayton, 30 January 1827 [probably 1828], Library of Congress MMC, mm79000172.
21 See, for example, Meade, op. cit., n. 2, pp. 22–30; Butler, op. cit., n. 3, pp. 26–31. The allegation shocked those who knew the young Benjamin: B. Korn, *The Early Jews of New Orleans* (1969) 187, quoting Jacob Florance.
22 Letter from Benjamin to Simon Stone, 15 November 1827, Library of Congress, op. cit., n. 7.

seeking re-admission.[23] Before receiving a response Benjamin travelled to New Orleans to make his fortune.

The Yale debacle caused a permanent estrangement from his father[24] and, it appears, his religious faith. Korn observed that while Benjamin never denied nor abandoned his Judaism, he showed no interest in it.[25] The port city was booming as ever increasing amounts of commodities moved down the Mississippi and into the Atlantic.[26] One of the great commercial metropolises of the mid-nineteenth-century world, New Orleans grew faster than any other city in America between 1830 and 1840. Such a city needed clever and enterprising young men to exploit its opportunities. It was also a city in which 'anti-Jewish prejudice was notable for its absence'[27] and 'every indication points to a broad-scale acceptance of Jews by both the Creole and Yankee societies of New Orleans'.[28] Salomon de Rothschild, visiting New Orleans in 1861, wrote 'what is really quite astonishing here ... is the high position occupied by our co-religionists'.[29] In the antebellum South, 'there was a direct causal relationship between the hospitable treatment accorded Jews and the abominable treatment meted out to blacks'.[30] A white minority feared for its own position and accorded a more favourable treatment to Jews. Anti-Semitism became more prominent after the Civil War as Jewish immigration increased.[31]

Benjamin likely worked for the notary Greenbury Stringer and banker Samuel Hermann.[32] In multilingual Louisiana, Benjamin learned French and Spanish. He studied law independently and was called to the Louisiana Bar in December, 1832. Shortly after, aged twenty-one, he married Nathalie St. Martin, then sixteen. The marriage was highly significant for Benjamin's future endeavours in law and politics. New Orleans in the 1830s was a city in transition. Its early settlers were French and Spanish and while the Louisiana purchase of 1803 placed it firmly within an American world, French

23 Letter from Benjamin to Jeremiah Day, quoted in Meade, op. cit., n. 2, pp. 29–31.
24 Evans, op. cit., n. 4, p. 22.
25 B. Korn, 'Judah P. Benjamin as a Jew' (1949) 38 *Publications of the Am. Jewish Historical Society* 153, at 171.
26 S. Marler, *The Merchants' Capital: New Orleans and the Political Economy of the Nineteenth-Century South* (2013) ch. 1.
27 Korn, op. cit., n. 21, p. 223.
28 id., p. 225.
29 S. Diamond (ed.), *A Casual View of America: The Home Letters of Salomon de Rothschild, 1859–1861* (1961) 115.
30 J.D. Sarna, 'Review of *The Jewish Confederates*' (2001) 89 *Am. Jewish History* 335, at 336.
31 A. Rockaway and A. Gutfeld, 'Demonic Images of the Jew in the Nineteenth Century United States' (2001) 89 *Am. Jewish History* 355, at 373. Other factors existed: E. Goldstein, 'Different Blood Flows in Our Veins: Race and Jewish Self-Definition in Late Nineteenth Century America' (1997) 85 *Am. Jewish History* 29.
32 Both witnessed Benjamin's marriage contract: Notarial Archives Research Center, New Orleans, Records of Louis Feraud, vol. 7, 58–58A, 12 February 1833.

Creoles[33] still maintained a powerful presence. The St. Martins were French Catholics who had fled to the United States following the Saint-Domingue slave uprisings. Nathalie's family was wealthy and prominent within the powerful French-speaking community. Importantly for a young attorney, her father, Auguste St. Martin, was the secretary of the Orleans Insurance Company and then president of the Orleans Navigation Insurance Company. Insurance generates legal work and Benjamin appears to have represented Auguste.[34] That the family were French Catholics helped Benjamin if not to assimilate within Creole society, at least to align himself with it. His law offices were always on the western edge of the Vieux Carré,[35] just within the French quarter but close to the increasingly important Americans. Judging by his court appearances, Benjamin had a significant client base within the French community. It has been said that the St. Martins allowed this marriage because Nathalie had scandalized society[36] but there are no discernible foundations for such a theory. For the St. Martin family, the 1830s were a vital point in New Orleans development as the political, legal, and commercial control of the city slipped from the French to the incoming Americans. A daughter's marriage to an American would have been advantageous for a prominent Creole businessman.[37] Benjamin himself was ever engaging and portraits reveal a handsome young man. Whatever the reason for the marriage, the relationship Benjamin had with his in-laws was a close one.

The Benjamin marriage was also unusual because they lived apart for most of their married life. Nathalie has been depicted as a shallow woman or a promiscuous profligate, and thus the spouse who caused this separation.[38] This depiction does a disservice to her. Creole women were rarely educated and, unsurprisingly, she has not left papers. The reasons behind her departure to Paris with their young daughter, Ninette, around 1845 have never been clearly explained. The Benjamins were married a decade before the birth of

33 The term 'creole' has assumed many meanings; it is used here in the sense applicable to the St. Martins, persons of French descent born outside France.
34 See, for example, *St Martin* v. *Peychaud*, First District Court, 19 February 1834, docket no. 11057, Louisiana Division City Archives & Special Collections, New Orleans Public Library; *Garnier* v. *Succession of Peychaud* (1836) 9 La 182, court records available at the Earl K. Long Library, The University of New Orleans, at <http://hdl.handle.net/123456789/11555>.
35 *Michel's New-Orleans Annual and Commercial Register for 1834* (1833) 20,195; *Gibson's Guide and Directory of the State of Louisiana and the Cities of New Orleans and Lafayette* (1838) 15, 195; *Michel & Co New Orleans Annual and Official Commercial Register for 1846* (1846) 81, 534.
36 W. De Ville, 'The Marriage Contract of Judah P. Benjamin and Natalie St. Martin, 1833' (1996) 37 *J. of the Louisiana Historical Association* 81, at 84.
37 See, generally, J. Tregle Jr., 'Creoles and Americans' in *Creole New Orleans: Race and Americanization*, eds. A. Hirsch and J. Logsdon (1992).
38 Butler, op. cit., n. 3, pp. 34–6; Meade, op. cit., n. 2, pp. 34–6; Evans, op. cit., n. 4, pp. 33–5.

their only child, to whom they were devoted. The decision to raise her in France was a rational one. The French in the Caribbean did have a practice of educating children in France and nineteenth-century New Orleans was not a healthy city, as contemporaries realized.[39] The humid, foetid, crowded port city was plagued by disease. Inhabitants particularly feared yellow fever, 'repulsive and treacherous ... its fatal ending is inexpressibly terrible'.[40] While this highly contagious disease was brought to the Americas with enslaved Africans and was transmitted by *Aedes aegypti* mosquitoes, in the nineteenth century it was thought that it was borne on or originating in the foul atmosphere of the bayous. Yellow fever, it was noticed, particularly attacked newcomers, notably Americans and Europeans.[41] Benjamin's mother died of it in 1847. There is also a suggestion that Ninette suffered from a 'lifelong disorder'[42] and may well have needed greater medical care.

Benjamin visited his family in Paris regularly.[43] He developed professional connections in Paris on these visits, something which gave him different perspectives and connections than Southern contemporaries. Benjamin remained close to Nathalie's father and particularly close to her brother, Jules, who accompanied him to a variety of places, despite his difficulties in speaking English.[44] In short, Benjamin's unusual marriage was one which gave him advantage as an attorney and served to broaden his connections and horizons later in life.

NEW ORLEANS ATTORNEY

It is striking how quickly and successfully Judah Benjamin's law practice developed. The nature of this practice has never been analysed and space limits this article to a few observations concerned with Louisiana law and Benjamin's cases. Louisiana then, as now, was a civil law jurisdiction. Benjamin's legal colleague, Christian Roselius, observed that:

> it is evident that the principal foundations of the laws of this State, in civil matters is, the Roman law ... hence ... the study of the Roman Law, in connection with our own Code, is indispensably necessary for a thorough understanding of the laws of Louisiana.[45]

39 *Commercial Directory* (1823) 226.
40 G. Cable, *The Creoles of Louisiana* (1884/2005) 301.
41 J. Carrigan, 'Privilege, Prejudice, and the Strangers' Disease in Nineteenth-Century New Orleans' (1970) 36 *J. of Southern History* 568.
42 Letter from Benjamin to Rebecca Levy, 29 September 1865, quoted in Butler, op. cit., n. 3, pp. 370–2 stating that he found Ninette 'in perfect health ... now radically cured ... and looking as blooming as a rose' (p. 371).
43 *Times*, 9 May 1884, 10.
44 W. Russell, *My Diary North and South*, ed. E. Berwanger (1988) recounts that Jules spoke English with difficulty (p. 130).
45 C. Roselius, 'Introductory Lecture (1854)' in *The Gladsome Light of Jurisprudence*, ed. M. Hoeflich (1988) 224, at 236.

157

The first Louisiana Digest of 1808 was a mixture of French and Spanish law and, in turn, provided that after the promulgation of the Code, the Spanish, Roman, and French laws in force in the state when Louisiana was ceded to the United States would remain in force for every instance not provided for in the Code.[46] After the Code of 1825, Louisiana courts still consulted the writings of Spanish and French jurists.

Billings suggests that the Louisiana Supreme Court played a conscious role in the development of Louisiana's civil heritage by establishing the requirements necessary to practise law. By 1840 prospective lawyers were required to undertake a course of legal studies composed of international law, Louisiana law, civil law (primarily Justinian, Domat, and Pothier), and the common law.[47] Benjamin, as a practitioner and an author, assumed a role in the development of nineteenth-century Louisiana law. In doing so, he drew upon a rich civilian heritage to apply the law to New Orleans's complex commercial and proprietary issues.[48] Benjamin's 1834 *Digest of the Reported Decisions* summarizes Louisiana law and its mixed heritage. Benjamin wrote *The Digest* to teach himself Louisiana law, for his 'personal convenience',[49] but, with the assistance of Thomas Slidell, published the work as a lawyers' reference. This was a purpose ably fulfilled.[50] Although Benjamin sought 'to present a full statement of every point or principle decided in every case',[51] the observations were more in the nature of brief rules arranged alphabetically than principles supported by reason or precedent and arranged within a coherent thesis. Although the scheme has a common law structure, it was concerned with how to apply legal rules from largely civilian legal systems within Louisiana.

Without records, it is difficult to ascertain with certainty the nature of the young attorney's practice. Some insight is provided by the law reports and

---

46 Article 3521. Louisiana is best described as a mixed-law jurisdiction. On the political and legal compromises presented in the formation of this jurisdiction, see V. Palmer, 'Two Worlds in One: The Genesis of Louisiana's Mixed Legal System, 1803–1812' in *Louisiana: Microcosm of a Mixed Jurisdiction*, ed. V. Palmer (1999) 23–40 and G. Dargo, *Jefferson's Louisiana: Politics and the Clash of Legal Traditions* (2009, revised edn.) chs. 6–7.

47 W. Billings, 'A Course of Legal Studies' in *A Law Unto Itself?: Essays in the new Louisiana Legal History*, eds. W. Billings and M. Fernandez (2000) 25.

48 Early-nineteenth-century Louisiana was characterized by attempts, beginning with the *Digest of 1808*, to limit the courts to law found within legislative enactments and to suppress the use of Roman, Spanish, and French law. The Louisiana Supreme Court, however, in *Cottin* v. *Cottin* (1817) and *Fowler* v. *Griffith* (1827) held that it could refer to the older sources of law and, after 1828, referred to its own cases as a means of applying the older sources of law. Benjamin and Slidell's *Digest* was thus a means by which this process could be facilitated.

49 Benjamin and Slidell, op. cit., n. 5, p. 1.

50 F. Jumonville, '"Formerly the Property of a Lawyer" – Books that Shaped Louisiana Law' (2009) 24 *Tulane European and Civil Law Forum* 161; Anon, 'Jurisprudence of Louisiana' (1846) 1 *Commercial Rev. of the South and West* 414, at 415.

51 Benjamin and Slidell, op. cit., n. 5, p. 1.

certain surviving legal documents. The exploitation of the natural resources of the land that drained into the Mississippi and the shipping of the resulting commodities required a sophisticated legal framework. Benjamin was an active and successful attorney in this commercial framework. The law reports record his presence in cases involving real property (including slaves), personal property, mortgages, probate and inheritance, negotiable notes, insolvency, insurance, shipping, and so forth. These cases also demonstrate Benjamin's knowledge of the Louisiana Code and the Spanish[52] and French[53] law underlying Louisiana law. Benjamin was also to employ the works of common law authors in his arguments.[54] The mixed nature of Louisiana law meant that cases could be considered and decided by reference to the common law with a civilian analysis long before such a practice occurred in England.[55] Benjamin seems to have excelled not only in his legal analysis but also in his legal oratory and ability to deal with witnesses.[56]

Benjamin's clients were largely commercial parties, corporations, such as the New Orleans Insurance Company,[57] and wealthy individuals, notably powerful Frenchmen. A question often relevant to the role of marginalized persons within law is their involvement with other marginalized persons. In Benjamin's case, the answer is ambiguous. One of his earliest cases was *Boisdere* v. *Citizens' Bank of Louisiana*[58] in which he represented free persons of colour and successfully denied attempts to prevent them from ownership of the bank's stocks. He also represented Genevieve Robert, a free woman of colour, in her attempt to claim a part of the estate of her deceased daughter.[59] These were, though, cases which involved large sums

---

52 See *Gasquet* v. *Dimitry* (1836) 9 La. 592; *Lyon* v. *Fisk* (1846) 1 La. Ann. 444; and *Succession of McGill* (1851) 6 La. Ann. 327.

53 See *Municipality No. 2* v. *Hennen* (1840) 14 La. 559; *McCargo* v. *New Orleans Ins. Co* (1845) 10 Rob. (LA) 202; *Harman* v. *Claiborne* (1846) 1 La. Ann. 342; *Shepherd* v. *The Orleans Cotton Press Company* (1847) 2 La. Ann. 100.

54 See *Tio* v. *Vance* (1837) 11 La. 199 (citing *Abbott on Shipping*; *Kent's Commentaries* and *Phillips on Insurance*) and *Lanfear* v. *Blossman* (1846) 1 La. Ann. 148 (citing *Chitty on Contracts*).

55 See the judgment of Garland J in *Wiggin* v. *Flower* (1843) 5 Rob. (LA) 406 in which he explained *Chitty on Contracts* in light of *Pothier's Traité du Contrat de Change* (Benjamin appeared as counsel).

56 A. Hall, 'Cross-Examination as an Art' (1893) 5 *Green Bag* 423, at 423. A contemporary parallel to Benjamin can be found in F.A. Mann, upon whom see G. Lewis, *F.A. Mann: A Memoir* (2013).

57 *McCargo*, op. cit., n. 53 is the principal case in which Benjamin represented the insurers in claims over the value of slaves emancipated by the British after the slaves revolted and took the ship to Nassau. Benjamin's clients were found not liable to pay partly on the basis that slavery was against the law of nature but was allowed by the law of nations.

58 *Boisdere* v. *Citizens' Bank of Louisiana* (1836) 9 La. 506.

59 *Robert* v. *Allier's Agent* (1841) 17 La. 4 and *Succession of Robert* (1842) 2 Rob. (LA) 427.

of money, where the individuals could afford good legal representation, and Benjamin's motivation was probably not altruism.

SUGAR MASTER

Benjamin was quickly recognized by contemporaries as:

> emphatically the *Commercial* Lawyer of our city, and one of the most successful advocates at our bar ... and holds a deservedly high place among the members of his profession'.[60]

This enormous success allowed him to enter the commercial activities of Louisiana. His most significant venture was the purchase, with Theodore Packwood, in December 1844[61] of the Bellechasse sugar plantation, six miles from New Orleans. The purchase included a hundred and eight named slaves. As a plantation owner, Benjamin had reached the apex of Louisiana society. He was a sugar master, one of a class of which managed to develop Louisianan sugar through a unique combination of an existing southern slaveholding with modern industrialist practices and plantation capitalism.[62] Benjamin took an active interest in the process, describing the sugar planter as 'manufacturer as well as agriculturist'.[63] Writing in *De Bow's Commercial Review*, he described how to most profitably grow, mill, and refine sugar using the new Rillieux vacuum system. He wrote to show how 'the industry and enterprise of our population shall succeed in developing to their full extent the resources which a bounteous Providence has lavished on this favoured land'.[64] This development came at enormous cost given its dependency upon slavery. Sugar is a labour-intensive crop to produce and the condition of the slaves forced to labour on the sugar plantations was a desperate one. In his unique account of Louisiana enslavement, Solomon Northup wrote that 'the oppressors of my people are a pitiless and unrelenting race'.[65] So severe was this treatment that the enslaved African population of Louisiana decreased.[66]

---

60 J. Whitaker, *Sketches of Life and Character in Louisiana* (1847) 27.
61 New Orleans Notarial Archives, vol. 12A D.L. McCay, act 263, 10 December 1844.
62 R. Follett, *The Sugar Masters Planters and Slaves in Louisiana's Cane World, 1820–1860* (2006) describes in detail the processes by which this was undertaken.
63 J. Benjamin, 'Louisiana Sugar' (1847) II *Commercial Rev.* 322, at 331.
64 id., p. 345.
65 S. Northup, *Twelve Years a Slave* (1853/2014) 175. The memoir was adapted by screenwriter John Ridley for the film, *12 Years a Slave*, which details the experiences of Louisiana slaves.
66 Follett, op. cit., n. 62, p. 77.

It is difficult to categorize the plantation owner as an outsider. A contemporary described Benjamin as 'by birth, and as his name imports, an Israelite' although with questionable adherence to 'the religion of his fathers';[67] such a description does not marginalize him. Benjamin was elected a Whig member of the legislature in 1842. Louisiana had particularly restrictive suffrage and office-holding requirements which meant that election was dependent upon the backing of the powerful,[68] and in New Orleans, this came from the French community. This indicates a high degree of social inclusion and very real political power. In 1853 the state legislature elected him to the United States Senate; Benjamin had already declined President Fillmore's nomination to the United States Supreme Court. It is said that Benjamin later remarked that had he been less ambitious he would have ended his days on the Supreme Court bench.[69]

The 1850s Senate was a challenging environment as the republic struggled with slavery. Russell, of the *Times*, wrote that Benjamin was 'the most brilliant perhaps of the whole of the famous southern orators'.[70] Benjamin spoke to support states' rights, notably the right to own slaves. While he had sold Bellechasse on entering the Senate he remained acutely conscious of the economic ramifications of slavery and the dependence of southern wealth upon it. As Benjamin observed the ownership of slaves was worth over four thousand million dollars and was a right guaranteed by the constitution.[71] Perceptive, calm, and reasoned, Benjamin's arguments were powerful because they took a variety of forms. He argued not only the economic and political expediencies of slavery but also its legal position.[72] Some have stated that the brilliance of his arguments led his opponents to personal attacks. Evans wrote that during debates about the extension of slavery into Kansas, Senator Wade from Ohio referred to Benjamin as an 'Israelite with Egyptian principles',[73] a point stated both before[74] and after[75] Evans. The context of Wade's speech makes it clear that he was addressing

---

67 Whitaker, op. cit., n. 60, p. 28. Later analysis confirms this, see Korn, op. cit., n. 25, p. 168.

68 J. Sacher, *A Perfect War of Politics* (2003) 12.

69 Neiman, op. cit., n. 4, p. 74.

70 W. Russell, *My Civil War Diary*, ed. F. Pratt (1954) 96.

71 J. Benjamin, Speech of Hon. J.P. Benjamin of Louisiana, on the Right of Secession (Senate of the United States, 31 December 1860) 15.

72 See, for example, the speech delivered on 11 March 1858, 'Slavery Protected by the Common Law of the World' in which he argued that the institution had come from England and had thus been protected under the United States constitution.

73 Evans, op. cit., n. 4, pp. 95–6.

74 B. Hendrick, *Statesmen of the Lost Cause* (1939) 173.

75 R.N. Rosen, *The Jewish Confederates* (2000) 64.

not Benjamin but the doughfaces, northern Democrats allied with southern Democrats.[76] The comments Wade addressed personally to Benjamin, who was not present in the chamber for most of the speech,[77] complimented him, referring to 'that plausible and beautiful style of which he is so completely master',[78] noting that he was 'the able and eloquent gentleman from Louisiana'[79] with an 'astute and gifted mind'.[80]

This is not to say that Benjamin did not suffer racist treatment during his political career. The many references to his 'Hebrew' or 'Israelite' origins indicate others viewed him as an outsider. The racism he encountered in the Senate likely took a far more insidious form than slurs hurled in debates, something apparent in an interaction with Jefferson Davis. In a debate about the purchase of firearms, Benjamin and Davis disagreed and the latter accused the former of misrepresentation.[81] Davis suspected Benjamin of advancing the mercantile interests of a client by seeking greater funds and accused Benjamin of being a 'paid attorney'.[82] Benjamin's reported responses were courteous but, off the record, he challenged Davis to a duel. Benjamin's actions constituted a defence according to the honour code of the day: an insider's actions. Davis privately admitted his error to Benjamin. Although earlier accounts of this event have Davis issuing a public apology in the Senate, the apologist was actually Senator Pearce who made a 'statement of fact' that his innocent mistake had caused the disagreement.[83] In short, it seems likely that Benjamin's Senate experiences were not ones of insults hurled on the floor but in dealing with the far less perceptible prejudices of those he referred to as his 'brother Senators'. A similar form of insidious anti-Jewish sentiment is clearly seen in the diary of the Confederate clerk, J.B. Jones.[84]

A significant aspect of Benjamin's Washington life was his practice before the United States Supreme Court. He was admitted to practice in 1848, in the same term as Abraham Lincoln. Benjamin appeared frequently and successfully before the Court. Benjamin represented clients from the south, notably Louisiana. The disputes were commercial cases of the sort he

---

76 *Congressional Globe*, 35th Congress, First session, 1115. Wade began stating that 'the doughfaces of the North ... are the most despicable of men. The modern doughface is not a character peculiar to the age in which we live, but you find traces of him at every period of the world's history' (p. 1115).

77 id., p. 1114.

78 id., pp. 1114–15.

79 id., p. 1115.

80 id.

81 id., pp. 2781–2.

82 Evans, op. cit., n. 4, p. 99, relying upon the notes of Thomas Bayard.

83 *Congressional Globe*, op. cit., n. 76, p. 2823. Davis replied to this statement but the reply takes the form of an explanation not an apology (p. 2824).

84 J. Jones, *A Rebel War Clerk's Diary,Vol. I* (1866) 118.

had taken in New Orleans: bankruptcy;[85] shipping;[86] estate and succession;[87] and land disputes.[88] One of his most prominent cases was the *United States v. Andres Castillero*,[89] a case concerned with the ownership of the New Almaden quicksilver mine in California. Benjamin and Reverdy Johnson appeared more frequently before the Taney Court than any other lawyers.[90]

When Louisiana seceded from the United States in January 1861 her senators left their seats. A recent re-appraisal of Benjamin argues that he accepted the inevitability of southern secession and willingly left the Union.[91] This marked the end of one political career for Benjamin and the beginning of another. It is with regard to Benjamin as a Confederate that the lack of personal papers providing insight into his thoughts and actions is most critically felt. It is highly doubtful that Benjamin would have wanted the Confederate states to engage in a lengthy war with the United States as he was clever enough to realize that a prolonged engagement was one the Confederacy could not win. Benjamin, the logical lawyer, likely thought that constitutional law favoured the Confederacy and that the great commodity purchasers of cotton, the United Kingdom and France, would recognize the new nation. Lacking personal papers, though, only a glimpse of this reasoning can be seen from his comments to others.[92]

Benjamin was central to the Confederate government. He was, in succession, the Attorney General, the Minister of War, and the Secretary of State. The pictorial depictions of the cabinet invariably display him beside or behind Jefferson Davis, the implication being that Benjamin guided the President. Benjamin's loyalty to Davis was great. The Confederacy was poorly equipped for war and this led to the loss of many lives at Roanoke Island. Rather than publicly expose this weakness, and Davis to censure, Benjamin assumed responsibility and suffered condemnation as the 'fat Jew sitting at his desk'.[93] The Civil War brought a spate of anti-Semitic attacks on Jewish figures. The most public of these was General Grant's order to expel all Jews from his department[94] but Jews were publicly blamed for

---

85 *Ingraham* v. *Dawson* (1857) 61 U.S. 486; *Jeter* v. *Hewitt* (1859) 63 U.S. 352; and *Adams* v. *Preston* (1859) 63 U.S. 473.
86 *Culbertson* v. *The Steamer Southern Belle* (1855) 59 U.S. 584; *Goslee* v. *Shute* (1855) 59 U.S. 463; and *Ure* v. *Coffman* (1856) 60 U.S. 56.
87 *McGill* v. *Armour* (1850) 52 U.S. 142 and *Poydas* v. *Treasurer of Louisiana* (1855) 59 U.S. 192.
88 *Foley* v. *Harrison* (1853) 56 U.S. 433; *Cousin* v. *Labatut* (1856) 60 U.S. 202; and *Spencer* v. *Lapsley* (1859) 61 U.S. 264.
89 *United States* v. *Andres Castillero* (1859) 67 U.S. 17.
90 H. Connor, *John Archibald Campbell* (1920) 83.
91 G. Cunningham, ' "The Ultimate Step": Judah P. Benjamin and Secession' (2013) 97 *Am. Jewish History* 1.
92 Benjamin told Russell that England was bound to recognize the Confederacy: Russell, op. cit., n. 70, p. 128.
93 Evans, op. cit., n. 4, p. 147.
94 See J.D. Sarna, *When General Grant Expelled the Jews* (2012).

many disasters that befell both sides. The diarist Mary Chesnut recorded that the mob referred to Benjamin as 'Mr. Davis's pet Jew'.[95] Benjamin's reception at a personal level was a different matter, though, for Chesnut also observed after meeting him that 'he is a Delphic oracle',[96] a man her husband thought the Senate's cleverest southerner.[97] Despite the anti-Semitic attacks on his character and the suspicions harboured by many Confederates, Benjamin worked ceaselessly for what he must have recognized early on was a 'lost cause'.

The end of the war found Benjamin in a particularly difficult situation.[98] Implicated in Lincoln's assassination, distrusted by many southerners in an anti-Semitic environment and with a reward for his capture, he stated that he would never be taken alive. Had he been caught, he stated later that year, 'they probably would have put him to death'.[99] His fears were real. The *New York Times* named Davis, Benjamin, and Breckenridge and thundered that 'the leading traitors should die the most disgraceful death known to our civilization – death on the gallows'.[100] The insider had become an outsider again.

BENJAMIN THE BRITON

Benjamin fled to Britain as a safe haven and it is possible that he did not consider himself a British subject.[101] He settled early on the idea of a legal career in England. He wrote to his sister that he was 'almost fixed in my purpose to practice my profession as barrister in London, but have not yet decided' as he ascertained the requirements for the admission of strangers.[102] His intention was reported in more definite terms in the *Solicitors' Journal*: 'it is said that Mr. Benjamin, ex-Secretary of State in the Confederate Government, intends joining the English Bar.'[103]

To outward appearances, Benjamin was a complete outsider when he arrived in Southampton in August 1865: 'it is difficult to imagine a position more apparently hopeless than his.'[104] At the relatively advanced age of

95 M. Chesnut, *Mary Chesnut's Civil War*, ed. C. Vann Woodward (1981) 288.
96 id., p. 542.
97 id., p. 288.
98 Gruss, op. cit., n. 4, pp. 964–70.
99 C. Pollock, 'Reminiscences of Judah Philip Benjamin' (1898) 10 *Green Bag* 396, at 397.
100 *New York Times*, 1 May 1865, at <http://www.nytimes.com/1865/05/01/news/the-importance-of-capturing-the-rebel-chiefs.html>.
101 In a letter to his sister, Benjamin wrote that he would probably have to be naturalized to become a barrister: Benjamin to Rebecca Levy, 29 September 1865, quoted in Butler, op. cit., n. 3, pp. 370–2.
102 id., p. 371.
103 *Solicitors' J. and Reporter*, 23 September 1865, 1002.
104 Anon, 'Judah P. Benjamin' (1889) 1 *Green Bag* 365, at 365.

fifty-five, Jewish, not only American but also a Confederate, and seemingly friendless in an alien land, the odds were against success. Even the intention to practise law seemed optimistic as he presented himself in a common law country having trained and practised in America's civil law jurisdiction. Appearances were deceptive and Benjamin made the most of any advantage offered. He began by utilizing the network he had established as Confederate Secretary of State. He went upon arrival to 17 Savile Row,[105] the residence of Henry Hotze, one-time chief Confederate propagandist formerly supervised by Benjamin. It was true that Benjamin was often proscribed for his previous advocation of slavery (curiously, few Britons seem to have realized that he had also been a major slave owner and this he kept to himself) but the Civil War had divided British allegiances. Benjamin was quick to accept sympathetic hands extended to him. A month after his arrival, Benjamin wrote that various members of parliament had called upon him, Benjamin Disreali offered assistance, and he would dine with William Gladstone.

Social contacts within political levels are not enough, though, on their own to overcome the various barriers Benjamin encountered on his arrival in London. While the legal profession in antebellum America was one into which a great diversity of men had entered, the same was not true of the English Bar. Here the advocates of the legal profession were overwhelmingly English, Anglican, and the sons of professional men or the landed aristocracy.[106] Successful barristers had generally attended a public school.[107] There was a 'near absence of the lower orders of society' and the sons of small shopkeepers were not represented amongst the Bar.[108] Jewish barristers were almost non-existent. On the face of it, the reception of a Jewish American lawyer, the son of a failed shopkeeper, was unlikely.

That Benjamin was a stranger was apparent to observers. He was described as a 'prince of the Secession',[109] 'of decidedly Jewish descent',[110] 'a little elderly man, snuffy and ill-shaven, with nothing to captivate men',[111] and one who spoke 'with a strong American accent'.[112] Analysing his establishment at the Bar it is clear, though, that this was made possible because he was Jewish and because he was a Confederate. Those factors which made him an outsider he utilized to move inwards. Describing himself

---

105 J. Witt, *Life in the Law* (1900) 160.
106 D. Duman, *The English and Colonial Bars in the Nineteenth Century* (1983) 9–15.
107 id., pp. 107–9.
108 P. Polden, 'The Legal Professions' in *The Oxford History of the Laws of England, Vol. XI* (2010) 1021.
109 *Law Times*, 17 February 1883, 278.
110 Pollock, op. cit., n. 99, p. 397.
111 R. Palmer, Earl of Selborne, *Memorials Part II. Personal and Political 1865–1895* (1898) 94.
112 Anon, *A Generation of Judges by their Reporter* (1886) 198.

as 'a Political Exile, proscribed for my loyalty to my own State',[113] Benjamin applied for admission to Lincoln's Inn in January 1866. He sought and received an exemption from preliminary examination. The Benchers then dispensed with their requirements as to terms and admitted Benjamin after a single term. While Sir Henry James stated at Benjamin's farewell banquet that 'from the first days of his coming he was one of us',[114] it is clear that there was resistance to his call to the Bar. A contemporary account of his 'unreasonable' call to the Bar wondered 'what peculiar claim Mr. Benjamin can have upon the Benchers of Lincoln's Inn'[115] in having almost all of his terms remitted.[116] Suspicions lingered that Benjamin's early call was attributed to Confederate sympathies at the Bar.[117]

At his farewell banquet, Benjamin thanked a number of Benchers for their assistance when he arrived. One was Baron Hatherley, then Page Wood VC. As an MP, Page Wood, a High Churchman and a Liberal, had led the debates about the removal of Jewish disabilities and was at the forefront in the admission of Lionel de Rothschild to the House of Commons. In Benjamin, Page Wood saw the opportunity of presenting the Bar with a gifted Jewish lawyer. His presence at Benjamin's call ceremony on 6 June 1866 was noted.[118] The first Jewish barrister, Francis Goldsmid, had been called in 1833. To practise before the Bar, students were required to swear an oath 'upon the true faith of a Christian'. The oath was anti-Catholic in origin and derived from legislation designed to bar from public offices those who would not take the Church of England sacrament. In Goldsmid's case, the benchers of Lincoln's Inn eventually agreed to allow him to dispense with the Christian phrase. Goldsmid, however, was not followed by many other Jewish lawyers[119] and this assists in the understanding of Page Wood's intervention.

As has been observed, Benjamin's England was one that accepted Jews in many ways. While prejudice, often most viciously displayed,[120] was still evident it was also the case that following their emancipation in the late 1850s, Jews were able to participate in political life. A significant portion of

113 *The Records of the Honourable Society of Lincoln's Inn, Vol. 5* (1991–2001) 133.
114 *Remarks of the Attorney General and the Response of Mr Judah P Benjamin at the Dinner in the Inner Temple Hall, London, June 30, 1883* (privately printed, undated) 6.
115 *Jurist*, 9 June 1866, 238.
116 The Benchers at Lincoln's Inn also considered an inquiry from Gray's Inn asking if they had called Mr Benjamin to the Bar without him having kept the required terms: *Records*, op. cit., n. 113, p. 140.
117 *Reynold's Newspaper*, 3 June 1866, 2.
118 *Daily News*, 8 June 1866, 8; *Jurist*, op. cit., n. 115.
119 See P.S. Lachs, 'A Study of a Professional Elite: Anglo-Jewish Barristers in the Nineteenth Century' (1982) 44 *Jewish Social Studies* 125 for a thorough examination of the subject.
120 See, for example, the treatment which could be accorded Jewish political candidates: M. Clark, *Albion and Jerusalem* (2009) 62–4.

the Anglo-Jewish community was 'irreverent, if not irreligious'[121] and Jews were emancipated Englishmen.[122] Benjamin, experienced in living within a gentile society, accustomed himself to this new environment. This gives credence to the view that his acceptance was conditioned upon his assimilation, but without an insight into Benjamin's own thoughts, it is impossible to prove that his assimilation occurred to gain acceptance.

Benjamin was able to find a place in the chambers of Charles Pollock, then a leading commercial barrister, through the intercession of his father, Chief Baron Pollock. It appears that Benjamin had James Mason take him as a guest to Lord Chief Baron Pollock's country house. Mason was the man Benjamin had sent to London as the Confederate envoy. After Benjamin spent several days charming the Pollocks, the father prevailed upon the son to take Benjamin, writing that he 'has no need to learn law, all he needs is to see something of the practice of our courts, and to obtain some introduction to the English Bar'.[123] Benjamin again employed Confederate links by choosing the Northern Circuit to practice; this included Liverpool where his knowledge of mercantile trade in American commodities was useful. As an anonymous American wrote, 'he seems properly to have joined the Northern Circuit, and the secessionist sympathizers at Liverpool ought to give him good business.'[124] *The Law Reports* indicate that this is what happened as Benjamin was soon representing firms involved in the cotton trade.[125]

Frustrated by what he regarded as the slow growth of his practice, Benjamin wrote a legal treatise to gain prominence at the Bar. While this was not an uncommon endeavour, it was uncommon for one of his age and experience. And as one who began as a civil law lawyer Benjamin seemed an intellectual outsider. In his usual fashion, though, Benjamin turned what could be viewed as weakness into strength. The full title of his work was *A Treatise on the Law of Sale of Personal Property; with References to the American Decisions and to the French Code and Civil Law*. By explicitly incorporating the law and jurisprudence of these other jurisdictions Benjamin was able to meet the needs of a legal profession that was transforming its law from one formulated on procedure to one based on substance.[126] Pollock thought that 'one great and early advantage held by Benjamin as a lawyer' was his knowledge of the civil law: 'the principles

---

121 id., p. 193.
122 id., p. 248.
123 Pollock, op. cit., n. 99, p. 397.
124 Anon (1866) 1 *Am. Law Rev.* 220.
125 See, for example, *United States of America* v. *Wagner* (1867) LR 2 Ch App 582; *In re Fraser, Trenholm, & Co* (1868) LR 4 Ch App 49; *Thomson* v. *Simpson* (1870) LR 9 Eq 497; and *Stringer* v. *The English and Scottish Marine Insurance Company* (1870) LR 5 QB 599.
126 The same process can be seen in the work of an English contemporary: C. MacMillan, 'Stephen Martin Leake: A Victorian's View of the Common Law' (2011) 32 *J. of Legal History* 3.

and practice of this great system of law Benjamin knew and appreciated thoroughly.'[127] But Benjamin was more than a civil lawyer for he already had a strong grasp of the common law. Not only had his years before the United States Supreme Court involved the common law, as was noted above, it is clear that his commercial practice in New Orleans involved large elements of the common law in conjunction with civil law and civilian jurisprudence.

Benjamin's treatise was enormously successful and was received with near universal acclaim: 'one of the most valuable legal publications of the year'[128] and 'entitled to rank in the highest class of text-books; and it is ... one of the most important contributions to legal literature which has appeared for many years.'[129] The treatise succeeded because Benjamin went beyond a compendium of cases and provided a dominant conception of the law of sale, constructed upon principles as elucidated in the cases. It was the construction of law by principle, particularly principles common to the Romans and civilians, which was so attractive to readers. As Sheldon Amos observed, the difficulty with most of the treatises of the age was that by failing to go beyond cataloguing the cases and avoiding any attempt to show the cases as a part of a larger, rational system of law, the treatise writers produced work which paralysed the originality of the student and dulled the energy of the practitioner.[130] By the end of Benjamin's career, the treatise was regarded as the definitive work on the subject: 'few works on English law have been so readily accepted and so universally used as "Benjamin on Sales".'[131]

Benjamin's incorporation of civil law into his treatise was to have very real effects on the development of the common law. Although this occurred as a part of a larger transformation whereby treatise writers adopted, in piecemeal fashion, the jurisprudence of civilians as an analytical and structural framework for English contract law, it is clear that Benjamin's work had its own specific impact on the common law. Two such instances can be seen in the doctrine of mistake in contract law[132] and the postal acceptance rules concerned with contractual formation at a distance.[133]

While Benjamin lamented the rate at which his practice grew, his contemporaries observed that it expanded rapidly.[134] What was the nature of this practice? While it might be thought that Benjamin would attract clients

127 Pollock, op. cit., n. 99, p. 398.
128 *Law Times*, 5 September 1868, 350.
129 *Solicitor's J. and Reporter*, 14 November 1868, 28.
130 S. Amos, *Science of Jurisprudence*, quoted in the *Law Times*, 15 June 1872, 111.
131 Pollock, op. cit., n. 99, p. 399. See, also, *Law Times*, 17 February 1883, 276 and 17 May 1884, 52; *Times*, 9 May 1884, 10.
132 C. MacMillan, *Mistakes in Contract Law* (2010) 230–8.
133 C. MacMillan, 'The Lousianan's Influence on British Law' in *Louisiana in European Legal History*, ed. J. Cairns (forthcoming).
134 Pollock, op. cit., n. 99, p. 399; Selborne, op. cit., n. 111, p. 95.

within the Jewish community, this does not appear to be the case. Indeed, Benjamin appears not to have had any active links within the Jewish community.[135] He was, in this regard, different from contemporary barristers George Jessel and Arthur Cohen. Benjamin's clients came largely from the commercial community. The nature of his early practice is less clear than his later one. From 1870, however, one finds an increase in the *Law Reports* cases in which he appeared as counsel and from 1872 he appears with enormous regularity.[136] In 1869, Benjamin was made a Queen's Counsel of the County Palatine of Lancaster, the limitation seemingly made so as not to offend the United States. In 1872 Baron Hatherley once again advanced Benjamin's career when, impressed by arguments in *Rankin v. Potter*,[137] a marine insurance case, Lord Hatherley conferred upon Benjamin a patent of precedence, taking rank over all future Queen's Counsel. The *London Law Journal* reported that the promotion 'will be viewed with satisfaction by the whole profession'.[138]

This advancement allowed Benjamin to specialize in appellate cases. The *Law Reports* indicate that Benjamin had come, in London, to specialize in the legal work which necessarily arose in the capital of a mercantile and trading empire. In this sense, the sort of law Benjamin was engaged in was similar to that he had practised in New Orleans. We find him active in cases concerned with shipping,[139] marine insurance,[140] admiralty matters,[141] credit and financing,[142] company law,[143] bankruptcy,[144] contract,[145] and the sale of goods.[146] Benjamin was, at times, involved in cases associated with landed

---

135 *Jewish Chronicle*, 9 May 1884, 16.
136 The figures are impressive: 9 cases in 1872, 20 in 1873, 33 in 1874, 31 in 1875, 53 in 1876, 38 in 1877, 25 in 1878, 36 in 1879, 37 in 1880, 29 in 1881, 26 in 1882, and 4 in 1883.
137 *Rankin v. Potter* (1873) LR 6 HL 83.
138 Reprinted in (1872–73) 7 *Am. Law Rev.* 387.
139 *Chartered Mercantile Bank of India v. Netherlands India Steam Navigation Company* (1882) 9 QBD 118; *Hopper v. Burness* (1876) 1 CPD 137; *Dahl v. Nelson, Donkin & Co* (1881) 6 App Cas 38; and *Jackson v. Union Marine Insurance Company* (1874) LR 10 CP 125.
140 *Rivaz v. Gerussi* (1880) 6 QBD 222; *Adamson v. Newcastle Freight Insurance Association* (1879) 4 QBD 462; *Lohre v. Aitchson* (1877) 2 QBD 501; *Inman Steampship Company v Bischoff* (1882) 7 App Cas 670; and *Rankin*, op. cit., n. 137.
141 *Borjesson v. Carlberg* (1878) 3 App. Cas. 1316; *The Onward* (1873) LR 4 AE 38; and *The M Moxham* (1876) 1 PD 107.
142 *Horne v. Rouquette* (1878) 3 QBD 514; *Swire v. Redman* (1876) 1 QBD 536; and *National Bolivian Navigation Company v. Wilson* (1880) 5 App Cas 176.
143 *Simm v. Anglo-American Telegraph Company* (1879) 5 QBD 188; *Twycross v. Grant* (1877) 2 CPD 469; and *Erlanger v. New Sombrero Phosphate Company* (1878) 3 App Cas 1218.
144 *Glegg v. Gilbey* (1877) 2 QBD 209; *Melhado v. Watson* (1877) 2 CPD 281; and *Campbell v. Im Thurn* (1876) 1 CPD 267.
145 *Cundy v. Lindsay* (1878) 3 App Cas 459; *Rhodes v. Forwood* (1876) 1 App Cas 256.
146 *Johnson v. Raylton* (1881) 7 QBD 438; *Borrowman v. Drayton* (1876) 2 Ex D 15; and *Reuter v. Sala* (1879) 4 CPD 239

169

interests, involving real property interests[147] and succession.[148] A surprisingly large number of Benjamin's cases were significant ones: *Cundy* v. *Lindsay*,[149] *The Franconia*,[150] and the case of the Titchborne claimant[151] are but a few examples.

Benjamin had an extensive practice before the Judicial Committee of the Privy Council and appeared in the lion's share of non-Indian Privy Council cases between 1877 and 1882.[152] During that time he appeared in cases from colonies and Dominions which were to become Australia, Canada, New Zealand, South Africa, India, Malta, China, Turkey, the Channel Islands, and the Isle of Man. Many of these areas were governed by a system of civil law and Benjamin's knowledge of civil law acted as an incentive to retain his services. Similarly, his knowledge of French and Spanish were important; he was retained in a large number of cases from Lower Canada where the governing law was civil law and the papers often in French.

AN INSIDER OR AN OUTSIDER?

As will be seen from this brief account, Benjamin was enormously successful in his endeavours. How, though did he transcend his origins on the margin of society – an impecunious, immigrant Jewish youth – to United States senator and successful Supreme Court counsellor? In answering this question, it is apparent that this success is attributable to Benjamin himself, a matter evident when he repeated this feat in transcending his status as political exile to the United Kingdom to the top of the Bar. At the same time, though, it is worth observing that although Benjamin was, by various factors marginalized, at the same time he lived in an era when he had the basic attributes (he was male and white) in which he could participate in civic society in the United States and the United Kingdom. This was a necessary precondition for success, without which all personal attributes would be meaningless.

What were the personal elements Benjamin deployed to enable him to transcend his status as an outsider? The first was undoubtedly his lifelong[153] capacity for hard work. Davis sought out Benjamin for the Confederate

---

147 *Neill* v. *Devonshire* (1882) 8 App Cas 135; *Gordon* v. *Gordon* (1882) 7 App Cas 713; and *Davis* v. *Treharne* (1881) 6 App Cas 460.

148 *Attorney General* v. *Noyes* (1881) 8 QBD 125; *Swinton* v. *Bailey* (1878) 4 App Cas 70; and *Taylor* v. *Graham* (1878) 3 App Cas 1287.

149 *Cundy* v. *Lindsay* (1878) 3 App Cas 459.

150 *The Franconia* (1876) LR 2 PD 8; *The Franconia* (1878) LR 3 PD 164.

151 *Castro* v. *The Queen* (1881) 6 App Cas 229.

152 G. Wheeler, *A Synopsis of all the Appeals Decided by the Judicial Committee from 1876 to 1891* (1893). Benjamin appeared in approximately 50 cases.

153 Meade, op. cit., n. 2, p. 11 recounts from a classmate that little Judah did not play at recess but prepared himself for his upcoming lessons.

170

cabinet because 'my acquaintance with Benjamin in the Senate had impressed me with the lucidity of his intellect, his systematic habits, and his capacity for labour'.[154] Pollock remarked about his English years that approached his tasks with the zeal and energy of a much younger man.[155] It is also seems likely that a part of Benjamin's success was his ability to delegate work and to manage others in the conduct of a greater matter. To his capacity for industry was coupled great intellect. There seemed little that Benjamin could not master and his intellectual abilities were multi-faceted. Benjamin was practical and chose to practise in an area of which he had great knowledge – mercantile trade. This was a knowledge acquired in boyhood and steadily built up:

> few men had a sounder or wider range of knowledge and experience of the law-merchant, including shipping, insurance and foreign trading, than Benjamin, long before he ever thought of leaving America.[156]

Industry, organization, and intellect were matched with exceptional oratorical abilities. As a barrister, he was thought to have 'extraordinary powers as a dialectician'.[157] He managed to adapt this skill to suit new conditions in England.[158] Lord Selborne noted that, as an advocate, he 'was quick, shrewd, and dexterous ... Benjamin did not disdain any sort of argument which an honest man could use, but urged them all with equal courage.'[159] The strength of Benjamin's cases lay in the advancement of a number of grounds to reach the same conclusion. These arguments were based upon reason and worked from general principles, principles Benjamin based upon the cases.

Above all else, though, it was Benjamin's personal abilities that allowed him to succeed. It is clear that many with whom he worked expressed anti-Jewish views and yet Benjamin ably withstood discriminatory treatment and prejudices. An example can be found in his client Prioleau whose letter book reveals anti-Jewish sentiment and yet he was happy to be represented by Benjamin.[160] He was frequently described as a *bon vivant*, a great wit, and an entertaining personality. His friend, Varina Davis, stated that Benjamin 'seemed to have an electric sympathy with every mind with which he came into contact'.[161] Lord Selborne described him as one whose 'kindly unpre-

---

154 J. Davis, *The Rise and Fall of the Confederate Government, Vol. I* (1881) 242.
155 Pollock, op. cit., n. 99, p. 399.
156 id.
157 Anon, op. cit., n. 112.
158 Henry James advised him not to reveal that he considered the judges' knowledge of the law inferior to his own: Meade, op. cit., n. 2, pp. 334–5.
159 Selborne, op. cit., n. 111, p. 96.
160 Letter to G. Trenholm, 22 October 1863, Business Records of Fraser, Trenholm & Company, Merseyside Maritime Museum, Liverpool B/FT/Box 8/178.
161 Letter to Francis Lawley, 8 June 1898, Lawley MSS, Pierce Butler Papers 56-10-2, Louisiana Research Collection, Tulane University.

tending manners made him a general favourite'.[162] Much of Benjamin's professional life was conducted against a backdrop of discord but he strove, as he explained, to always maintain 'the most courteous manner' and that:

> I have endeavoured, upon all occasions, that my manner towards my brother Senators should be such that whilst we differ in opinion ... there should be left no sting behind in the debates which might occur between us, that none but the kindliest and best feelings may exist.[163]

Benjamin's engaging manner and sociability acted to advance his interests and smooth the path to his acceptance in a wide range of circles. An aspect of his personality was perseverance in the face of adversity.

Benjamin was able not only to overcome adversity, but also to turn what could be seen as weaknesses into strengths. Those factors that might have marginalized him were matters that he turned to his advantage. This is clearly seen in his passage into the English Bar. He established himself through a combination of his Judaism and his Confederate support. He advanced his professional work in such a way as to take advantage of his civilian learning rather than be inhibited by it. As can be seen in this brief biography, Benjamin cannot truly be described as an outsider. He was not marginalized from power, wealth or influence. That he was different from others was also the key to his success. If we compare Benjamin's fate to that of other Confederates, the fact that he was an outsider, one who had a different world-view and different connections meant that he was able to withstand the collapse of the Confederacy and to begin anew. Judah Benjamin was to a great extent the master of his own destiny and not one marginalized by others.

162 Selborne, op. cit., n. 111, p. 96.
163 *Congressional Globe*, op. cit., n. 76, p. 2824.